ECO-INNOVATION

ECO-INNOVATION

WHEN SUSTAINABILITY AND COMPETITIVENESS SHAKE HANDS

Dr Javier Carrillo-Hermosilla,

IE Business School, email: Javier.Carrillo@ie.edu

Dr Pablo del Río González

Institute of Public Goods and Policies (IPP), email: pablo.delrio@cchs.csic.es

Dr Totti Könnölä[*]

*Institute for Prospective Technological Studies (JRC-IPTS),
email: totti.konnola@ec.europa.eu*

*The views expressed are purely those of the authors and may not in any circumstances be regarded as stating an official position of the European Commission.

First published 2009 by
PALGRAVE MACMILLAN

Palgrave Macmillan in the UK is an imprint of Macmillan Publishers Limited, registered in England, company number 785998, of Houndmills, Basingstoke, Hampshire RG21 6XS.

Palgrave Macmillan in the US is a division of St Martin's Press LLC, 175 Fifth Avenue, New York, NY 10010.

Palgrave Macmillan is the global academic imprint of the above companies and has companies and representatives throughout the world.

Palgrave® and Macmillan® are registered trademarks in the United States, the United Kingdom, Europe and other countries.

ISBN-13: 978–0–230–20206–1

This book is printed on paper suitable for recycling and made from fully managed and sustained forest sources. Logging, pulping and manufacturing processes are expected to conform to the environmental regulations of the country of origin.

A catalogue record for this book is available from the British Library.

A catalog record for this book is available from the Library of Congress.

10 9 8 7 6 5 4 3 2 1
18 17 16 15 14 13 12 11 10 09

Printed and bound in Great Britain by
CPI Antony Rowe, Chippenham and Eastbourne

Dedication

To our families

Contents

Foreword

A warm welcome to this book which states the case for sustainability and shows companies struggling for real and fair competitiveness how to introduce the concept of eco-innovation as a management tool and the primary model.

Recent events in the global economy inescapably demonstrate the need for a new model of development; one which ensures improvements in the quality of life for current and future generations and for a larger proportion of the world's inhabitants. This is what sustainability is all about. This requires reconsidering the whole system and calls for innovation in sustainability and governance, since the two go together. It does not mean just any innovation; rather innovation with a purpose, innovation to make progress in sustainability – in short, eco-innovation, the key operational concept of this book.

This book is about bringing a new logic – the logic of sustainability – to business via eco-innovation, offering a leading edge to those who are convinced that sustainable business is about doing business both now and in the future. It is about applying 'the economy of permanence', it is about delivering product-services packages in a way that is effective (what society and people actually need or demand) and efficient (with as little use of resources and environmental degradation as possible), leaving society, via demand management and fiscal systems, to take care of the 'sufficiency principle', that is, how much is enough in terms of use of natural resources without impeding the development of future generations.

Many of us have argued tirelessly that a new development is necessary, possible and timely. It is now inevitable. We have no other choice but to introduce the required changes and particularly – this is something we tend to overlook – the conditions for change or the appropriate rules of the game. This is the key to providing real advantages, to providing rewards in market terms too – competitive advantages – for companies which introduce eco-innovation as a leading concept and management tool. If we do not pay sufficient attention to this in the present situation of financial crisis, we may once more underestimate the need to establish this institutional framework or the conditions for change.

As the book notes, Michael Porter has already stated the case for countries introducing stricter environment-promoting eco-innovation into business, possibly resulting in higher competitiveness ratings. Similarly, the Dow Jones Sustainability Index stated the case for higher returns for companies at the cutting edge. The question is how to retrieve those arguments in order to transform the current crisis into an opportunity and how to establish the conditions for change at a global level too. As one well-known NGO has been stating for some time: 'From climate change to a climax for change'.

The authors provide the theoretical and empirical basis and tools for applying eco-innovation as a management instrument to deliver higher competitiveness. Therefore, I will focus on the conditions for change, the business environment – what the authors call the institutional framework –, which must be developed to ensure that the market economy works towards sustainability, reducing the impact of those, in the financial sector too, who take abusive short-term benefits and transfer costs or externalities to the rest of society and to future generations. This institutional framework must also pave the way for the doers of good, that is, those at the cutting edge of eco-innovation – the eco-innovators.

This book demonstrates that we have the management tools for businesses to deliver product-services packages with the understanding that it is probably better from a sustainability perspective to have products delivered as part of a service to society rather than the other way round, which is usually the case. It is only a matter of ensuring that this time we do not overlook the key point of creating the conditions to really turn this into an advantage.

We need to set a real Agenda for Change, where the key references must be sustainability and governance, using existing instruments of the market economy, within limits, to ensure efficient allocation of resources once basic needs are covered and once proper costs are internalized. This involves realizing that, perhaps, an appropriately run market with proper taxation can help or encourage businesses to **increase efficiency**, or at least do things more efficiently in terms of use of resources (the efficiency principle), and it may even help them, as this book identifies, to **do the proper things** (the effectiveness principle), while a greater effort from the regulators is required, particularly via taxation, **not to overdo things** (the sufficiency principle), that is to say, to rationalize.

Many attempts have been made to establish an institutional framework at EU level and it may be of interest to review them. The main barriers to making the market work for sustainability and to promoting eco-innovation should be considered, with the aim of establishing the institutional framework that this book urges, so as to enable sustainability and competitiveness to go together. At the European Council of March 2005, eco-efficient innovation was recognized as a potential economic driver in the Lisbon Strategy. The 'Clean, Clever, Competitive' project started during the Dutch presidency (second half of 2004) already pointed to the fact that many existing programs focused on the supply side (R&D) of the innovation market. The conclusion was to turn attention to the demand side of the market too and thus to some policy initiatives and to the institutional framework.

Following a mandate by the European Council to engage in dialogue with businesses and other relevant stakeholder organizations, a group of experts was assembled (I had the opportunity to be one of them) which came up with recommendations for European leaders. Some of the statements are worth mentioning and commenting in connection with this book.

- Eco-efficient innovation (doing more or, I should say, doing enough with less) reconciles the apparently conflicting goals of more economic growth and employment and less pressure on the environment by finding new solutions other than the traditional compromises between the two. For Europe eco-efficient innovation as a brand is a tremendous opportunity to define its competitive edge in the world.
- Taking profitability as a main driver, barriers to introducing eco-innovation into the market should be tackled as the move into the market for eco-innovations is not spontaneous. Several barriers to introducing eco-innovation into the market remain, linked particularly to limited reliability, risk and benefits evaluations in relation to mainstream products and services, difficulties securing venture capital and credit for introducing them into the market, uncertainty about the consistency of mid- to long-term government policies and the failure of the market to afford the environment and resources the value they deserve.
- Removing barriers with market-oriented measures will encourage business and improve European competitiveness. If market failures and related barriers are properly addressed, business will seize the opportunity and Europe's position in the world market will improve. Eco-innovations are a window of opportunity for Europe, but urgent action must be taken as our competitors are not unoccupied either.

In order to improve the market prospects of eco-innovations, five courses of action were advocated and they are more pertinent than ever before as we need to rethink the market economy. We need medium- and long-term approaches and scenarios to ensure predictability for businesses, we must foster knowledge and ability, create and lead public markets as a launching customer, offer appropriate incentives to end users and, of course, encourage useful customer information.

A reshuffling of the market was considered and has become a key challenge since we have seen that voluntary action alone cannot produced the desired results in terms of sustainable growth and improved competitiveness. Stragglers and short-term interests cannot define the markets. Shaping a sustainable and competitive market framework is ultimately a political responsibility while leaving room for bottom-up initiatives which encourage a learning process.

The conclusions of these recommendations which are very encouraging in relation to the aims and content of this book are clear: eco-innovation is an economic driver, enhancing competitiveness, and a key factor in Europe to achieving sustainable development which requires perspective, a common will and common action, including measures to improve the demand side of the market and measures to stimulate demand market signals which will also encourage more investment in the supply side of the innovation market.

More recently, in February 2008 the EEB (European Environment Bureau) and the SSNC (Swedish Society for Nature Conservation) issued a report exploring the possibilities of an EU approach to 'ecodesign'. Once again, it called for the establishment of a proper name, including legal moves to ensure that ecodesign becomes the leading factor in designing the product-services packages of the future.

This book could not come at a better time or with a better purpose and content as we are, and will be, struggling to find a change of development model at every level in which sustainability must be the primary reference and sustainable businesses the key agents – the real makers of a real economy, with eco-innovation as the main driver.

This book demonstrates that there are tools available to enable companies to deliver eco-innovative product-services packages that satisfy the needs and demands of society in a more effective and efficient way. It also makes a clear call for establishing the appropriate institutional and legal framework for the market to work towards sustainability and to reward those who are more sustainable.

I would like to express my gratitude and offer my congratulations to the three authors for their stimulating and timely work.

Domingo Jiménez Beltrán
Former Executive Director of the European Environment Agency
26 October 2008

CHAPTER 1

Introduction

1.1 SUSTAINABILITY VERSUS COMPETITIVENESS?

The concept of sustainable development and the general understanding that the environment and the economy are interdependent have aroused increasing interest in recent years amongst political powers and society. The debate about this issue began in the early 1970s, following the publication of D.H. Meadows' book *Limits to Growth*, a critique of which was subsequently written by H.S.D. Cole. The discussion – developed and enlarged upon by many other authors in that decade – centered upon whether ongoing economic growth would inevitably lead to environmental degradation and the collapse of society on a global scale. It was partially concluded – though the debate still remains open – that economic development could be sustained on an unlimited basis provided that it was adapted to take into account that, at the end of the day, it depends on the environment and that cleaner ways of consumption and production would be adopted.

The concept of sustainable development as such was indelibly stamped on the international agenda with the publication in 1987 of the *Brundtland Report*.[1] This document accepts that the Earth's resources are, in principle, sufficient to meet humanity's long-term needs; the key issues to be debated being the unequal territorial distribution of the natural support capacities and the analysis of the ineffective and irrational use of such resources.

Although different international institutions and countless state governments have since devoted great attention to analyzing and developing 'sustainable policies', it must be said that economists have not yet reached a clear consensus on how sustainability-related ideas should be formulated. The outcome is that dozens of definitions of sustainability concepts have been published.[2] The diversity of these definitions and the conflicts between them are a clear indication that sustainability is a complex concept that everyone is willing to support but that no one has managed to define in a consistent manner. However, most of said definitions are underpinned by a generally accepted idea: sustainable development meets the needs of the present without compromising the ability of future generations to meet their own needs. In short, it suggests a trade-off between present-day well-being and the future well-being of members of society.

Parallel to the aforementioned debate, over the last decade there has been considerable discussion about the relationship between businesses and the natural environment.[3] There is no doubt that the way companies organize their manufacturing processes and the characteristics of the products and services they launch have a critical impact on our environmental surroundings. It is also broadly accepted that businesses can cause environmental problems and that they are called on to play a decisive role in their solutions. Integrating the demands of sustainability in a business, however, is a challenge for management, since it implies fundamental changes in some of the ways the company is run.[4] These changes will depend on companies' assessment of their potential benefits and risks. Moreover, unclear effects of environmentally-driven investments on the financial future of the company bring great uncertainty for decision-makers at board level.[5] The difficulties experienced by firms when moving towards corporate sustainability raise the question of how environmental and social management can be better integrated with economic business goals.[6]

The relationship between environmental sustainability, economic performance and competitiveness has been debated strongly for many years and still remains unclear. The many available studies, prepared from a theoretical as well as an empirical perspective, have yet to reach a definite consensus thus far. This literature gives us two main views of the link between environmental and economic performance, which give rise to rather different perspectives on this relationship. They are:

1. The 'traditionalist', or neoclassical, view of a trade-off between environmental performance and competitiveness.[7] According to this view, the purpose of environmental regulation is to maximize social welfare, making polluting firms responsible for the costs of the negative externality they produce, thereby correcting the market failure. As a consequence, environmental policies may have an adverse impact on competitiveness, insofar as this regulation imposes additional costs to firms. This burden may be of particular concern in industries with substantial environmental impact, where the share of environmental costs in total production costs is considerably higher than for the manufacturing sector on average.[8] A defensive business strategy and the adoption of end-of-pipe technologies may be expected.[9]

2. The 'revisionist' view adopts a more dynamic perspective of the relationship between sustainability and competitiveness, and assigns a central role to technological change and innovation. Better environmental performance can lead to lower production costs and enhance competitiveness through efficiency, productivity and new market opportunities.[10] According to the so-called 'Porter Hypothesis',[11] stringent environmental regulation could force polluting firms to seek innovations to reduce the cost of compliance and production, improving the firm's competitiveness and leading to a positive relationship between environmental and economic performance. Additionally, companies can obtain 'first mover advantages' by marketing the innovation itself and through the creation of new markets or market segments.[12] Hence properly designed environmental policies may help firms discover their inefficiencies and sources of comparative advantage, promoting innovation and creative thinking.[13]

Setting aside these theoretical discussions, and in more practical terms, it is clear that technological development and institutional considerations play an important role in the transition of the economic system towards sustainability.[14] In other words, technological change is probably a necessary, albeit insufficient, condition for achieving sustainability. Institutional changes, including changes in routines, social norms, formal regulations, etc., are needed not only to induce the required technological changes, but also to encourage behavioural changes at all levels of society in more sustainable directions.

Today's major environmental problems, such as climate change, the destruction of the ozone layer, loss of biodiversity, the degeneration and erosion of soil and water pollution are characterized by their delocalization, considerable uncertainty, irreversibility and extreme complexity in terms of consequences and the likelihood that they will occur. The increasingly wide spectrum of environmental issues makes it necessary to adopt a preventive approach to the link between manufacturing activities and said environmental quality. Additional factors in this equation include uncertain scales and duration, which may lead to irreversible damage, and growing social preferences for environmental quality. The nature and scale of present-day environmental problems call for innovation as a solution. In short, it is clear that in order to improve the quality of the environment without limiting economic activity, concerted efforts must be made to encourage **eco-innovations**.

1.2   TOWARDS SUSTAINABILITY AND COMPETITIVENESS THROUGH ECO-INNOVATION

The aforementioned urgency for change has led to increasing application of the term 'innovation' in environmental management and policy. Despite the promise of eco-innovations, the term is also used in diverse contexts with different underlying connotations that may eventually diminish its practical value.

In this book we understand innovation to be a systemic technological and social change process which consists of the invention of an idea for change and its application in practice. Expanding on this definition of innovation, we define eco-innovation as referring to an innovation that improves environmental performance. Basically, innovation refers to the change in the way something is done. Hence, for the purposes of characterizing innovation – including eco-innovation–, we consider addressing change as a useful starting point.

Fundamentally, just like any innovation, different dimensions of change in the case of eco-innovations can be identified which together explain factors of success or failure.

Eco-innovation is most commonly related to technological change in production processes and products. This has been addressed in many engineering oriented studies and books. Furthermore, eco-innovation can be considered a change in the behaviour of individual users or organizations, which has been addressed in both management and policy related literature. Eco-innovation has also been studied as a strategic perspective to renew the business. In practice, these dimensions are often intertwined, which is why we attempt to address them together – an approach that has not been sufficiently considered before.

Therefore, in this book we shall develop a conceptual framework to characterize different kinds of eco-innovations and arrive at the respective implications for their management and governance. We shall identify and describe different dimensions for studying innovation processes which address environmental issues – namely the design, user, product/service and governance perspectives.

When these dimensions are addressed together, they form a comprehensive but not exhaustive framework for the analysis of eco-innovation. Ultimately, the success of eco-innovations in providing new business opportunities and contributing to a transformation towards a sustainable society depends on the interplay of these different dimensions and the engagement of related key stakeholders in the innovation process. Thus, we hope that the framework offered in this book may operate as a practical tool for the management and governance of eco-innovations.

1.3   HOW TO READ THIS BOOK

We have written this book with different kinds of readers in mind. Given the wide array of contexts and uses of the term 'eco-innovation', we recommend taking a look at Chapter 2 before moving on to other chapters, as it describes our own approach to eco-innovation. We develop a general framework termed 'Dashboard of Eco-innovation' addressing design, user, product-service and governance dimensions of eco-innovation. The dashboard is referred to again in other chapters, especially in the case description of eco-innovations in Chapter 6.

Some readers may find it useful to continue on to Chapter 3, which addresses the barriers that eco-innovation faces both in its development and application. This perspective is relevant given the fact that many promising eco-innovation initiatives face techno-institutional barriers. Overcoming such barriers requires a profound understanding of the existing established practices in both policy and management which hinder the breakthroughs of eco-innovation. For readers interested in the role of policy in this challenge, Chapter 4 is a comprehensive review of diverse policy approaches and rationales that are available to promote eco-innovation. Hence, this chapter attempts to meet the challenge posed in Chapter 3 on barriers to eco-innovation.

In turn, those looking for means of promoting eco-innovation in business are likely to pay closer attention to Chapter 5, which looks at eco-innovation from the viewpoint of the corporate management. What can management do to take up the eco-innovation? The chapter answers this question by exploring the main dimensions of eco-innovation proposed in Chapter 2 and offers a comprehensive set of advanced tools for addressing eco-innovation in business.

Chapter 6 offers a series of cases on eco-innovation which help the reader reach conclusions on how and when eco-innovation can become successful. Through these case descriptions, the chapter also reflects the diversity of eco-innovations and respective different policy and management efforts. Hence, reading the cases is likely to lead the reader to refer back to earlier phases and make connections between the chapters. Indeed, eco-innovation is often a combination of various factors driven by both the private and public sector. Finally, Chapter 7 closes the book and identifies future challenges for us all.

CHAPTER 2

What is eco-innovation?

2.1 INTRODUCTION

The scale of environmental problems, coupled with social inequalities and competitiveness challenges within the global economy, have raised increasing awareness of the need to change and renew existing technological production and social behavioural patterns. At best, such awareness may produce innovative responses that gradually move society along a more sustainable path. Analytical tools for such transformation have been developed in the field of environmental management, namely within frameworks such as eco-efficiency,[1] industrial ecology[2] and design for environment[3] and more recently within the concept of eco-effectiveness,[4] natural capital and bio-mimicry.[5] Furthermore, the urgency for change has led to increasing application of the term 'innovation' in environmental management and policy. Despite the promise of eco-innovations, the term is also used in diverse contexts with different underlying connotations that may eventually diminish its practical value. Most commonly eco-innovation refers to new technologies that improve economic and environmental performance but also some definitions include organizational and social changes for improving competitiveness and sustainability and its social, economic and environmental pillars (see Box 2.1).

The definitions of eco-innovation seem to be quite general meaning that many kinds of innovation can be defined as eco-innovations. This raises the important issue of further classifying eco-innovations in order to better understand their specific characteristics.

Towards this, for instance, Andersen[6] has recently drafted a classification that entails key types of eco-innovations reflecting their different roles on a (greening) market: Add-on eco-innovations, Integrated eco-innovations, Alternative product eco-innovations, Macro-organizational eco-innovations, and General purpose eco-innovations. Still, although several classifications of eco-innovations have been proposed (Box 2.1), there exist only a few attempts to

Box 2.1   Definitions of eco-innovation and sustainable innovation

- *'Eco-innovation is any form of innovation aiming at significant and demonstrable progress towards the goal of sustainable development, through reducing impacts on the environment or achieving a more efficient and responsible use of natural resources, including energy.'*

  Competitiveness and Innovation Framework Programme (2007 to 2013), European Commission.

- *'Eco-innovation is the creation of novel and competitively priced goods, processes, systems, services, and procedures designed to satisfy human needs and provide a better quality of life for all, with a life-cycle minimal use of natural resources (materials including energy, and surface area) per unit output, and a minimal release of toxic substances.'*

  Europa INNOVA Thematic Workshop, Lead Markets and Innovation, 29–30th June 2006, Munich, Germany.

- *'Eco-innovation is the process of developing new products, processes or services which provide customer and business value but significantly decrease environmental impact.'*

  Fussler, C. and James, P. (1996) *Eco-innovation: A Breakthrough Discipline for Innovation and Sustainability* (Pitman Publishing).

- *'[Eco-innovation is] Innovation which is able to attract green rents on the market.'*

  Andersen, M.M. (2002) 'Organising Interfirm Learning – as the Market Begins to Turn Green', in de Bruijn, T.J.N.M. and Tukker A. (eds), *Partnership and Leadership – Building Alliances for a Sustainable Future* (Dordrecht: Kluwer Academic Publishers), 103–119.

- *' "Sustainability-driven" innovation is "the creation of new market space, products and services or processes driven by social, environmental or sustainability issues." '*

  Arthur D. Little (2005) 'How Leading Companies are Using Sustainability-Driven Innovation to Win Tomorrow's Customers'.

- *'Sustainable innovation as a process where sustainability considerations (environmental, social, financial) are integrated into company systems from idea generation through to research and development (R&D) and commercialisation. This applies to products, services and technologies, as well as new business and organisation models.'*

  Charter, M. and Clark, T. (2007) *Sustainable Innovation* (The Centre for Sustainable Design).

conceptualize eco-innovation and provide structured approaches for its management and governance.

In this chapter, we shall develop a conceptual framework to characterize different kinds of eco-innovations and arrive at the respective implications for their management and governance. We shall identify and describe different dimensions for studying innovation processes which address environmental issues – namely the design, user, product/service and governance perspectives. Last, at the end of the chapter, the different dimensions are gathered together in the *Dashboard of Eco-innovation* which will be used in the following chapters.

2.2   DEFINING ECO-INNOVATION

Any attempt to understand eco-innovation can benefit considerably from the emergence of a stream of innovation studies covering a wide range of different disciplines, such as institutional and evolutionary economics and technological change theories, industrial economics, systems analysis and operations research, sociology and political sciences, actor-network and communication theories, organizational change and knowledge management, among others. However, the effective use of different disciplines in the management of eco-innovation also calls for a coherent theoretical framework.

There is extensive evolutionary literature on technological change and related drivers and barriers.[7] Such approaches have been extended recently to cover institutional aspects too, such as legislation, norms, standards and routines.[8] This evolutionary viewpoint – addressing both technological and social change – offers a useful framework for micro-level management and macro-level economics and systemic innovation policy. The increasing application of this approach is largely based on the way it conceptualizes innovation: (1) it acknowledges innovation as an endogenous phenomenon within the economy and (2) it characterizes innovation as knowledge, whose creation and exploitation is highly dependent on available resources such as capabilities and time.

On the basis of these premises, we understand innovation to be a technological and/or social systemic change process which consists of the invention of an idea for change and its application in practice. Expanding on this definition of innovation, we define eco-innovation as referring to an innovation that improves environmental performance. While it is namely environmental impacts that define eco-innovation, economic and social impacts play a crucial role in its development and application and hence determine its diffusion path and contribution to competitiveness and overall sustainability. Indeed, there are many factors affecting eco-innovation and only one of those is environmental motivation (for example, others are the characteristics of the sector and the existence of technological opportunities). Furthermore, from the social point of view, it does not matter very much if the initial motivation for the uptake of eco-innovation is purely an environmental one. This approach avoids the discussion over whether the innovation was initiated or adopted as a result of environmental motivation.[9]

However, agreeing on the actual improvement of environmental performance is not always easy. Environmental performance comprises different dimensions such as resource use and the impacts on water and air. For instance, the use of catalytic converters in combustion engines reduces volatile organic compound emissions but increases CO_2 emissions due to lower fuel efficiency. In this case, the environmental improvement depends on how one values different kinds of environmental impacts and the use of resources. Therefore, just like environmental performance, eco-innovation too is a value-based concept open to discussion about its impacts on society. Furthermore, innovation once regarded as environmentally friendly can subsequently be considered even harmful if information about its negative impacts is received. For example, Chlorofluorocarbons (CFC, HCFC), which are compounds containing chlorine, fluorine and carbon were once widely used in industry, for example as refrigerants, propellants, and cleaning solvents. Only after decades of use was it discovered that they had an adverse effect on the ozone layer and climate change. Today, their use has been prohibited by the international Montreal Protocol. Similarly, the combustion engine car was initially thought to provide environmental benefits by replacing horse traffic and thus reducing dung-related problems in city centers. Only much later did the harmful impacts of emissions produced by combustion engines and other negative impacts of car traffic come to be understood.

Basically, innovation refers to the change in the way something is done. Hence, for the purposes of characterizing innovation – including eco-innovation –, we consider addressing change as a useful starting point. Here, we distinguish between radical and incremental changes which are brought about by eco-innovation or which are essentially required for its successful application and diffusion within society:[10]

- Incremental changes refer to gradual and continuous competence-enhancing modifications that preserve existing production systems and sustain the existing networks, creating added value in which innovations are rooted.
- Radical changes, in contrast, are competence-destroying, discontinuous changes that most often seek the replacement of existing components – or entire systems – and the creation of new networks, creating added value.

Distinguishing between the two can be complicated, however, due to the fact that what is radical at one level of analysis of the system may appear incremental at a higher level of analysis.[11] The shift from hard disk drives to flash memory, for example, can be radical for disk drive manufacturers, but incremental for the larger personal computer value network in which memory is an embedded component. Nevertheless, it has been suggested that only 10 per cent of all new innovations produce radical changes.[12]

2.3   DIMENSIONS OF ECO-INNOVATION

Evolutionary economists consider that innovation arises through a systemic process that refers to the interconnectedness of different actors and internal and external factors influencing the innovation process. Typically, innovation emerges through a complex interplay of supply and demand. Due to this systemic nature of innovation, it is worth exploring the multiple dimensions of the innovation process including both causes and effects.

Fundamentally, just like any innovation, in the case of eco-innovations different dimensions of change can also be identified which together explain factors of success or failure. Therefore, we shall look at different dimensions of innovations; first design issues, then user and product service perspectives and finally the role of governance.

2.3.1 Design dimensions of eco-innovation

The design stage of product and process development, recognized as a key for determining costs and profitability, is also an unparalleled window of opportunity to address environmental objectives. During this early stage, key materials, process, and energy source decisions largely determine the environmental impacts of a product for its entire life-cycle. Integration of environmental factors into design is an emerging trend known as design-for-the-environment (DfE), eco-design, or life-cycle design.[13] While pollution prevention, cleaner production and eco-efficiency[14] have provided DfE with approaches on minimizing negative environmental impacts, eco-effective management[15] has been conceptualized to offer an alternative perspective which, in contrast, encompasses maximizing positive impacts on the environment.

Indeed, in view of the environmental perspective, it is possible to distinguish two different design perspectives on innovations:

- The first perspective is to consider human actions incompatible with the natural environment, referring to negative impacts of human-made systems such as agricultural and industrial production and transport systems. Hence, environmental management should focus on minimizing such impacts on the environment.
- The second perspective is to consider incompatible human actions as 'design failures' and to focus on re-designing human-made systems towards positive impacts on the environment and society, for example through the remediation of polluted land and water systems or the reforestation of areas suffering desertification.

With these two perspectives of negative and positive impacts on the environment (or more specifically on the eco-system comprizing both the natural environment and human-made systems and activities), we can construct a design framework for eco-innovation. Incremental vs. radical change is located on the horizontal axis and the negative vs. positive impact on the vertical axis. The resulting framework suggests that re-design for positive impact combined with radical change lead to, at best, ecological, social and economic sustainability. More specifically, within this framework, three different design approaches can be defined to identify the role and impacts of the eco-innovation (see Figure 2.1), including:

- Component addition
- Sub-system change
- System change.

Component addition (development of additional components to improve environmental quality, for example 'end-of-pipe' technologies): Component level changes aim to minimize and repair **negative**

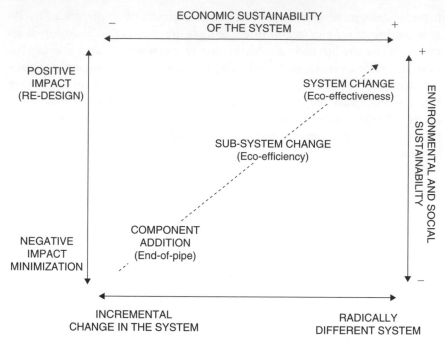

Figure 2.1   Design framework for eco-innovation in view of radical and incremental change and negative and positive impacts on the environment. The highest sustainability and competitiveness benefits are likely to occur in the top right-hand corner of the figure

Source: Authors' own figure.

impacts without necessarily changing the process and system that produces the problem. If the innovation is an additional component to the system, commonly referred to as 'end-of-pipe' technologies, it is likely to produce extra costs to the process. End-of-pipe technologies are used to curb the environmental impacts of existing industrial and transport systems, such as air emission filters and plant effluent treatment. Since the industrial revolution, the implementation of these technologies has produced major improvements in local air quality and water purification, particularly in industrialized countries and similar opportunities exist in many developing countries. However, if these technologies do not change the fundamental process, they will only solve part of the problem. For example (see Box 2.2), catalytic converters reduce the toxicity of emissions (nitrogen oxides, monoxide, hydrocarbons) from an internal combustion engine, but increase fuel consumption and CO_2 emissions, the major factor affecting climate change. The catalytic converter is an add-on solution adopted instead of a cleaner and more efficient combustion engine offering fuel economy benefits as well as low-emissions. When existing production systems cannot be changed quickly enough, the component addition type of eco-innovation can be a valuable tool for dealing with the problem. For example, as discussed in Chapter 6 of this book, carbon capture and storage is an approach to mitigating global warming by capturing CO_2 from large point sources such as fossil fuel power plants and storing it instead of releasing it into the atmosphere. It may prove to be a powerful mechanism for curbing fossil fuel-based carbon emissions and for combating climate change. In other words, these type of technologies may allow us to 'gain time' in order to wait until the existing dirty technologies embedded in large and expensive infrastructures have exhausted their useful lives and it is economically attractive to replace them with cleaner alternatives.

Sub-system change (for example, eco-efficient solutions and the optimization of sub-systems): The aim is to improve environmental performance through sub-system changes leading to increased efficiency of human-made systems such as power plants or cars. The goal is to reduce **negative impacts** by creating more goods and services while using fewer resources and creating less waste and pollution. This approach is crystallized in the term eco-efficiency, which was coined by the World Business Council for Sustainable Development (WBCSD) in its 1992 publication *Changing Course*.[16] This concept describes a vision of the production of economically-valuable goods and services while reducing the ecological impacts of production. In other words, eco-efficiency means producing more with less (fewer raw materials, less energy, fewer toxic substances, etc.). The concept of eco-efficiency provides practical action-oriented guidance on how to combine environmental issues in business. Eco-efficient markets are rapidly growing and thousands of companies can attest to the major benefits of its application. Eco-efficiency aims to make the old, destructive production system less so. But its goals, however admirable, are insufficient due to the limitations related to the concept. Reduction, re-use and recycling curb rates of pollution and depletion but do not stop these processes. For example (see Box 2.2), improvements in combustion engine efficiency have led to major improvements in the fuel consumption of vehicles. However, at the same time, the number of vehicles and total fuel consumption have continued to increase, along with their harmful environmental impacts. This problem has been defined as the 'dilemma of the N-curve';[17] increases in environmental efficiency are combined with efficiency gains with the reduced cost of driving leading finally to more driving. Hence, eco-efficiency improvements may not lead to sustainability since they tend to be easily erased by subsequent growth processes, provoking a rebound effect in the economy. This dilemma may affect both the component addition and the sub-system change approaches, more than offsetting the environmental contribution of these design changes. Thus, while eco-efficient solutions may be competitive in the short-term, they are likely to maintain existing unsustainable production and behavioural patterns, which are detrimental in the long-term to both the economy and the environment.

System change   (re-design of systems, for example towards eco-effective solutions): Changes in the system and its components and sub-systems are designed with a view to both their **negative and positive impacts** on the ecosystem. This approach builds on the analogy between natural and socio-technical systems elaborated in industrial ecology;[18] how industrial systems should incorporate principles exhibited within natural ecosystems and shift from linear (open loop) systems – in which resource and capital investments move through the system to become waste – to closed loop systems where wastes become inputs for new processes.

   The first two perspectives discussed above (component addition and sub-system change) consider human actions incompatible with the natural environment, referring to the negative impacts of human-made systems. This third perspective, in turn, focuses on re-designing human-made systems towards biocompatibility. The designed change contributes to the re-design of the whole system towards greater biocompatibility and added value for the provided service, product or process. Biocompatibility refers to the quality of human-made systems, for example materials not having toxic or otherwise harmful effects on biological systems. For example, materials such as lead and mercury are harmful to and hence incompatible with organisms.

   The idea of taking into consideration the positive impacts of human activities as a design criteria has been particularly developed in connection with the concept of eco-effectiveness that addresses such system-level aspects.[19] *Eco-effectiveness* seeks to design industrial systems that copy nature and its healthy abundance. An eco-effective solution maximizes biocompatibility and product or service usefulness together. Here, the central design principle is *waste equals food*. Within this concept, the systemic approach to environmental design leads to two alternative design perspectives:[20] 1) 'closed cycles', referring to the design of the uptake of products back to industrial production processes at the end of their useful life to produce equally or more valuable new products and 2) 'open cycles', referring to the design of products that are biodegradable and become nutrients to new cycles within the ecosystem. Further on the automobile example, both perspectives are represented in Ford's 'Model U', a car running on renewable energy and designed to be disassembled, and returned to the soil or to industry (see Box 2.2).

Eco-innovation is most often related to the design dimension which largely defines what kinds of impacts the innovation has on the environment. In this discussion, eco-innovation is typically linked to concepts of end-of-pipe technologies and eco-efficiency which provide practical action-oriented guidance on how to combine environmental issues in business and to curb rates of contamination and depletion – but not to stop these processes. Eco-effectiveness brings in a new perspective which tackles designing a product which may return to industry and whose materials are used to make equally or more valuable new products. To sum up, the design of eco-innovation consists of three different dimensions: component additions, sub-system changes and system changes. The characteristics and examples are provided in Table 2.1 and Box 2.2.

Table 2.1   Three design dimensions of eco-innovation and their characteristics

Dimensions of eco-design	Characteristics	Examples
Component addition	Development of additional components to reduce negative impacts on the environment, for example end-of-pipe technologies.	Chimneys. Plant chemical waste treatment. Carbon sequestration and storage in connection with fossil fuel-based power plants.
Sub-system change	Contributes to the environmental performance improvement of the sub-system to reduce negative impacts on the environment, for example eco-efficient solutions and the optimization of sub-systems.	Efficiency improvements in energy, water and raw material use in manufacturing. Building insulation. Washing machines with low water consumption. Energy-efficient home appliances.
System change	(Re-)design of the system in view of its impacts on the eco-system, taking into account the positive and negative impacts on the environment, for example with eco-effective solutions.	Closed industrial production cycles for example in the textile industry. Hydrogen-based renewable energy systems.

Box 2.2   Example: design framework for the automobile eco-innovation

Around 70 million automobiles are produced yearly and there are around 210 million automobiles running only in Europe. The production, usage and dismantling of the automobile have relevant impacts on the environment and competitiveness.

Component addition

Catalytic converters reduce the toxicity of emissions (nitrogen oxides, monoxide, hydrocarbons) from an internal combustion engine, but increase fuel consumption and CO_2 emissions, the major factor producing climate change. Catalytic converter is an add-on solution adopted instead of a cleaner and more efficient combustion engine offering fuel economy benefits besides low-emission.

Sub-system change

Improvements in the combustion engine efficiency have created major improvements in the fuel consumption of the vehicles during the recent decades. However, at the same time, the number of vehicles and the total fuel consumption have continued to increase together with their harmful environmental impacts.

System change

Ford Motor Company's 'Model U' (following Ford's famous 'Model T') provides all the convenience and functionality of a normal car, but has designed out many of the environmentally damaging aspects. Its components are made and assembled so that they can be separated when the car is disassembled, and returned to the soil or to industry; polymers and metals recovered and recycled at the same level of quality or better, for reuse in generation after generation of vehicles; engines running on energy that's derived from the sun, and producing no pollution. Clearly its commercial success would go a long way to eliminating many of the environmental issues surrounding the car industry.

2.3.2 User dimensions of eco-innovation

In order to develop eco-innovations, companies should also have the competence to involve users so as to benefit from their creativeness and to ensure that they will accept and take up new products and services. Users play a key role not only in applying innovations but also in identifying, making improvements and developing new innovations. It has been demonstrated that many users – both individuals and firms – develop new products to serve their own needs. Some of these are subsequently adopted by manufacturers and sold as commercial products. Thus, user innovation can greatly influence the rate and direction of innovation in some industries and service providers,[21] towards environmentally benign practices. So it may be crucial for companies to know which users are capable of contributing in the different phases of the innovation process and how to interact with them.

User development:

Von Hippel[22] defines users as firms or individual consumers that expect to benefit from using a product or a service. In contrast, he differentiates manufacturers who expect to benefit from selling a product or a service. A firm or an individual can have different relationships to different products or innovations. Von Hippel uses the example of Boeing as follows:

> The Boeing is a manufacturer of airplanes, but it is also a user of machine tools. If we were examining innovations developed by Boeing for the airplanes it sells, we would consider Boeing a manufacturer-innovator in those cases. But if we were considering innovations in metal-forming machinery developed by Boeing for in-house use in building airplanes, we would categorize those as user-developed innovations and would categorize Boeing as a user-innovator in those cases.

Furthermore, a review of empirical studies reveals that some users are very active in the innovation process by taking on the roles of inventors and (co)-developers.[23] This phenomenon has been apparent in areas such as scientific instruments,[24] CAD software[25] and sporting equipment.[26] Users have also played an important part in developing eco-innovations – in particular, car sharing to reduce urban traffic has led to new businesses that encourage efficient use of car fleets. The spread of environmental management systems and, more generally, environmental awareness among companies has led to the search for eco-innovative solutions too. For example, Wal-Mart, the largest grocery retailer in the US, has opened three stores as experimental laboratories. These stores were constructed using recycled building materials and energy-saving lighting methods. Features include a 100 per cent integrated water-source heating, cooling and refrigeration system, motion-sensing LED lights and an advanced daylight harvesting system. The application of these features means consuming 20 per cent less energy than regular stores. New partnerships have produced a truck designed with forward-thinking aerodynamics, transmission, tyres, a high-efficiency auxiliary power unit and emissions controls in order to make the fleet 50 per cent more energy efficient by 2015.

As stated above, studies have shown that many users engage in developing or modifying products. However, when considering the radical nature of user-driven innovations, the aforementioned studies reveal that the new products have a rather low to medium degree of innovativeness. This observation might be explained by the specific barriers to users in the context of radical innovations. Cognitive limitations may prevent users from delivering valuable inputs. In the idea-generation phase, users can be 'functionally fixed' to their current use context and therefore unable to develop radically new ideas. It may also be difficult for users to evaluate concepts and prototypes of radical innovations as no reference products exist. Nor might users be able to provide valuable inputs due to the high technological complexities involved. On the other hand, users are not always willing to contribute to radical innovation projects. This lack of motivation can stem from high anticipated switching costs and from the fear that existing knowledge will become obsolete.

In order to systematically involve users in the innovation process, firms need a special competence to identify which users are capable of providing valuable inputs in innovation projects and to engage them in innovation activities.[27] The lead user methodology[28] seeks to identify and involve progressive users in the idea generation and development phase. Lead users differ from ordinary users in two respects. First, lead users encounter needs months or years before the bulk of the marketplace. Second, lead users derive significant benefits from obtaining a solution to those needs and, therefore, are highly motivated to engage in the new product development process.[29]

Table 2.2 Dimensions of user innovation

Dimensions of user innovation	Characteristics	Examples
Development	Innovation is initiated and/or developed by the users.	Retailers, for example Wal-Mart, energy efficient building and transport solutions. Car-sharing networks.
Acceptance	Changes in user behaviour, practices and processes are crucial to the dissemination of the innovation.	Sorting household waste as part of waste recycling.

User Acceptance: User behaviour plays a crucial role in the application of eco-innovations and their resulting impacts on society. The pace and scale of the adoption of an innovation ultimately makes the difference between its being successful or not. Already in the 1970s, Midgely[30] addressed the different types of user behaviour in the uptake of innovations. According to his study, only 2.5 per cent of users could be classed as innovators. Taking up new innovations is closely related to the relationship between the innovation and the values and routines in the society that it is addressing in its adoption process. Hence, acceptance of the eco-innovation and the changes required in user behaviour can be considered key dimensions for characterizing the eco-innovation.

To sum up, user dimensions of eco-innovation comprise development and acceptance. Characteristics and examples are provided in Table 2.2.

2.3.3 Product service dimensions in eco-innovation

The generation of eco-innovation largely depends on the benefits received by the innovator to improve their competitiveness and their aspirations regarding improvements in sustainability performance. The way companies create added value (for example the business logic) with their products, processes and services can play a crucial role in the innovation process and its impacts on the environment.[31] Successful innovation must provide higher value or reduce costs and, ultimately, either increase revenues from existing customers or attract new customers. In the context of probing the market viability of sustainable services, Halme et al[32] identify four key dimensions, comprising:

1. added value for customers or users
2. competitive advantage over other alternatives
3. required capabilities and resources of the providers, and
4. financing and the formation of income flow.

To be radical, product service (or business model) innovation requires a redefinition of the product service concept and how it is provided to the customer.[33] Mont[34] and Williams[35] propose the application of a 'product service system' for developing sustainable business models. It refers to 'a system of products, services, supporting networks and infrastructure that is designed to be: competitive, satisfy customer needs and have a lower environmental impact than traditional business models.' The approach focuses on the delivery of a 'function' to the customer that might, in practice, mean the provision of combinations of products and services that are capable of 'jointly fulfilling users needs'.[36]

Product service eco-innovation calls for particular consideration of overall business strategy and logic, including the convergence of supply chains. In doing so, the focus on management and operations shifts from short-sighted local optimization to the entire supply chain during the production, consumption, customer service and post-disposal disposition of products.[37] This stresses the relevance of a supply chain perspective in eco-innovation. In practice, the relations between different actors creating added value in products, processes and services can be characterized as value networks rather than value chains.[38] For the purposes of the overarching framework for eco-innovation, we consider two product service dimensions crucial: first, the change in product service deliverable and second the change in the value network processes (see Table 2.3).

2.3.4 Governance dimension of eco-innovation

Eco-innovations, particularly when they are radical and require techno-institutional system-level changes,[39] are difficult to achieve because the prevailing system may act as a barrier to the creation of a new system and the diffusion of innovation.[40] Such prevailing conditions have been documented in the emergence of numerous technologies, including the automobile, electricity and the personal computer. If the system has become socially and economically pervasive, or if

Table 2.3 Product service dimensions of eco-innovation

Product service dimensions of eco-innovation	Characteristics	Examples
Change in product service deliverable	Changes in the product service delivered and changes in the perception of the customer relation.	Interface Inc. transformed its business from selling carpets to offering a service package including renting carpets and their maintenance to provide office comfort.
Change in value networks and processes	Changes in the value-networks (value-chain and other relations) and processes which enable the delivery of the product service.	Certified forest management that commits the whole value chain to implement sustainable practices.

there are other justifications for its maintenance, such as national security, government may intervene and encourage system expansion through a variety of mechanisms including subsidies, incentives or outright ownership.[41] Ultimately, they also dramatically intensify the barriers to eco-innovation. Overcoming such lock-in conditions may require major governance innovation both in the private and public sectors.

Environmental governance innovation refers to all new and applied institutional and organizational solutions for resolving conflicts over environmental resources. Such solutions can deal with one or combined functions of environmental governance, including: exclusion of unauthorized users; regulation of authorized resource use and the distribution of the respective benefits (market-based instruments); provisioning and the recovery of costs; monitoring; enforcement; conflict resolution; and collective choice.[42] From the view point of a company, the governance dimension challenges the management to renew its relationships with other stakeholders, in particular with the government. Hence, managers are invited to explore the wider role of business in society. Corporate governance and management systems can be both drivers and barriers to eco-innovate.

Governance institutions can be considered to have at least three functional tiers: 1) operational, 2) collective choice and 3) constitutional.[43] Multi-level governance solutions may emerge because an upper level of governance is established to coordinate lower-level

Table 2.4   Governance dimension of eco-innovation

Governance dimension	Characteristics	Examples
Governance	Environmental governance innovation refers to all new and applied institutional and organizational solutions for resolving conflicts over environmental resources both in the public and private sectors.	European Technology Platforms (industry-led stakeholder platform to set and implement European research and development agendas). Environmental management systems.

solutions, or because lower levels of governance are established to implement higher-level strategies.[44] Radical innovations in governance have emerged, in particular, where industrial federations and overarching institutions have been created through bottom-up processes to coordinate the functioning of governance solutions.[45] The opposite – top-down processes – in turn, create many formal multi-level governance solutions. Such bottom-up and top-down processes can also come together, as is the case of the global regime to mitigate climate change and its national and regional implementation efforts. Characteristics and examples of governance dimension of eco-innovation are provided in Table 2.4.

2.4   DASHBOARD OF ECO-INNOVATION

Expanding on the above discussion, eco-innovation is often a combination of the dimensions of design, product/service business model, user and governance innovations. While the importance of the dimensions in eco-innovation processes varies, eco-innovation – by definition – should have a positive impact on the environmental performance of the system of which it forms part. Hence, the design dimension is decisive to determining the environmental impacts of the innovation and labelling it eco-innovation.

However, the actual innovation processes leading to design changes are also likely to emerge from other innovation dimensions. Therefore, the dimensions can be considered equally important in the management of eco-innovation. When the aforementioned dimensions – including three design dimensions, two user dimensions, two product/service dimensions and one governance dimension – are addressed together, they form a comprehensive but not exhaustive framework for the analysis of eco-innovation (see Table 2.5).

Table 2.5 Framework for characterizing eco-innovation

Dimensions of eco-innovation	Characteristics
Design dimension	
1 *Component addition*	Development of additional components to improve environmental quality, for example end-of-pipe technologies.
2 *Sub-system change*	Improvement of the sub-system to reduce negative impacts on the environment, for example eco-efficient solutions and the optimization of sub-systems.
3 *System change*	Re-design of systems to be compatible with ecosystems, for example towards eco-effective solutions.
User dimension	
4 *Development*	Innovation is initiated and/or developed by the users.
5 *Acceptance*	The changes in user behaviour, practices and processes for the application of the innovation.
Product service dimension	
6 *Change in product service deliverable*	Changes in the product service delivered and changes in the perception of the customer relation.
7 *Change in value chain process and relations*	Changes in the value-chain process and relations that enables the delivery of the product service.
Governance dimension	
8 *Governance*	Environmental governance innovation refers to all new and applied institutional and organizational solutions for resolving conflicts over environmental resources both in the public and private sectors.

With the eight different dimensions of eco-innovation now identified, it is worth addressing their relative importance to better characterize the eco-innovation. For this purpose, we propose the assessment of the relative change occurred in each dimension of the innovation process, using the Likert scale with five levels of scores; 1 being an incremental change and 5 a radical one. In this context, zero constitutes no change. If the dimensions are presented together with the scores of change, it is possible to construct a dashboard to visualise the characteristics of each eco-innovation (Figure 2.2).

When an eco-innovation is assessed in all eight dimensions using the Likert scale, the given grades can be connected to produce an area characterizing the eco-innovation. Below, by way of an example, we take the vacuum waste collection system to illustrate the use of the framework in defining the dimensions of eco-innovation (see Box 2.3).

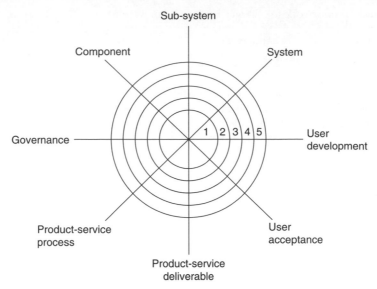

Figure 2.2   Eco-Innovation Dashboard for the assessment of the occurred change in eight dimensions of eco-innovation. The scores 1 to 5 refer to the Likert scale from incremental to radical change. The greater the area produced the more radical and systemic the eco-innovation can be characterised
Source: Authors' own figure.

Box 2.3   Example: the vacuum waste collection system (see also a complete case description in Chapter 6)

The Automated Vacuum Collection system, also called 'pneumatic refuse collection', transports waste at high speeds through underground tunnels to a collector where it is compacted, sealed in containers and then carted away. The system is based on pneumatics (from the Greek 'pneumatikos', coming from the wind), which means the use of pressurised gas to do the desired work. Pneumatic transfer systems are employed in many industries and recently in waste collection too, to move municipal and commercial solid waste. The waste is sucked to a centrally located waste transfer station.[46] To achieve this, an underground network of pipes is required, reaching distances of up to 1.5 km. Resources can be collected from a variety of drop-off points throughout a single building or even a residential development area, including restaurants and shopping complexes. Working on the principle of under-pressure suction, the system comprises several collection points linked by steel piping to a central collection station. Refuse is deposited, either indoors or outdoors, into an inlet and temporarily stored in a chute on top of a discharge valve. When full, the inlets are emptied one by one using a computer control system that switches on the fans – an air inlet valve is also opened to allow transport air to enter the system. The bags fall by gravity into the network of pipes and are sucked to the collection stations at a speed varying between 20–25 m/s, depending on the density of the waste. The refuse enters the station via a cyclone, whereby the transport air passes through dust and deodorant filters before it is released, and the refuse falls into a compactor that packs it into a sealed container.

Dimensions of eco-innovation	Grade (1–5)	Description
1 *Component addition*	4	New patented components enable the development of the vacuum system for sorting and collecting waste.
2 *Sub-system change*	5	Vacuum systems have been used in many fields. However, the vacuum waste collection system is a radically new approach in waste collection compared to conventional waste collection.
3 *System change*	3	Vacuum systems radically change the way the waste is sorted and collected, hence, they also provide partial solutions to sorting, reusing and recycling waste.
4 *User Development*	3	The development of the system has been done through active piloting in the municipalities to offer a radically different system of waste collection.
5 *User Acceptance*	3	Households and industrial users have to change the way they sort and dispose of waste.
6 *Change in product service deliverable*	3	Vacuum waste collection requires a different way of organizing the sorting and collection of waste, which improves the local environment in terms of the reduction of noise, odours and visual pollution.
7 *Change in product service process*	5	The vacuum system builds on radically different technologies, expertise and partners throughout the value chain compared to conventional waste collection.
8 *Governance change*	2	Requires some changes in the waste management practices of the client. Local governments often play a decisive role in demand articulation and permissions and financing the required capital investments.

When the dimensions of the eco-innovation are plotted on the eight axes, the framework can be visualised in the Eco-innovation Dashboard (Figure 2.2). Locating the grades of the extent of change in different dimensions helps characterize the eco-innovation. When the given grades are linked on the board, they produce an area that provides a quick overview of eco-innovation in view of the extent of change in eight dimensions:

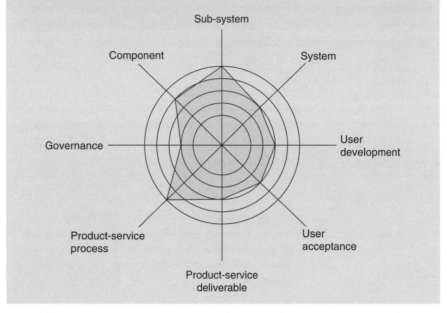

2.5   DISCUSSION

This chapter has defined eco-innovation as an innovation that improves environmental performance. Building on evolutionary economics, innovation is devised as a systemic change process that brings into the analysis different actors and factors influencing the success or failure of the innovation. Therefore, we argue that it is also crucial to the management of eco-innovation to understand the wider context in which the innovation occurs.

This chapter has sought to provide relevant starting points to analyze the role of eco-innovations not only from its design dimension but also regarding user participation, the development of new product and service concepts and governance innovation.

It is worth noting that the assessment of changes occurring in the eco-innovation process is subjective, not only because of incomplete information but also because of interpretations and the use of the graded scale of changes. Still, the characterization provides support for management and policy to understand the specific nature of each eco-innovation, set development priorities and engage stakeholders crucial to its success. Furthermore, this helps management to identify required internal competences. For instance the design dimension may place emphasis on science and engineering, user dimensions on marketing and communication, product/service dimensions on business management and strategy and governance dimension on policy expertise and corporate governance. The competences needed vary according to the different characteristics of the eco-innovation in question.

Ultimately, the success of eco-innovations in providing new business opportunities and contributing to a transformation towards a sustainable society depends on the interplay of these different dimensions and the engagement of related key stakeholders in the innovation process. Thus, we hope that the Dashboard of Eco-innovation may operate as a practical tool for the management and governance of eco-innovations.

CHAPTER 3

Barriers to eco-innovation

3.1 INTRODUCTION

Although many potentially significant eco-innovations exist, many of them leading to competitive gains and social and environmental benefits, they are underused, that is, they do not diffuse easily and quickly in the economy. Many factors (barriers and/or absence of drivers) contribute to this.

The key question is, then, why firms do not adopt eco-innovations developed by others or why do they not develop their own eco-innovations. There is no easy answer to this question because there is probably not one single factor at play, but rather several of them which are context-specific (that is, they depend on the country and the sector) and their impact is felt at different levels (barriers to specific environmental technologies and more general obstacles), negatively affecting virtually all types of eco-innovation practices. Some barriers are common to other general innovations, whereas others are specific to the environmental protection component which characterizes eco-innovations.

In general, eco-innovations encounter a double difficulty in appearing and diffusing in the market and society, that is, they are subject to a double market failure (double externality).[1] In addition to the negative externality of pollution, which leads to an under-provision of eco-innovations, that is, below the social optimum level, technological change in general has good public features, which also leads to a lower level of development and diffusion of technologies:

- The *technological change externality* is related to the fact that a firm developing or implementing a new technology (for example artifacts, software or management systems) generates benefits to others while incurring all the costs. The innovation process leads to spillover effects. If some firms can take advantage of the innovation results of others, then those companies will have the incentive to reduce their own innovation efforts. In other words, there is a dynamic market failure in the innovation process due to the public good nature of knowledge, whose production is expensive but whose reproduction is not.

- The *environmental externality* is related to the fact that, when negative environmental externalities have not been internalized, the investment rate in environmental solutions are likely to be lower than the social optimum level. The fact that eco-innovation practices lead to a reduction in environmental pressures which does not translate into a lower private cost compared to conventional practices is one of these general barriers. In other words, the social benefit of environmental innovations cannot easily be transformed into benefits for the pioneering entrepreneur.[2] Since these reductions are not valued by the market, which does not internalize those negative environmental externalities, eco-innovations have an additional difficulty in being developed and adopted.

In addition, there is a certain tendency to use old solutions (both technological and organizational solutions) out of habit, because users are familiar with them and often distrust the new ones, given their lack of experience with them. Furthermore, single barriers are usually a necessary, though not sufficient, condition for non-adoption. It is their systemic interplay which provides sufficient conditions for entrenchment. The literature has termed this the problem of techno-institutional 'lock-in'.

Innovations are applied in connection with existing systems. This means that there are different kinds of compatibility requirements for new applications in view of existing technologies and institutional structures. This favours the solutions that are already widely used in the markets. Particularly, technologies and their production, distribution and application may enjoy the different dimensions of increasing returns such as learning economies, network and co-ordination effects, economies of scale and adaptive expectations.[3] For example, investment decisions are often linked to earlier investments and experiences on the performance of technologies. Existing services and technologies are deeply embedded in wider social and technological systems. This creates economic, technological, social, cognitive, cultural and political barriers for innovations.

Indeed, our own research,[4] using a broad-based, co-evolutive view of the process of technological and institutional change, has revealed that clean technologies face complex obstacles caused by the presence of increasingly high uptake performance due to economies of scale, learning and network effects which arise from the integrated and systemic nature of the deployment of these technologies (see Box 3.1). The obstacles are related to one another and to past decisions.[5]

Box 3.1   The concept of 'technological lock-in'

Technological lock-in refers to macro level forces that create systematic barriers to the diffusion and adoption of efficient and sustainable technologies. The term arises from the recognition that achieving greater environmental quality without limiting productive activity requires efforts to promote innovation in clean technologies. Nevertheless, there is a growing consensus on the potential for environmental improvement that could be achieved through the diffusion of the clean technologies that already exist, in particular in terms of improved energy efficiency and the consequent reduction in the emissions associated with the use of fossil fuels. The question then becomes: What is holding back the diffusion of these existing technologies? The debate basically rests on the cost of transition to these new technologies. This is an issue which has been approached from two opposing perspectives: 1) aggregate economic models (a top-down approach); and 2) engineering studies (a bottom-up approach). According to various authors, both approaches rely on excessively simplistic assumptions about the dynamic of energy substitution and the process of technological change. A broader and evolutionary view of the process of technological change shows how an important barrier to the diffusion of clean technologies arises from the fact that the economic system can be locked-in to technology standards which are potentially environmentally inferior.

This lock-in is due to the existence of significant increasing returns to adoption of energy technologies, produced by economies of scale, learning and networks, arising out of the integrated and systemic nature of these technologies. Under these conditions, the same distribution of technologies and user preferences can lead to different structures in the breakdown of the user market, depending on how things start out. The system therefore has a multiplicity of equilibria which, when expressed in terms of market shares, can be interpreted as a succession of spontaneous or de facto standards. Spontaneous standards emerge as a result of internal market processes and not as the result of a coordinated action by its participants. Early superiority, however, is no guarantee of long-term suitability. Thus, in the presence of increasing returns, apparently inferior designs can become locked-in to the production system in a historically dependent process in which circumstantial events determine the winning alternative.

Source: Carrillo-Hermosilla, J. (Lead Author); Dontje J. (Topic Editor) (2008) 'Technological lock-in', in Cleveland C.J. (ed.) *Encyclopedia of Earth* (Washington, D.C.: Environmental Information Coalition, National Council for Science and the Environment) [First published in *the Encyclopedia of Earth*, 17 November 2006; Last revised 2 April 2008; Retrieved 6 November 2008]. http://www.eoearth .org/article/Technological_lock-in

In contrast to these general barriers which tend to affect all eco-innovations, other obstacles might be more specific to technologies, services or firms. For example, if expensive machinery has recently been adopted by one company, it is unlikely that this firm will implement a new cleaner process in the short-term.

From the perspective of the firm, which is a potential adopter of an eco-innovation, the barriers can be grouped into three categories.[6] Some of these barriers (or lack of drivers) are clearly related to the 'external environment' surrounding the firm, that is, the absence of pressures to eco-innovate by key social actors (including consumers, policy makers, NGOs, etc.). The 'institutional environment' including public policies, laws and organizations may not provide the necessary impetus for firms to engage in eco-innovation practices.

Sometimes, the external impetus exists, but the barriers are mostly related to different characteristics and aspects of the company, that is, there are conditions within the firm which hinder eco-innovation. For instance, firms may not have the necessary financial resources to invest in these practices or they may lack the technological competency to either absorb eco-innovations developed by others or to develop their own eco-innovation. They may also not attach much importance to environmental issues and, thus, not consider their development and adoption attractive.

Finally, another set of factors is largely related to the techno-economic characteristics of eco-innovations themselves. For example, these might be too expensive or are incompatible with the existing production process in the firm.

Of course, it is actually very difficult to single out any of these factors, because they do not operate in isolation and are often related to one another, whilst also interacting and/or reinforcing one another. For example, the technology to be adopted might be very expensive (techno-economic factor) but could be partly related to the lack of internalization of negative environmental externalities as a result of the absence of appropriate environmental policies. The absence of a proactive environmental strategy on the part of the firm (that is, the lack of priority given to environmental problems, an internal factor) is partly due to an institutional environment that does not consider environmental issues a key social priority. Therefore, this lack of institutional impetus translates into a low incentive to engage in eco-innovation by firms.

Additionally, some of the relevant barriers to eco-innovation may fall into several categories. For instance, the fact that many eco-innovations are more expensive than their conventional competitors is related to the lack of internalization of negative environmental externalities. Therefore, this could be considered a techno-economic barrier but it can also be viewed as a barrier related to the lack of environmental policies leading to such internalization.

The specific characteristics of the different types of eco-innovations lead to barriers arising at different levels – from the higher or systemic level – whereby different barriers are combined, to the lowest, more specific level, often represented as the barriers to incremental eco-innovations. Clearly, the more systemic the type of change required by eco-innovation, the greater the interrelation between different types of barriers.

Therefore, the singling out of specific barriers in the next sections is done for illustrative/descriptive purposes, in order to highlight the main forces at play, but their interactions should be taken into consideration when analyzing the obstacles to eco-innovation. The remainder of this chapter is dedicated to discussing these barriers in more detail, according to the three categories mentioned above and following the approach taken by Del Río.[7]

3.2   HOW CAN WE CLASSIFY THE BARRIERS TO (AND DRIVERS OF) ECO-INNOVATION?

Although at a systems level we can consider the existence of economic, technological and institutional barriers, this distinction is too general and, at the level of specific eco-innovations, we can distinguish the three main categories mentioned in the previous section (factors that are internal and external to the firm and technological features), following Del Río.[8] The many papers published on the subject also provide a discussion of all these barriers, although this discussion is usually ad-hoc, that is, not structured according to main groupings.[9]

However, this is not the only possible classification of barriers and other proposals have been made in this respect. For example, Kemp and Volpi[10] distinguish between endogenous and exogenous factors.[11] Montalvo[12] distinguishes between government policy, economics, markets, communities and social pressure, attitudes and social values, technological opportunities and technological capabilities and organizational capabilities. Ashford[13] states that there are three broad factors ('elements') which are deemed necessary and sufficient for technological change to occur: willingness to change, the opportunity/motivation to change, and the capacity to change. These factors affect one another but each is determined by more fundamental factors. Our classification is compatible with those proposals and encompasses all the factors (drivers and barriers) considered in the existing literature. It groups those factors into three categories (factors internal to the firm, factors external to the firm and characteristics of the eco-innovations).

Therefore, our starting point is that, when deciding to adopt an environmental technology, firms are influenced by several socio-economic and institutional actors and factors. The interaction of these 'external' forces with the capacities, competencies and characteristics of the firm and the main techno-economic features of the technologies to be adopted leads to the adoption (or not) of a specific environmental technology, in a process that is mediated by the benefits, costs and risks of development and adoption (see Figure 3.1).[14] These three sets of factors often result in a slow and rather incremental environmental technological transition, with eco-innovations competing with 'conventional' innovations.[15] The following sections provide a detailed discussion of each factor.

3.2.1 Internal factors affecting the development and adoption of eco-innovations

3.2.1.1 *Characteristics of the firm*

- *Financial situation.* Eco-innovations often involve significant disbursements by companies, which may not be paid back in the short-term. Therefore, those firms in a better financial position are more

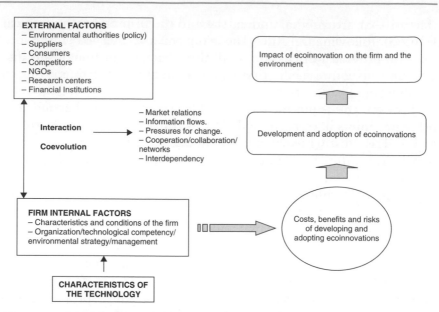

Figure 3.1 Interrelation and interaction between the actors and factors for the development and adoption of eco-innovations
Source: Adapted from Del Río, P. (2005) 'Analysing the factors influencing clean technology adoption: a study of the Spanish pulp and paper industry' *Business Strategy and the Environment*, 14, p. 24.

likely to engage in eco-innovation. Competing business priorities and, particularly, pressure to obtain short-term profits, might also reduce the incentives for eco-innovation (except in the case of win-win technologies). This pressure is especially strong for small enterprises.

- *Size of firms*. Small firms are usually organizations with a lower endowment of financial, human and technological resources than larger firms. Therefore, they may lack the internal expertise to develop eco-innovations or do not have the internal funds necessary for the purchase of innovations developed by others. Thus, they are less likely to engage in eco-innovation.[16] In addition, they may suffer from disadvantages of scale (due to the indivisibility or lumpiness of the innovation).[17] This means that a larger firm size is usually correlated with more radical clean technology adoption because to make good use of these technologies a minimum optimal size of the installation might be required.[18]

- *Position in the value chain*. The situation of the firm in the supply chain may influence its propensity to adopt an eco-innovation. This refers to the final or intermediate character of the company's products. For the same level of pressure from external forces (see pp. 40–6), firms which are at the end of the production process (e.g., those selling final demand products) are more likely to experience pressure from environmentally-responsible final consumers. Firms selling intermediate products could also experience pressure from purchasing firms, especially if these have followed a very proactive environmental strategy and try to reduce the environmental impacts of their products from cradle to grave (that is, throughout the whole production process).

- *Age of the firm.* The influence of this variable could be ambiguous. On the one hand, old firms tend to have accumulated more knowledge, technological and human capital (particularly tacit knowledge) and, thus, they could be considered more capable of developing eco-innovations in-house. In this sense, this variable is clearly related to the technological competency of the firm (see pp. 36–8). On the other hand, there is likely to be more technological and cultural inertia in older firms, which have used the same routines for years. This makes them less willing (and capable) to engage in the strategic, organizational and technological changes required by eco-innovation, especially regarding the most radical ones.

- *Multinational or local character of the firm.* Again, this variable may have contradictory impacts. On the one hand, firms belonging to multinational groups are likely to have more resources (financial, technical and human) to either develop or adopt eco-innovations.[19] On the other hand, they might feel constrained in their decision-making processes because they have to follow the instructions of the parent company.[20] This could either stimulate or restrict the adoption of eco-innovations. In extreme cases, some argue that 'ecodumping' could occur, that is, multinationals send the most polluting technologies to their subsidiaries in countries with lower environmental standards, although the empirical evidence for this is very limited.[21]

- *Export-oriented production.* Firms exporting a large share of their production to environmentally-conscious markets in other countries could be more pressed to develop or adopt eco-innovations.[22] This is so if consumers in those countries are more environmentally conscious (in case of final demand products), if the firm sells intermediate products to purchasing firms which have adopted a proactive environmental strategy leading to the reduction of environmental impacts all along the product life-cycle and/or if the environmental regulations of the country where the products will be sold are more severe than those of the country where the goods are produced and, thus, require some changes to be made.

- *Characteristics of the sector*. Sometimes it is not the characteristics of the firm itself, but certain features of its sector which affect the firms' propensity to eco-innovate, including the market structure, position in the supply chain and technological opportunities in the sector.[23] The position in the value chain has already been dealt with above, whereas the issue of technological opportunities will be tackled in section 5.4. With respect to market structure, Volpi and Kemp[24] observe that changes in market structure (entry) are likely to affect clean technology diffusion. However, the general literature on innovation is ambiguous with respect to which type of market structure leads to a higher probability of innovating. This ambiguity is replicated in the case of eco-innovation. On the one hand, firms in a monopolistic setting 'must fear less imitation from competitors and gain more from scale economies associated with innovations'.[25] On the other hand, 'large monopolistic firms have less incentives to innovate, whereas small firms in competitive markets are forced to 'be better' than their competitors by developing new products. As a result the effect of the firm's size on its innovation activities is undetermined from a theoretical perspective.'[26]

3.2.1.2 Technological competency (absorption capacity)

Eco-innovations require significant skills at the firm level, either to develop or adopt them.

Developing eco-innovations …   Eco-innovations are a special form of technological knowledge, one that leads to a reduction of the environmental impacts of the company while simultaneously enhancing its competitiveness. Therefore, in order to develop eco-innovations, firms need skilled human capital, which is a function of R&D investments. Horbach[27] empirically shows that the improvement of the technological capabilities ('knowledge capital') of firms by R&D or further education of the employees triggers environmental innovation. These capabilities comprise the physical and knowledge capital stock of a firm to develop new products and processes. In a study of the Canadian pulp and paper industry, Doonan et al[28] found out that environmental education of employees was a major determinant of environmental performance.

… adopting eco-innovations   In order to adopt eco-innovations, a trained workforce and expertise should also be present, in order to properly install and adapt the newly purchased equipment to the major techno-economic features of the company, but also in order to operate

the new equipment and to maintain it. It has been found that 'plant managers are often unwilling to invest in clean technologies because they do not have the in-house technical capacity, skilled technicians or engineers to operate clean technologies'.[29] As observed by Montalvo,[30] major factors inhibiting the adoption of new cleaner production processes include 'insufficient availability of expertise in clean production (eco-design), the current training and clean technology capacity building at the sector level and the insufficient understanding and experience in cleaner production project development and implementation.'

Previous investments in R&D by the firm are likely to have a positive impact on the adoption of eco-innovations, because this investment increases the knowledge of the firm, which is key to engaging in information flows to be aware of the existence of potential eco-innovations relevant for the firm and to be able to implement it within its pre-existing production process (absorptive capacity).

Engaging in collaboration and information flows, ¿cause or effect? A key aspect of the technological competency to develop and adopt eco-innovations and use technological opportunities offered by the market depends on the creation of relationships and the formation of strategic alliances with actors across the production chain (customers or suppliers) and on the use of collaboration networks with research institutions in order to outsource the acquisition of knowledge needed for the innovation process.[31]

Of course, relationships take place between actors in the supply chain with quite different power and, thus, the respective influence may be a driver of or a barrier to eco-innovation. As observed by Montalvo,[32] the capacity to engage with and influence suppliers of technology, materials and inputs has been reported as a strong determinant of innovation, especially in industrial sectors close to large retail chains.

Engaging in collaboration partnerships and information flows is thus crucial to eco-innovate, although this may be a chicken and egg situation, because a pre-existing technological capacity and competency makes such engagement more likely.

Box 3.2   Technological competency: what do the empirical studies say?

Some empirical studies have already shown the impact of lack of technological competency on the development and adoption of eco-innovations, focusing on clean technologies. For example, lack of awareness/understanding of cleaner production principles was found to be a barrier against the uptake of cleaner production practices in South African industry.[33] Visser et al[34] also established empirically that education and training of potential adopters was essential in this respect. The Environmental Technology Action Plan (ETAP) of the European Union illustrates this relevance with an example in the construction sector, where the diffusion of the most advanced energy-saving technologies is dependent on small local fitters and repair companies (ETAP 2004). Fresner et al[35] empirically established that the level of technical training, the experience and the age of the workers had an equally significant impact on the correct adoption of best available technologies (BATs) in Austria. Sartorius[36] found out that the availability of technical capacity in the firm was a key element in the decision to develop and adopt stationary fuel cells. In an analysis of the implementation of BATs in the Italian galvanic industry, Cagno and Trucco[37] found out that the technical and operational know-how of firms was one of the two critical elements for BAT implementation (the other being the profitability of those technologies).[38]

How can technological competency be improved? Technological competency can be enhanced, according to Ashford[39] by both: (1) increases in knowledge or information about cleaner opportunities, partly through formal Technology Options Analysis, and partly through chance or intentional transfer of knowledge from suppliers, customers, trade associations, unions, workers, and other firms as well as reading about environmental and safety issues (all leading to increased technological diffusion); and (2) improving the skill base of the firm through educating and training its operators, workers and managers, on both a formal and informal basis.

3.2.1.3 Environmental strategy and organizational factors of the company. Attitude of managers towards change, environmental protection and innovation

Eco-innovation often requires a corporate culture which is favourable to change in general and is particularly proactive regarding environmental protection and innovation. This is because eco-innovation is often a risky practice from an innovation perspective and because one of the attributes of eco-innovations is the environmental protection dimension, which must be highly valued internally by the firm in order to engage in this type of innovation, especially in the absence of stringent environmental policies encouraging the uptake of eco-innovations.

Ashford[40] observes that a company culture with a strong resistance to change would make engaging in eco-innovation unlikely. 'Changing the attitude is more idiosyncratic to a particular manager or alternatively a function of organizational structures and reward systems'.[41] There might be some inertia in managers: 'the syndrome "not in my term in office" describes the lack of enthusiasm of a particular manager to make changes whose benefit may accrue long after (s)he has retired or moved on, and which may require expenditures in the shortor medium term'.[42] Cultural change within the innovating organization is a factor encouraging greener innovations.

A necessary internal condition is the tendency to be environmentally proactive. In other words, a corporate management commitment to environmental issues would contribute towards the engagement in eco-innovation practices. A proactive environmental strategy has to be adopted, environmental goals have to be set up (including a written environmental policy) and an organizational structure with clear environmental responsibilities has to be implemented. There are several possible approaches of the firm with respect to environmental management:[43] including passive, reactive and proactive.[44] This is a challenge for the firm. When these preconditions are absent then environmental responsibilities are not defined and adoption of eco-innovations is not likely to be considered.[45] Similarly, Visser et al[46] also found that the company strategy and the vision of the CEO and the management team were decisive to engaging in eco-innovations.

In this context, a strong organizational inertia to keep doing things as they have traditionally been done in the past may exist and act as a powerful deterrent to eco-innovation. Indeed, in general, those innovations that preserve work practices and organizational structures will be the most likely to succeed.[47] Lack of suitable eco-innovation management models, particularly those applicable to emerging markets may be a powerful barrier.[48] Therefore, corporate strategy and organizational changes in this context are not an easy task and require a high degree of leadership by the firm's managers. Montalvo[49] observes that committed CEOs must have a high degree of self-efficacy and leadership, not only to sell the notion to shareholders but also to orchestrate behavioural change within the firm. In an empirical study of the Canadian pulp and paper industry, Doonan et al[50] found out that involvement of the firm's higher level management was one of the most relevant determinants of environmental performance.

One of the internal changes required is the adoption of environmental management systems (EMS), although, again, it might be a chicken and egg situation: the environmental orientation of the firms is reflected in the implementation level of EMS which, in turn, is one important determinant for firms' environmentally-related innovation activities. In the same vein, Wagner[51] interprets the existence of EMS certification as a signal of firm competencies (that is, environmental strategy related to competency). He considers ten dimensions of EMS implementation, including written environmental policy, procedure for identification and evaluation of legal requirements, initial environmental review, definition of measurable environmental goals, program to attain measurable environmental goals, clearly defined responsibilities, environmental training program, environmental goals are part of a continuous improvement process, separate environmental/health/safety report or environmental statement and audit system to check environmental program.

In addition to EMS, other relevant organizational-related factors have been identified in the literature: whether firms inform consumers about environmental effects of product and production processes, if market research on the potential of green products is carried out, if firms use ecolabelling or carry out product recycling, if firms have implemented life-cycle assessment and if firms carry out benchmarking activities.[52]

3.2.1.4 Other internal pressures: employees

Worker demands for a cleaner working environment may influence the adoption of eco-innovation practices which also lead to a reduction of pressures on the external environment. In turn, the senior staff may try to increase the morale of employees by demonstrating greater environmental awareness.[53]

3.2.2 External factors affecting the development and adoption of eco-innovations

Eco-innovations are developed and adopted by firms as a result of the interactions of actors. Firms are embedded in a social, institutional, economic and cultural context from which they receive stimuli and disincentives for change. These incentives can take the form of direct pressures to eco-innovate, but information flows, cooperation/collaboration/networks and market relations may also enhance the uptake of eco-innovation practices.[54] Collaboration networks facilitate the flow of information on eco-innovations, reducing the risks involved in adoption.

This context comprises actors and institutions as well as the relationships between them and with potential eco-innovation firms. More specifically, the process of eco-innovation involves the following socio-economic and institutional actors:

- *Public policy* has traditionally been signalled as the major driver and barrier for eco-innovation. This has often been related to environmental policy, albeit innovation policy (in the form of R&D support and subsidies for cleaner technologies) might also provide a significant stimulus. Eco-innovative behaviour is generally and usually related to the level of ambition of environmental policy.[55] Environmental policies can be highly diverse. They may prescribe a specific conduct in the form of a requirement to adopt a certain technology (technology standards), to keep the environment surrounding the production facility below certain pollution thresholds (environmental standards) or to keep emissions and discharge levels from the installation within certain limits (emissions standards). All these rules are often termed 'command-and-control' regulations. In contrast to these direct regulations, other instruments provide an economic incentive for firms to behave in a more environmentally sound manner. These 'market-based' or 'economic' incentives include taxes, emissions permits and subsidies. A third group of instruments include information and education measures (targeted at citizens in general, consumers and/or firms), VAs (whereby a sector agrees with the environmental authority to cut pollution by a certain percentage within a certain time frame, without sanctions in case of non-compliance, but with an (implicit or explicit) threat that a direct regulation will be imposed in this case), and environmental management systems (see Box 3.3).

It is important to take into account that, although environmental policy may lead to changes in energy costs, waste costs, landfill costs, etc., which in turn influence the attractiveness of a new technology, there may be other factors from the regulation environment also having an effect on those costs and sometimes working in opposite directions. For example, this could be the case of the process of the electricity market liberalization process, with unclear impacts on the uptake of renewable energy technologies.

Furthermore, sometimes it is not the existence of a particular regulation which is a major factor encouraging eco-innovations but rather

Box 3.3   Environmental management systems and eco-innovation

Environmental management systems (EMS), which can be regarded as an environmental policy instrument or an (organizational) eco-innovation in its own right, have already been mentioned in Chapter 2, and involve a set of internal practices which allow firms to be more aware and control the potential environmental impacts of their production activities. EMS allow the identification of cost-savings, positively affecting environmental innovations.[56] In addition, adopting an EMS could improve the environmental visibility of the firm which, in turn, could positively influence the adoption of eco-innovations.

However, an empirical debate remains open on the extent to which EMS influence the development and adoption of eco-innovations and on the types of eco-innovations that are more and less stimulated by these instruments.[57] Nevertheless, the established EMS may lead to excessive focus on incremental improvements rather than radically different eco-innovations. Könnölä and Unruh[58] describe the emergence of EMS lock-in as a path dependent evolution occurring within the context of the larger quality management paradigm. While EMS may produce improvements in environmental performance, EMS may also constrain organizational focus to the exploitation of present production systems, rather than exploring for superior innovations that are discontinuous. The authors even question the exuberant private and public sector support for EMS implementation and instead recommend an ambidextrous management approach which integrates foresight and broader stakeholder collaboration in the environmental management practice. EMS dominantly seeks to incrementally improve the environmental performance of current development path, ultimately extending the life of traditional industrial processes that emerged over 100 years ago. If resolving the complex global environmental problems requires new and discontinuous solutions, then it appears new tools beyond EMS will be required to really change course.

Another relatively recent controversy is the one concerning the incentive to eco-innovate provided by either economic or command-and-control instruments. Although the general wisdom has traditionally been that economic instruments provide a greater stimulus to eco-innovate, the jury is still out on which instrument is more dynamically efficient in different contexts and circumstances.[59]

the prospects of a stringent or ambitious environmental regulation.[60] As observed by Kivimaa,[61] innovations are often developed in anticipation of future policies or as side-effects of existing policies. Therefore, anticipation of a new regulation might be a key driver of eco-innovation.

In addition, the relevant regulation is not only the one applied in the country where the firm is located, but in other countries as well, especially for those firms whose production is export-oriented. For example, Visser et al[62] found that most of the eco-innovations they studied were indirectly triggered by (the expectation of) new regulations in frontrunner countries, which were regarded as indications of future market changes. Lanjouw and Moddy[63] also found out that innovation in a country responds to regulations in other countries.

- The *general situation of the economy* (income and welfare effects) is another potential influential variable in this context. A weak economic climate may be a barrier to the uptake of eco-innovations, because these are usually regarded as paying off in the medium to long run, while the costs of development and implementation are mostly incurred in the short-term. This means that, in a context of competing innovations (eco-innovations and 'normal innovations'), limited resources for eco-innovation and a precarious economic situation, it is likely that only innovations leading to short-term results will be developed and adopted. This is normally not the case with eco-innovations (except in the case of so-called win-win technologies, which provide short-term benefits for the environment and for adopting firms alike).

- *Lack of information.* Case studies have shown that a lack of information on the existence of eco-innovations as well as on their real costs and benefits are a key barrier to eco-innovations.[64] This might be a particularly serious problem in the case of small and medium enterprises (SMEs), which often suffer this barrier to a greater extent. Given their lack of technological, human and financial resources, these firms have to make a greater effort to be aware of the existence of eco-innovation practices and usually rely on equipment suppliers. Industrial associations, chambers of commerce and technological platforms have also played a role in many European Union countries as key information providers on environmental regulations and the ways to comply with them, including environmental technologies.[65] The ability to engage in relevant information flows for eco-innovation also depends on variables within the firm and, particularly, on the company's technological competency/capacity. Firms previously investing in R&D or with a highly-trained and skilful human capital base are more likely to profit from those information flows.

- *Suppliers*. Relevant actors in this respect include both input as well as equipment suppliers. Both are key sources of technical information, as empirically found by Del Río[66] for equipment suppliers and Luken and van Rompaey[67] for input suppliers. However, the role of equipment suppliers is much more relevant as a driver of eco-innovations and as a barrier to certain eco-innovation types. This is especially so in the event that the company decides to purchase an eco-innovation rather than to develop it in-house. In this context, the role of suppliers might not only be as a key information provider, but also as an effective collaborator in the adaptation of the technology to the characteristics of the existing production process. Furthermore, some eco-innovations are even developed jointly between the firm and its equipment suppliers. Berkhout[68] distinguishes in this regard between 'abatement technologies' (corresponding to what we have termed 'end-of-pipe'), which are usually bought in from specialist suppliers, process technologies, which are developed through partnerships between capital goods suppliers and leading producers, and product changes, which are managed in-house as a critical source of competitive advantage. Equipment suppliers are a key element of the supply side of eco-innovations.[69] This might be problematic if, as stressed by the European Commission in the Environmental Technology Action Plan (ETAP),[70] it is difficult to disseminate them because distribution channels for new technologies are not as good as those for established technologies.

- *Final consumers/industrial clients/public customers*. In contrast to the 'supply-push' provided by the previous actors, firms may receive the stimulus to eco-innovate in the form of a 'market pull' from other actors in the supply chain. This might be the case both from final consumers (when the company produces final demand products) as well as from industrial clients (if the firm manufactures intermediate products, that is, products which are purchased by other firms). Empirical evidence shows that pressure to eco-innovate increases in product market segments that are close to final consumers.[71] Low consumer and purchaser awareness of environmental problems may act as a significant barrier to eco-innovating. It might be the result of a lack of information on the impact of the consumption of specific products and/or simply a lack of interest in the environmental aspects of a product compared to other aspects of the products (including price and quality).[72] At least in Europe, there is a tendency towards growing environmental awareness on the part of society in general, and, thus, consumers, although lack of standardized information on the environmental impacts of most products (such as eco-labels) does not facilitate this driver.[73]

- *Competitors.* Good environmental performance of competitors may motivate plant managers to adopt eco-innovations to improve their own environmental reputation and keep up with their competitors.[74] In the case of clear win-win eco-innovations, not adopting the new technology/practice when competitors have done so would result in a loss of competitiveness. On the other hand, the vested interests of powerful but less innovative competitors can impede or delay the innovation process.[75]

- *Industrial associations.* In many instances, and together with the chambers of commerce, these are the main source of information on eco-innovation alternatives. Luken and van Rompaey[76] observe that there is some evidence of the influence of business associations on a plant's environmental behaviour and clean technology adoption. Del Río[77] empirically shows the relevance of this factor in the case of eco-innovations in the Spanish pulp and paper sector.

- *Environmental NGOs and green parties.* Environmental NGOs may be a source of direct and indirect pressure on the development and adoption of eco-innovations. Direct pressure on firms is unlikely, however, except in some visible cases concerning multinationals.

- *Civil society* (larger public). The social awareness factor can be an important driver, and interacts with other drivers as well. Firms may want to demonstrate social awareness by being innovative in environmental performance. This in turn may improve the image and the general performance of the firm. Public acceptance of particularly visible large eco-innovations requiring substantial infrastructure is key for their success. For example, some not-in my-back-yard (NYMBY) effects can lead to the rejection of eco-innovations, as seems to be the case with wind farms in the UK.[78]

- *Research centers.* The relationship between research centers and firms may contribute to the development and diffusion of eco-innovations. The technological knowledge of research centers may be very useful for the development of eco-innovations. However, it is the joint development of eco-innovations which is likely to be more successful, because firms are in the best position to know their market needs and demand behaviour.

- *Financial institutions.* Access to finance is a crucial variable to invest in eco-innovation practices, either for those developed in-house or for those purchased from equipment suppliers but especially for highly capital-intensive eco-innovations. The EU Environmental Technology Action Plan (ETAP) states that difficult access to finance in the form of a lack of adequate venture capital, in particular for SMEs and start-ups, represents one of the most relevant barriers to the rapid market development of environmental technologies.[79] In this context, the problem is especially acute for SMEs, which tend to have comparatively more difficulties than larger firms in accessing finance and probably more pressure to obtain short-term profits. Insufficient availability of the venture capital required to move from the drawing board to the production line is particularly problematic for SMEs to engage in eco-innovation.[80] Access to finance is probably more difficult for eco-innovation than for 'normal' innovations. In this respect, Montalvo[81] observes that there is a certain bias in financial institutions against capital availability for cleaner production investments.

3.2.3 Characteristics of the technologies

Existing technologies are rigid and resistant to change.[82] There is some inertia in continuing to do things the way they have usually been done and to stick to the existing technologies. Certain features of the technologies (eco-innovations) contribute to this inertia.

- *Costs and cost-savings.* Some clean technologies are so-called win-win technologies, that is, they lead to a reduction in environmental impacts while simultaneously saving costs for the firm (in the form of a lower energy or material consumption, for instance). In this case, the likelihood that these technologies are adopted is higher than when those cost savings are not present. However, even in the case of win-win technologies, they may fail to be adopted, due to information or other reasons which prevent managers from looking for these opportunities, as argued by the 'Porter Hypothesis' (see Chapter 1). Thus, cost-savings in materials or energy might be a significant driver for eco-innovation whereas a high (initial or variable) cost compared to competing technologies would be a great deterrent. The relevant cost comparison is between the total average costs of the new technology (variable and fixed) and the variable average costs of the existing technology. Given that the existing technologies are already paid off (at least partially) and that there are no further fixed costs to incur, there is a lower incentive to adopt the new technology. Its higher fixed cost is only partly offset in the event that the new technology has a lower variable cost. Something similar occurs when there are two eco-innovation alternatives from which to choose, an incremental and a radical one. The variable costs could be similar, but the fixed costs tend to be much greater in the case of radical technologies, because they usually involve a much greater investment, that is, the up-front costs tend to be higher.

Although the possibility of cost savings is very important in the introduction of cleaner technologies, the problem is that, sometimes, it is not really an issue of costs, but of perception of those costs. Often, firms are not able to recognize the cost saving potentials (for example, energy or material savings) of environmental innovation.[83]

- *Potential benefits (greater revenues)*. Clean technologies may also lead to tangible and intangible benefits.[84] The exploitation of a green image may increase revenues as a result of the higher sales or a higher price of the products (if consumers are willing to pay a 'premium' for cleaner products). Intangible benefits, such as improvements in the quality of products, in the image of the firm and in the motivation of the staff may also result from adoption of eco-innovations.[85]
- *Complexity of eco-innovations*. Eco-innovations may have several degrees of complexity.[86] This may affect the probability of their being adopted by firms. A complex eco-innovation may require additional training for the existing workforce or it may increase the need for specialized, highly skilled human resources in the company[87] or it may require a closer relationship between the equipment (technology) supplier and the firm.[88] All these aspects increase the difficulty of implementing the technology in the firm and/or increase the costs of doing so. This barrier is especially strong in the case of radical eco-innovations, which are often complex technological systems made up of interdependent parts. Replacing one part involves the substitution of the whole system, which is expensive and makes such replacement unattractive.[89]
- *Compatibility with the existing system*. New eco-innovations may not fit easily into the existing production system of the firm, that is, they involve some degree of rupture with the existing system. In contrast, technologies which represent mere additions to current technologies ('drop-in innovations') such as EOP are more likely to

be adopted than technologies which are more difficult to integrate into existing production processes.[90] If the new technology entails a change in some key component of this system, then this will reduce its attractiveness. The potential changes are many, and include changes in the physical stock (that is, equipment goods), the human capital stock (the hiring of new, more skilled employees is required) and in external relationships (with clients or suppliers). Eco-innovations involving a lower degree of rupture with the existing system and fitting in with the traditional manner of doing things by the company (routines), are more likely to be attractive for potential adopters.

- *Existence of an installed base.* The existence of an installed base in the form of recent investments may be a powerful deterrent for investing in eco-innovations, especially regarding the capital-intensive ones. This means that eco-innovations are more likely to be adopted if they do not involve the scrapping of investments already made. When the adoption of eco-innovations follows the normal capital cycle of the firm (that is, they are adopted when the existing investments have already been depreciated), they are more likely to be adopted. Therefore, the age of the existing (physical) capital stock influences the uptake of eco-innovations. Previously installed technology has empirically been found to have a dampening effect on adoption.[91]

- *High up-front costs.* Related to the previous factors, eco-innovations that do not require major initial investments are more likely to be adopted. Initially high capital investments in the new technology (that is, in capital goods embodying the clean technology) act as a powerful deterrent for eco-innovations, especially for SMEs.[92] The reason is that these firms are unlikely to have the financial resources or they may have other priorities on which to spend those resources, which are perceived as more urgent for the short-term survival of the firm. This 'short-term' thinking (which is not an exclusive attribute of SMEs) works against eco-innovations, which often require long pay-back periods. The exception is win-win eco-innovations, which are paid off in the short-term.

- *Complementary innovations.* The existence of complementary innovations in the firm facilitates the uptake of eco-innovations. Eco-teams and environmental management and auditing systems are regarded by Kemp and Volpi[93] as examples of complementary innovations for clean technology diffusion. Colombo and Mosconi[94] were the first to provide evidence on the relevance of complementarity between different technologies within the same firm.

- *Sectoral technological opportunities.* Technological alternatives and eco-innovations opportunities are likely to differ per sector. In other words, part of the available stock of cleaner technologies is likely to be sector-specific.

  The sector's characteristics do not only have a direct influence on the existence of technological opportunities, they also determine the innovativeness of the sector and, thus, the likelihood that eco-innovations will be developed and adopted.[95] In this context, Ashford[96] argues that the capacity to change may be influenced by the inherent innovativeness of the firm as determined by the maturity and technological rigidity of particular product or production lines. The heavy, basic industries (usually the most polluting), change with great difficulty, especially regarding core processes.[97] Berkhout[98] observes that in process industries operating within rather inflexible technological trajectories and where resource productivity and competitiveness are already strongly aligned, the scope for introducing radically novel resource-saving technologies may be limited. These sectors' differences may translate into a different impact of the drivers and barriers, which have been discussed throughout this section.

- *Expectations of cost reductions and quality improvements.* Technologies in general (e.g., not only those reducing the impacts on the environment) improve and their costs are reduced as a result of several processes: spillovers from the R&D investment process elsewhere, cost-competition between suppliers, learning effects and economies of scale. The potential for cost reductions is usually greater the less mature the technology is. If a firm hopes that a certain eco-innovation will reduce its costs or improve its quality in the future, then it will wait until those changes occur, for example as a result of initial adoption by others. In other words, expectations of cost reductions and improvements may lead to delays in the uptake of eco-innovations, since early adopters suffer the risks and higher costs associated to immature technologies.

- *Criteria for assessing the new technologies.* Also, the evaluation of technologies is usually undertaken with the criteria used to evaluate the old ones. This may make the new technologies look unattractive because the advantages of the new technology may not be considered.[99]

The aforementioned factors discussed in this chapter are unlikely to work in isolation from each other. It is rather the interplay and interaction of different barriers and drivers going in different directions which has an influence on the final development, innovation and adoption of environmentally-sound practices and technologies. Combinations of factors are likely to be present, leading to feedback mechanisms and reinforcing effects.

On the other hand, the incidence of given factors (drivers and barriers) is likely to be different for different types of eco-innovation (that is, incremental versus radical), firms (large versus small), sectors and countries. For example, environmental regulation is usually considered to be the main driver behind the development and adoption of EOP technologies, whereas the financial constraint is especially dramatic for SMEs. In general, the more radical the technologies, the more relevant are the different factors as a barrier to eco-innovation and the greater the relevance of the systemic interplay of those barriers as an obstacle to eco-innovation.

In this context, a recent but growing current in the literature on the subject has focused not on the drivers and barriers for specific appliances, but rather on a more aggregated level of analysis, that is, on 'environmental innovation systems'. Indeed, some authors argue that focusing on micro-level, individual technologies is problematic because:

1. it is liable to miss dynamics across the wider techno system that may be more significant
2. studies are faced with the far from trivial problem of distinguishing between a clean and a dirty techno (a single dimension of environmental performance is typically highlighted and little account is taken of the broader system impacts that a new clean technology may have); and
3. the emphasis on discrete technologies leads to a focus on new investment and substitution of one technology for another, and a lack of attention to processes of incremental innovation.[100]

Berkhout[101] observes that the institutionalist analysis of technical change is concerned with linking between several levels of change, that is, micro, meso and macro. Again, the co-evolution of technical and institutional systems is stressed.

Finally, we wouldn't like to end this chapter without mentioning the complementarity between technological and social eco-innovations. Eco-innovations may be technical and social, they reinforce each other and are necessary for each other. Radical eco-innovations require simultaneous technological and social change.[102] However, since a deeper analysis of the determinants for non-technical innovations is more complex,[103] we have focused on technical eco-innovations in this chapter.

CHAPTER 4

Policy strategies to promote eco-innovation

4.1 INTRODUCTION

The previous chapter analyzed the different drivers of and barriers to eco-innovation. In this chapter the aim is to identify those policy features and measures that can be implemented in order to help remove those barriers (or encourage the drivers) and enhance the uptake of eco-innovations. In order to do so, we have taken into account the theoretical and empirical literature on environmentally sound techno-institutional change, as well as certain policies currently implemented in the EU, the US and elsewhere.[1] After justifying in section 4.2 why eco-innovation should be promoted publicly, section 4.3 outlines the policy approach to promote eco-innovations. Section 4.4 is devoted to the pinpointing of specific measures, whereas the following sections (4.5 and 4.6, respectively) discuss the most appropriate measures for tackling specific barriers to eco-innovation and how different types of eco-innovations are more likely to be promoted with different instruments. The chapter closes with some concluding remarks.

4.2 WHY SHOULD ECO-INNOVATION BE PROMOTED PUBLICLY?

On the one hand, Chapter 3 showed that eco-innovation provides several socio-economic and environmental benefits. Therefore, society and firms could be better off with greater diffusion of these innovations. A firm's competitiveness could be enhanced when an eco-innovation is adopted by the company.

However, it was also argued that the market by itself (and with some exceptions) does not inspire the diffusion of eco-innovations. Although some eco-innovations are certainly very attractive from a business perspective – and they are adopted –, others are not and, thus, they need a certain stimulus. In addition to market failures (the negative externality of pollution and other environmental damage and the positive externality of R&D (spillovers)),[2] there are other barriers preventing the uptake of eco-innovations. Policy measures are needed to ensure that these barriers are removed and those externalities addressed.

Nevertheless, the direct public promotion of eco-innovation may not be a panacea, because it could also lead to technological failures or to crowding out of 'normal' innovations which nonetheless are social welfare-improving. It is thus generally recognized that policy is better at creating the 'context' conditions, rather than pushing specific eco-innovations and that economic instruments (rather than direct regulation) are more suitable for this task.[3]

4.3   WHAT SHOULD THE MAIN ELEMENTS OF A POLICY APPROACH TO PROMOTE ECO-INNOVATION BE?

Innovation should be redirected towards more sustainable paths. A review of the empirical literature reveals that environmental policy in general has an impact on the rate and direction of eco-innovation, regardless of the type of instrument applied.[4] The relevance of public policies in encouraging sustainable technologies was pointed out more than 30 years ago by Kneese and Schulze,[5] who argued that in the long run, perhaps the most important criterion on which to judge environmental policies is the extent to which they spur new technology toward the efficient conservation of environmental quality.

Two main sets of elements of a policy to promote eco-innovation can be distinguished. On the one hand, the design of an appropriate eco-innovation policy should contain some general features (the 'framework conditions') which could be more conducive to eco-innovation. On the other hand, this policy should be implemented through the use of specific measures that are likely to be more effective in this regard. This section focuses on the first aspect. Some recommendations regarding the general framework conditions are provided, whereas the specific instruments are discussed in the next section.

4.3.1   Acknowledge the wide array of barriers to environmental techno-institutional change

As observed by Gunningham,[6] achieving efficient and effective regulation and encouraging innovation is a far more complex activity than mainstream neoclassical economists believe(d) it to be,[7] requiring a much broader range of strategies, tailored to a much more extensive range of motivations and harnessing a much wider range of social actors. The mix of instruments for environmental protection is very much determined by the context in which firms operate.[8] An effective policy to promote eco-innovation should take into account the different types of barriers that prevent eco-innovations from being adopted, already considered in Chapter 3. Only if these barriers are identified will policy makers be able to influence the rate and direction of eco-innovations, without necessarily picking winners. The greater intensity of some obstacles over others leads to the recommendation of specific instruments although, as argued in the previous chapter, barriers are usually not present in isolation and, thus, an instrument combination is normally the most effective policy approach, which brings us to the following point.

4.3.2   *Combine different policy approaches (instrument mix)*

Since there are different types of barriers to eco-innovation and obstacles are likely to interact and to be interrelated, different types of instruments should be combined. Nevertheless, when applying certain instruments it should be taken into account that specific instruments interact between one another, leading to synergies or conflicts. Indeed, in the real world, measures are usually applied in combination to exploit their respective benefits and the synergies between them.[9] This would either enhance or reduce the effectiveness of specific instruments.

More specifically, measures belonging to the realms of environmental and innovation policy should be used simultaneously and better integrated in order to improve the coherence and effectiveness of public policy. As suggested by Del Río[10] and Kivimaa and Mickwitz,[11] it is necessary to include environmental protection considerations in innovation policy and technology promotion concerns in environmental policy and, thus, there should be a better coordination between public agencies with environmental and technological responsibilities. Innovation policy is usually insufficiently oriented towards eco-innovation, while environmental policy hardly acts as a pull for innovation to lead to the emergence of new products and processes with an environmental impact.[12] The promotion of eco-innovation would benefit greatly if possible conflicts between both types of policies were mitigated.

4.3.3 Make static and dynamic efficiency compatible

Some authors observe that there might be a trade-off between achieving quick environmental results and encouraging radical eco-innovation.[13] Of course, it should not be forgotten that the aim of environmental policy is not only (or even primarily) to promote eco-innovation, but to protect the environment and do so at a reasonable cost to society. Therefore, innovation is only one criterion for environmental policy and it must be added to rather than replace the more traditional criteria of effectiveness, efficiency and equity.[14]

However, there is not necessarily a conflict between the two goals. Indeed, eco-innovation is a necessary tool for reducing environmental pressures stemming from production and consumption activities. Therefore, public policies should be judged by their (cost) effectiveness in terms of environmental improvement and eco-innovation,[15] but there is also a need for government authorities to focus explicitly on technological change (rather than implicitly through a change in the economic framework conditions).[16] In other words, in addition to identifying which policy instruments are better at encouraging (cost) effective environmental protection and eco-innovation, it should be considered how eco-innovation could be promoted in a way that contributes to cost effective environmental protection.

4.3.4 Acknowledge the limitations of public policy as a driver

The main assumption in this chapter, as well as in environmental techno-institutional change literature, is that policy can encourage the adoption and diffusion of eco-innovations. Given the existence of market failures and other barriers, relying on the effectiveness of policy is key if we aim to remove or mitigate these barriers in order to facilitate the uptake of eco-innovation.

However, public policy may have severe limitations as regards influencing the factors which impede the uptake of eco-innovations and, in other cases, it may certainly lead to failures, i.e., counterproductive results when trying to pick winners. Indeed, the history of technology is full of experiences where public policy led to the 'wrong' technologies.

Kemp[17]already warned some time ago that one should be careful in using regulation for promoting innovation because technology can not be moulded into a pre-defined, socially desirable shape. Therefore it is difficult to design instruments that are either effective in achieving a set goal or outcome, or efficient in terms of costs or technology choice.

There are two major reasons why regulation may have a limited impact on environmental technological change: the design of environmental regulation depends on the existence of technological alternatives and there might be a problem of regulatory capture.

The design of environmental regulation is usually decided by considering the existing technological capacity to reach those targets (that is, it is endogenous to technological changes) and usually does not result in a sufficient incentive to develop the most radical types of eco-innovations. This is so because governments rarely mandate the use of environmental technologies, which allows firms to comply with environmental regulation, in the absence of their demonstrated economic viability.[18] Regulations are often based on available solutions which may stifle innovation.[19] Ashford[20] observed that in the early 1970s, most environmental, health, and safety regulations in the US set standards at a level attainable by existing technology.

On the other hand, regulatory capture is likely to discourage eco-innovation, i.e., existing interest groups may be particularly effective in influencing environmental regulations that are either not stringent enough to stimulate eco-innovations or that encourage existing but not radical eco-innovation types.[21]

Finally, there are some situations in which regulation is not necessary because social pressures and other factors are more effective. For example, Gunningham[22] found out that community and environmental advocacy groups tend to act as effective watchdogs and de facto regulators, pressuring companies into beyond-compliance environmental performance.[23]

4.3.5 Tackle all the stages of the eco-innovation process

Eco-innovations are the result of a complex process which involves all the stages of technological change: invention, innovation and diffusion. The traditional, linear perspective has been to look at those stages separately, following a 'logical continuum' from invention to diffusion. In contrast, the systemic perspective on technological change stresses the interrelations and mutual feedbacks between stages. While it is true that in order for there to be diffusion there has to be a previous inventive activity, it is also true that some inventions and innovations occur in the diffusion stage. For example, von Hippel[24] highlighted long ago the role of users in the innovation process. Others have found out that post-adoption technical challenges provide a stimulus for innovative activity.[25]

The implications for an eco-innovation policy of this conceptualization of the innovation process are straightforward: instruments should foster eco-innovations in all the stages of the technological change process, although some instruments may be more effective at tackling certain stages than others. Note that supporting one particular stage would have synergistic effects on the other stages because, according to the systemic approach, those stages are interrelated. Therefore, it is important to take into account that, although all those stages are part of the same (eco-innovation) process, each probably requires a different policy approach, including a specific set of instruments, that is, a one-size-fits-all policy approach is probably not appropriate. In other words, what is effective at encouraging eco-innovations at an early stage is unlikely to be effective at later stages. It should also be identified what part of the eco-innovation process shows the greatest weakness. For example, the problem may be a lack of eco-innovation ideas due, for example, to a lack of incentive or vision by managers. Or, perhaps, the problem could be one of bringing already developed eco-innovations to the market (that is, commercialization).

4.3.6   Adapt the policy measures to the maturity of the eco-innovations

The previous point also implies that a policy approach to eco-innovation should take into account the degree of maturity of specific eco-innovations, and apply instruments accordingly. Obviously, some eco-innovations are relatively immature. For example, they may have a great potential for cost reductions and quality improvements which has not been fully exploited. If this is so, R&D investments and protected niches which allow the innovations to diffuse and achieve their potential are particularly suitable. It is usually believed that technology-push measures (such as subsidies for R&D investments) are more effective at earlier stages of the technological change (or eco-innovation) process whereas demand-pull (such as ecolabelling or public procurement) would be more effective at later stages.[26] All this brings us to the following points.

4.3.7   Simultaneously apply supply-push and demand-pull measures

Encouraging eco-innovations at different stages of the innovation cycle usually requires the combination of supply-push and market-pull measures. Governments must consider how to support technology development (supply push), for example through R&D subsidies, as well as encouraging demand through market creation (demand-pull) for environmental technologies.[27] For example through public procurement. In this context, and considering that these suffer from the aforementioned double externality problem, technology policy instruments represent a useful complement to environmental policies[28] and potential complementarities and synergies in fostering environmental technological change exist in this regard. Some experts have focused on either the supply or demand sides of eco-innovations. For example, the analysis and recommendations of the CCC report,[29] which is the consensus outcome of the assessments of an expert group based on their experience, focus on the demand side of eco-innovations, in the conviction that strengthening it will stimulate the respective supply and make the programs already underway on this side of the market more effective. It suggests five courses of action for governments and public authorities within the framework of what it calls the 'on-going/continuous competitiveness improvement cycle':

1. defining a clear, common standpoint and direction
2. promoting knowledge and ability
3. creating and leading/guiding markets by means of public procurement
4. offering pertinent incentives to end-users, and
5. promoting information of use to consumers.

The BLUEPRINT report,[30] which was the outcome of a series of five workshops on the integration of science, technology and environmental policy attended by over 100 participants from the realms of research, politics and business, upholds an approach combining supply-push instruments, such as R&D incentives, and demand-pull instruments, placing emphasis on the creation of markets. The appropriate combination of push and pull policy approaches have been looked for, for instance, in the lead markets initiative of the European Commission (see Box 4.1).

4.3.8 Combine general measures to promote innovation with others specific to eco-innovation

Since some of the barriers to eco-innovation are also general barriers to 'normal innovations', some measures to promote eco-innovation are likely to be similar to those which would promote innovation in general. For example, creating an appropriate environment for innovation is as important for innovations in general as for environmental innovations (eco-innovations). However, in addition, other

**Box 4.1　A Lead Market Initiative in markets
for renewable energy**

Among the six chosen markets for the LMIs in Europe, markets for renewable energies have been identified. The set of policy instruments that have been planned to implement in these markets:

Legislation: promote the Internal Market in renewable energies by removing barriers to the integration of renewable energy sources in the EU energy system.

- Replace current legislation (for example Renewable Electricity Directive) with measures that: allocate the 20 per cent renewable energy target amongst the Member States; require national action plans that set out pathways and to standardize EU guarantee of origin regimes to enable EU-wide flexibility in meeting national targets; create the framework for opening the market for guarantees of origin; set out environmental sustainability criteria; anticipate future qualifications and skills needed to favour the uptake of renewable energy sources.
- Remove barriers for renewable energy development and simplify authorization procedures.
- Remove planning and certification barriers to the uptake of renewables; incorporate renewable energy in building codes; provide guidelines for authorization procedures; eliminate red tape for SMEs.

Public procurement: increase the share of renewable energy purchased by the public authorities.

- Establish a network between public purchasers of renewable energy to apply the Commission guide on public procurement for innovation; identify via that network good practices in the field of procurement of renewable energy and promote their application across the EU.

Standardization, labelling and certification: reap the benefits of the EU internal market through a coordinated approach for standard setting and labelling on technologies for energy generation and transmission.

- Continue the process of adopting minimum energy performance standards (eco-design requirements) in the form of implementing

Directives for 20 priority product groups including boilers, water heaters, consumer electronics, copying machines, televisions, standby modes, chargers, lighting, electric motors and other products.

- Ensure that appropriate measuring methods will be developed on time through CEN/CENELEC or other appropriate means. Products that do not meet the agreed minimum requirements may not be placed on the market (c.f. EEAP Priority).
- Develop European sustainability standards in the value-chain for production of renewable energy in Europe.
- Begin with the creation of a biofuels sustainability regime in the new renewable energy Directive. In line with the Biomass Action Plan, consider the extension of the regime to other areas.

Complementary instruments: mobilize public and private financing: Promote the exchange of experience in financing from such funding mechanisms as the EU Structural Funds, European Investment Bank initiatives specific to renewable energy – workshops, networks, and so on. Strengthen the EU support through, for example, CIP-IEE, LIFE+, FP7, or Structural Funds to bridge the gap between successful demonstration of innovative technologies and effective market entrance.

- Develop the state of the art business cases for an effective supply chain in different renewable energies.
- Anticipate the future qualifications and skill needs to uptake innovation in renewable energy and to enable its fast implementation.
- Support the internationalisation of renewable energy technologies.
- Further investigation and identification of the barriers hindering the commercialisation of renewable energies.

Source: European Commission (2007) Communication 'A lead market initiative for Europe', COM(2007)860 (21.12.2007), Annex 1 – Thematic Action Plans.

measures should necessarily be more focused on the promotion of eco-innovations. This is related to the double externality problem (see Chapter 3). The 'technological side' of the double externality problem calls for general innovation measures (probably, those in the technology-policy category),whereas the 'environmental side' calls for specific measures to stimulate eco-innovations (mostly those in the environmental-policy group) given the lack of internalization of negative environmental externalities, which discourages eco-innovations.

Of course, proposing effective general innovation or more-focused eco-innovation policies depends on an analysis of what the most relevant factors influencing eco-innovation are, that is, specific factors influencing innovation in environmental technologies or barriers to innovation in general.

4.3.9 *Prioritize measures higher up the eco-innovation hierarchy*

What type of eco-innovations should be promoted? In principle, given the definition of eco-innovation provided in Chapter 2, all types of eco-innovations might result in a net benefit for the environment as well as in an enhancement of the competitiveness of the firm. This would include even those alternatives lower down the eco-innovation hierarchy (that is, EOP technologies). Indeed, Frondel et al[31] and Oosterhuis[32] point out that a certain amount of end-of-pipe technologies will remain necessary to curb specific emissions which cannot easily be reduced with cleaner production measures. This is also probably the case with carbon capture and storage (CCS) in the climate change mitigation debate.

However, it was also shown in Chapter 2 that not all eco-innovations have the potential to contribute to those two goals equally. In particular, those categories higher up the eco-innovation scale are preferable and should be prioritized.[33] What does this imply for the policy approach to be implemented? It is likely that the barriers to eco-innovation are more difficult to eliminate when we consider eco-innovations higher up the eco-innovation hierarchy. For example, the adoption of more radical eco-innovations may lead to significant changes in the production process of the firm. In contrast, EOP technologies are easier to integrate into the existing production processes.[34]

Furthermore, the barriers to more radical types of eco-innovations are likely to be more systemic and related to a wide array of factors. This makes the combination of policy measures probably more relevant in the case of these eco-innovations as a way of facilitating their introduction than in the case of EOP technologies. To sum up, if barriers differ according to environmental technology type and there is a superiority of certain environmental technologies over others, then policy measures should be adapted to those barriers in order to more effectively promote specific technologies.

Policies should also aim to encourage system innovation (such as integrated mobility or industrial ecology) because those eco-innovations may provide factor 10 improvements in environmental impact compared to the factor 2 improvements associated with incremental changes or factor 5 improvements of partial system design.[35]

4.3.10   *Avoid lock-in to suboptimal technologies*

Policy makers should try to mitigate the risk of lock-in when supporting eco-innovations. This means that favouring eco-innovations lower in the hierarchy can result in a reduced willingness to adopt eco-innovations higher up the hierarchy. This can be a result of the conflict between the short-term cost-effectiveness (or effectiveness) of environmental policy measures aimed at correcting a certain environmental problem (which could mandate the urgent adoption of an EOP) and the dynamic efficiency of those measures, which might call for the encouragement of radical eco-innovations. Therefore, policy makers should be cautious that some measures which allow the reduction of pollutants in the short-term and do this at relatively low costs by encouraging the uptake of eco-innovations which are at the bottom of the eco-innovation hierarchy (EOP technologies) may discourage the development and adoption of radical eco-innovations. However, this conflict may be difficult to circumvent in the case of environmental problems which may require an urgent solution. These demand the implementation of short-term compliance periods, leaving insufficient time available to develop long-term, innovative solutions and often resulting in EOP technologies.

4.3.11   *Maintain diversity and flexibility of possible alternative technological trajectories*

Policies makers should build up institutions awarded of risks of path-dependence in public policies, which ensure economic choices flexibility and diversity of alternative trajectories, and which guarantee the possibility to change from previous trajectory if learning outcomes show it has to be done.[36] According to Kemp,[37] in order to prevent adherence to suboptimal technologies, policies should stimulate the widest possible range of technological solutions and remain flexible with respect to technological choices. Notwithstanding, as pointed out by Godard,[38] public intervention tackles two contradictory goals here: 1) reducing uncertainty and controversy to clarify the future and thereby promote private investments; and 2) maintaining an open universe of options to stimulate innovation and avoid a premature lock-in to suboptimal technologies.

4.3.12 Consider appropriate timing when implementing policies

Technological changes in general and eco-innovations in particular, especially in mature sectors, are more likely to be adopted when the existing technologies and productive equipment are already paid off or when they are at the end of their useful life.[39] The implication is that policy makers aimed at encouraging eco-innovations should take the capital cycle of the firms in a sector into account, and adapt to this 'window of opportunity'[40] when proposing measures.[41] If policies are not implemented to fit with existing investment and innovation cycles, there might be serious limitations to encouraging eco-innovations, especially radical ones.

4.3.13 Combine a sector-specific perspective with cross-sectoral measures

It is likely that the specific characteristics and structure of sectors influence the rate and direction of environmental technological change.[42] The innovativeness of a particular sector depends on factors such as the maturity of the sector, the maturity of the dominant technology, scale, capital intensity, R&D intensity of the industry and competitiveness.[43] For example, heavy industries change with difficulty.[44] Therefore, a better understanding of technological trends at the sectoral level is a necessary precondition for a better understanding of the impact of environmental regulation on technological change.[45] For example, regulation is likely to be an important driver of environmental technologies in emissions-intensive mature sectors.[46] The relevance of the characteristics of the sector for innovation has long been stressed by innovation economics, which has highlighted the role of 'sectoral systems of innovation'.[47] In addition, market structure, which tends to differ according to sector, may influence the rate of technological change in general and the rate and direction of environmental technological change in particular. Finally, environmental technological opportunities tend to be sector-specific.[48]

Therefore, a sectoral perspective on policy measures to promote eco-innovations is likely to be important. The above implies that instruments to promote environmental technological change effectively should take those characteristics of sectors into account, that is, if industry characteristics are important determinants of firms' technological strategies, then we may expect that different policy mechanisms may be more effective in promoting eco-innovation in specific industries than other instruments.[49] Notwithstanding, adopting a sectoral perspective does not rule out the implementation of cross-sectoral measures. In addition to fostering sector-specific eco-innovations, policy strategies should be devised to promote cross-sectoral eco-innovations (including nanotechnology, biotechnology, ICTs, and so on).

4.3.14 *Prioritize win-win eco-innovations*

Win-win eco-innovations are those with very short pay-back periods, that is, they reduce costs or increase revenues in the very short-term and, thus, the investment is recovered quickly. Although these eco-innovations exist in virtually all sectors of the economy and they would be very attractive from both a firm's and a social perspective, several barriers to their adoption exist (see Chapter 3). Obviously, since they are clearly beneficial to the firms adopting them as well as to the environment, they should be developed, innovated and adopted first, with some policy push in the form of information provision. If, as argued by Montalvo[50] 'in order to foster environmental innovative behaviours, it is a primary condition to reduce the level of conflict between the firm's self-interest (that is, profit making and survival) and the social interest that embodies environmental protection', the promotion of win-win innovations reduces this apparent conflict to a minimum.

4.3.15 *Focus on design elements*

When considering policy approaches to promote eco-innovation, the discussion should go beyond the debate on the choice of specific instruments and include other relevant aspects.[51] Indeed, the almost exclusive emphasis on instruments has been criticized by some authors. For example, Ashford[52] and Jaenicke et al[53] argue that too much attention has been paid to the selection of a specific instrument ('instrumentalism') while their design features, which are relevant for their implementation, have been disregarded. Empirical studies on the relationship between public policy and environmental innovation show that the success of policies aimed at eco-innovation is not dependent only on the specific policy instruments used but, also, on whether the instrument has been designed, implemented and coordinated in an accurate manner. Therefore, in addition to the instrument chosen, some features of the regulation determine the effectiveness and efficiency of environmental policy, such as the setting up of long-term objectives and accurate timings, the combination of policy instruments, the frequent interactions (cooperation) among actors (firms and regulators), regulatory flexibility and certainty and policy approaches adapted to the specific characteristics of the sector.[54]

Certain specific design elements of a given instrument may be more successful than others in promoting eco-innovation. Although each instrument has strengths and weaknesses, their capacity to influence eco-innovation depends on their details[55] and how these details stimulate industry-generated information, provide economic or political incentives, reduce long-term uncertainties and lend flexibility. For example, emissions trading schemes with permits being auctioned instead of grandfathered are traditionally regarded as providing a greater stimulus to environmental technological change.[56]

4.3.16   *The stringency of regulations is key for radical eco-innovations ...*

The stringency of regulation has been shown to have a clear effect on the rate and directions of eco-innovations.[57] Indeed, Frondel et al[58] argue that policy stringency is more important than policy instrument choice. According to Ashford,[59] a regulation is stringent either:

1. because compliance requires a significant reduction in exposure to toxic substances,
2. because compliance using existing technology is costly, or
3. because compliance requires a significant technological change.

The more ambitious the environmental targets (or the tax rate, in the case of environmental taxes), the more likely it is that eco-innovations will be developed and adopted. On the other hand, it must also be taken into account that the difficulty, or even impossibility, of reaching a very demanding target or 'high hanging fruit' might deter subsequent efforts to innovate.

A high level of stringency may be particularly relevant for stimulating radical eco-innovations, that is, eco-innovations higher up the eco-innovation hierarchy. Lenient environmental regulations are unlikely to correct the environmental or technological dimensions of the double externality problem. Although the stringency level can be part of any instrument, certain measures are traditionally regarded as 'soft', like voluntary standards and information dissemination, albeit these instruments should be usefully combined with others in any eco-innovation strategy.

Stringency is not only related to the level of ambition of the environmental targets, it is also related to the effectiveness of enforcement of environmental regulation. Obviously, regulated profit-maximizing business corporations take costly measures to improve their performance only when they believe that legal non-compliance is likely to be detected and harshly penalized.[60]

4.3.17   ... but within long-term compliance periods ...

Setting stringent and clear targets does not mean that firms should not be allowed to comply with those targets in a flexible manner. A key flexibility element is setting long-term compliance periods in order to promote radical environmental technological changes. Long-term policy targets may facilitate the inclusion of environmental improvements in innovation activities. However, an excessively long-term policy target may be counterproductive in terms of eco-innovation. For example, van Soest et al[61] show that, as future technological advances are inherently uncertain and investments in new technology are, at least partly, irreversible, it may 'pay' to postpone investments in energy saving and wait for the arrival of improved varieties. This behaviour might be even more marked under long-term compliance periods. As observed by Kemp,[62] significant process innovations are likely to occur in response to stringent regulations that give firms in the regulated industry enough time to develop comprehensive strategies. On the contrary, short-term compliance periods may stifle innovation and diffusion of clean technologies because they induce swift changes in firms and require companies to adopt already existing well-proven and costly technological measures which are non-innovative and of an incremental nature (EOP technologies). These technological alternatives are detrimental to the firm's competitiveness.[63]

4.3.18   ... which limit uncertainty for investors in eco-innovations

Uncertainty is a major factor inhibiting investment in general and investment in eco-innovations in particular because their development requires long-term horizons and the costs of their adoption are usually recovered in the medium- and long-term. Uncertainty can arise from a number of sources: unclear or imprecise regulations, ambiguous regulations, rapidly changing regulations and lack of coordination between different regulatory bodies.[64]

By increasing predictability and reducing uncertainty, regulation can stimulate eco-innovation. Predictability is defined by Bernauer[65] as the degree to which future regulation and its properties can be foreseen. For example, if policy sends a message to firms that, over time, they will have to increasingly internalize their environmental externalities, eco-innovation would be more likely to occur.[66]

Perhaps, uncertainty is a double-edged sword because too much uncertainty certainly constrains innovation, but too much certainty may also have a negative impact in this regard.[67] Indeed, Ashford[68] sees the benefits of some uncertainty due to regulation, arguing that too much certainty will stimulate only minimum compliance technology. The COM report[69] also points out that overly detailed regulations may reduce the scope for innovation, thereby discouraging it.

4.3.19   The style of regulation is a relevant variable

Some authors have put the emphasis on the 'style of regulation' as a factor influencing environmental technological change.[70] According to Jaenicke et al,[71] innovation-friendly policy styles are based on dialogue and consensus, are decisive, proactive and ambitious, open, flexible and knowledge-oriented. This leads us to the following point.

4.3.20   Promote a cooperative, participative approach between actors

An eco-innovation friendly policy style mostly refers to whether the regulation is the result of a participatory approach between the regulators and the regulated or whether this relationship is confrontational. One would expect that a more collaborative relationship between firms and regulators, based on trust, would lead to an open exchange of information which, in turn, would result in a more supportive attitude to eco-innovation in firms (taking into account the limitations of the latter and the specific barriers to eco-innovation) on the part of policy makers and a lower perceived risk on the part of firms when investing in this type of innovation.

Clayton et al[72] stress the importance of dialogue between firms and government, 'both to solve problems and to ensure that cleaner solutions may be more generally disseminated and adopted. Critically, such dialogue may allow firms to disclose important information about their operations to regulators and in turn allow regulators to utilise the expertise and innovative ability of industry in formulating solutions'. Indeed, several empirical studies have shown that dialogue and collaboration between government and industry is a crucial factor determining the success (effectiveness and efficiency) of an environmental-technology oriented policy.[73]

For example, the EU Environmental Technology Action Programme (ETAP) has followed this approach of 'involving different stakeholders'. Preliminary conclusions on its functioning reveal that the mobilization and involvement of industry and relevant stakeholders is key to improving the development and uptake of environmental technologies.[74] One of the priority actions in this regard has been to launch technology platforms bringing together researchers, industry, financial institutions, decision-makers and other relevant stakeholders to agree on long-term research agendas with concrete deliverables.[75]

Blazejczak and Edler[76] found that Swedish policy was the most innovation-friendly in the pulp and paper sector as it was characterized by a search for consensus in combination with ambitious long-term goals.[77] The Danish model of local authority regulation and the National Environmental Plan in the Netherlands are initiatives in the direction of collaboration between regulator and regulated firm around environmental goals. These experiences suggest that partnerships with regulators and sector-wide agreements can play a key role in enabling firms to respond more positively and constructively to regulatory pressure.[78]

The case study on the automobile industry carried out by Wallace[79] also shows that the more confrontational policy style in the US and other countries has not spurred eco-innovation to the same extent as in consensus-based policy regimes, as in the Netherlands. One of the interactive instruments used in the Netherlands is the Target Group Policy, where collective environmental targets for industry sectors are set through an interactive process between government and industry associations, which later co-ordinate the abatement efforts of their members.[80]

However, Oosterhuis[81] does not find evidence that the Dutch consensus-based approach has encouraged radical technological changes. Furthermore, the institutional and cultural context may make it difficult to apply the cooperative Dutch approach to other countries. As stressed by Parto,[82]

The complexities of the environment-economy relationships disallow one-size-fits-all solutions to similar environmental challenges in different contexts. It would be naïve to expect that the Dutch or the German deliberative policy styles could be readily adopted by other countries since there are fundamental differences among the modes of governance and stages of economic development that characterize the different nation states. To be successful, an environmental policy has to resonate with the formal and informal institutions through which governance is exercised. The long tradition of democratic and participatory modes of governance in Nordic and western European countries is not present in many countries experiencing similar environmental challenges.

On the other hand, the cooperative, consensus-based approach can also be negative for eco-innovation, insofar as information asymmetry between regulated and regulator and the negotiation process between them can lead to a low level of stringency and, thus, negatively affect the uptake of eco-innovations. Indeed, an excessive influence of firms on regulators (for example, as a result of lack of technical knowledge of the latter or a stronger negotiation position of the former) could indeed lead to regulatory capture, whereby softer instruments (such as VAs) or 'hard' instruments with non-ambitious targets are implemented.[83] This political economy aspect has been suggested by different authors.[84] For example, Kemp argues that there is always the risk of strategic behaviour on the part of industry which may claim that it is impossible to develop technology that is both environmentally superior and economically feasible. In turn, Ashford observes that 'there is increasing evidence that "cooperative" approaches may often actually impede the needed changes and transformations – especially if government processes are unduly influenced or even captured by the problem industries'. This author argues that dialogue and consensus on their own, while useful, are unlikely to prove sufficient to transform an industry into a sustainable one.

4.3.21 Combine sticks and carrots

Although there is a widespread belief that the coercive forces of environmental regulation play an essential role in stimulating environmentally sound technological changes, public administration can also play a complementary role as a facilitator or 'change agent' for eco-innovations. Thus, different roles for policy makers can be envisaged: that of a sponsor, planner, regulator, matchmaker, alignment actor and a 'creative game regulator'.[85] A shift in the role of regulators is implied, from seeing them as an external force compelling firms to adopt certain behaviours, to seeing them as promoting and reinforcing a shift in the internal climate and perspectives of the firm (leading to a culture in which environmental goals are linked to competitive goals).[86]

The main policy implication is that the 'stick' provided by regulation should be combined with other instruments ('carrots') which positively influence the uptake of environmental technologies in a non-coercive manner. Sticks involve a direct requirement to change the environmental (and, thus, technological) practices of firms. Regarding carrots, governments can use information, communication, encouragement, peer pressure, and education strategies to convince firms and the public of the need for change.[87] Indeed, the regulator can play a role in promoting and organizing exchanges of information among firms and between firms and other sources of knowledge.[88]

4.3.22   *Adopt a supply-chain, life-cycle, multi-media perspective*

In contrast to the dominant approach, which has mainly focused on single sectors, firms or specific technologies (with the notable exception of Mazzanti and Zoboli and IPTS[89]), more emphasis should be put on the analysis of the whole 'supply chain' of specific products.[90] This approach would provide a more complete picture of the environmental impacts related to production and consumption activities and may be useful for the design of effective environmental policy measures aimed at reducing those impacts. For example, the government can try to encourage large firms to help their suppliers and distributors adopt cleaner production, as done in Taiwan, where the government promotes the creation of so-called 'corporate synergy systems', which are essentially networks for sharing technical information.[91]

Actually, a supply chain perspective involves the adoption of a life-cycle approach to the environmental problems caused by products 'from cradle to grave'. A life-cycle perspective forces a range of innovations to be considered simultaneously, and to be evaluated against the impacts during all phases of a product's life, including production, use and disposal.[92]

In turn, adopting a supply chain and life-cycle perspective involves taking into account all the possible environmental impacts of technologies. Thus, policies should adopt a multi-media approach. As observed by Norberg-Bohm,[93] 'policies that are single-media are likely to result in fragmented responses in which firms move pollutants from the air and water to the land. A multi-media perspective, which asks firms to consider all environmental impacts simultaneously, is more likely to stimulate green technological innovations, as the shifting of pollutants is illuminated and

Table 4.1   Elements of a policy approach promoting eco-innovation

- Acknowledge the wide array of barriers to environmental technological change
- Combine different policy approaches (instrument mix)
- Make static and dynamic efficiency compatible
- Acknowledge the limitations of public policy as a driver
- Tackle all the stages of the eco-innovation process
- Adapt the policy measures to the maturity of the eco-innovations
- Simultaneously apply supply-push and demand pull measures
- Combine general measures to promote innovation with others specific to eco-innovation
- Prioritize measures higher up the eco-innovation hierarchy
- Avoid lock-in to suboptimal technologies
- Maintain diversity and flexibility of possible alternative technological trajectories
- Consider the appropriate timing when implementing policies
- Combine a sector-specific perspective with cross-sectoral measures
- Prioritize win-win eco-innovations
- Focus on design elements
- The stringency of regulations is key for radical eco-innovations ...
- ... but within long-term compliance periods ...
- ... which limit uncertainty for investors in eco-innovations
- The style of regulation is a relevant variable
- Promote a cooperative, participative approach between actors
- Combine sticks and carrots
- Adopt a supply chain, life-cycle, multi-media perspective

Source: Authors' own table.

also because the total cost of a large number of single, end-of pipe treatments becomes clear'. Similarly, Ashford[94] argues that 'one justified criticism of traditional regulation is that it is fragmented on a media-specific basis. Air, water and waste regulation evolved as separate systems and uncoordinated regulatory requirements do create disincentives for holistic, prevention-oriented technological change.'[95]

Table 4.1 summarizes the previous discussion on the main features of a policy approach to promote eco-innovation.

4.4   WHAT TYPES OF SPECIFIC MEASURES ARE OUT THERE?

Measures to facilitate eco-innovation can be grouped into three large categories: environmental policy instruments, technology policy instruments and other measures. This section describes those measures and their potential role in promoting eco-innovation.

4.4.1 Environmental policy instruments

Traditionally, environmental policy instruments have been grouped into three categories: command-and-control (CAC) instruments, market-based instruments and a miscellaneous category.

4.4.1.1 Command-and-control (CAC) instruments

These instruments encompass different types of measures. In general, they can either require the adoption of a specific technology to address a given environmental problem (technology standards) or rather require that firms maintain their environmental impacts within acceptable levels (performance standards). The discussion on the eco-innovation impact of CAC regulation has focused on these two areas. It is generally believed that either of the CAC instruments are less effective at stimulating eco-innovation than market-based instruments.[96] In turn, a widespread belief is that technology-based standards provide a weaker incentive to eco-innovate than performance-based standards because the latter allow for greater scope in determining how to achieve the regulatory goal.[97] Technology standards specify the technology that has to be adopted by the firms in a sector, and thus they are rigid since they provide little incentive to apply or develop other technologies. Performance standards require firms to keep emissions or discharges within specific limits (emissions standards) or to keep the concentration of pollutants within acceptable limits (environmental standards), but both allow firms to comply with the requirement however they deem best, that is, they do not require firms to adopt a specific technology and, thus, provide a certain leeway to eco-innovate.

Norberg-Bohm[98] gives two main reasons why performance standards have been a limited force for green innovation. First, they are generally based on existing technology, and thus promote diffusion rather than innovation. Second, they are implemented by requiring polluting entities to obtain a permit to pollute. Although firms are allowed to comply using any technology, this is the exception rather than the rule because permits are easier to obtain when the technology used as a basis for the standard is employed. Thus, performance standards often act as de facto technology standards. Similarly, Ashford[99] argues that it might be difficult to distinguish between the two types of standards, because what appears to be a performance standard may *de facto* be a technological standard, because only one technology can allow firms to comply with the performance standard.

For example, performance standards might be based on levels of performance which could be achieved with the installation of best available technologies. Performance standards designed in this way are not structured to require firms to search for novel means of improving environmental performance, as is reported to be the case in Canada.[100]

However some authors challenge the view that market-based instruments are more effective at stimulating innovation. For example, based on a case study on the German power industry, Oosterhuis[101] observes that 'direct regulation may also be a powerful instrument in spurring eco-innovation (provided that the standards set are tight and challenging) because firms may have an interest in developing cleaner technology if they can expect that that technology will become the basis for a future standard (for example BAT), so that they can sell it on the market'. That is to say, direct regulation can play a positive role in inducing environmental innovation under certain conditions.[102]

All in all, certain design elements of the standards may be more conducive to eco-innovation than others. For example, when using standards it is important that the regulator gives industry enough time to develop solutions that are environmentally benign and meet important user requirements.[103]

4.4.1.2   Market-based instruments

Market-based (also called incentive-based) mechanisms encompass a wide variety of instruments, but these can be summarized into taxes (or, more generally, fiscal measures), tradable permit systems, subsidies, deposit-refund schemes (product take-back regulation) and awards.

- *Taxes* require regulated entities to pay a certain amount of money for each unit of pollutant emitted or discharged to the environment (that is, the tax rate). Thus, firms have an incentive to develop or adopt an eco-innovation in order to reduce total payments. These savings have to be compared to the costs of investing in R&D to develop the eco-innovation or with the costs of the new equipment (machinery) embedding the eco-innovation.
- In a *tradable permits scheme*, the regulator sets an environmental target (that is, a certain level of emissions) to be attained by a given date, and issues a number of permits equal to the amount of pollution (emissions) allowed by the target. Those permits can be

distributed to the regulated firms freely (based on the level of pollution, that is, emissions of the firm in a reference year). But companies may also be required to pay for those permits in an auction. Either way, firms have an incentive to eco-innovate in order to reduce their pollution and either sell the permits not needed to other firms or reduce the need for permits they have to buy. Again, the costs of purchasing or developing the eco-innovation have to be considered.

- *Subsidies* have also been used in order to promote eco-innovation. They can take the shape of an investment subsidy (that is, a single payment to firms developing or adopting an eco-innovation, which covers up-front costs partially or totally) or a production subsidy (that is, support is given per unit of production achieved with the new eco-innovation[104]). Of course, this instrument would tend to encourage the adoption of eco-innovation, although it could also encounter some problems. For example, its additionality may be very low, that is, firms would have adopted the eco-innovation even if a subsidy was not granted.[105] This windfall profit for adopters cannot be justified either on environmental or on economic grounds. Furthermore, subsidies may encourage market entry of firms in the sector.[106]

- *Deposit-refund schemes and product take-back regulation.* Deposit-refund system consists of a 'deposit', which a front-end payment for potential pollution, and a 'refund' which is a guarantee of a return of the deposit upon proving that the pollution did not take place.[107] On the other hand, product take-back regulation seeks to reduce waste disposal and develop recycling markets by requiring manufacturers to manage the end-of-life disposition of products they produce.[108] According to Türpitz,[109] its effectiveness is limited to those companies that are interested in taking back their own products after the utilization phase or making money in recycling them.

- *Government awards* can be considered another economic instrument. For example, in Taiwan, awards are given every year to companies that demonstrate the best improvement in environmental performance through adopting clean techniques[110] (see also Box 4.2).

These instruments have usually been praised for their superiority over CAC instruments in relation to the encouragement of technological innovation because they provide a continuous economic incentive to

Box 4.2   Japanese Top-Runner Program

When the Kyoto Protocol was entered into force and greenhouse gas reduction goals were established, strengthened energy conservation measures were specified as leading measures to counter global warming. Japan consequently revised the Energy Conservation Law in April 1999 with the goal of strengthening the legal underpinnings of various energy conservation measures. As a staple energy conservation measure for the residential and commercial sector and the transportation sector, the Top Runner Program was introduced to advance energy efficiency of machinery and equipment:

- METI standards for 21 energy-using products.
- The 'top-runner' regarding energy efficiency becomes the basis of the product standard (weighted average).
- Efficiency standard becomes mandatory for national producers and importers once the target year is reached.
- 'Name and shame' approach is used as an intermediate instrument.
- Combined regulations: Green Procurement Law (2001), green automobile tax, annual awards for energy efficient products, energy label and support for innovative retailers.

The fulfilment of the standards is generally very positive. Several products have achieved the standard before the target year (air conditioners, cars, computers, videotape recorders). Increased competitiveness of the products has confirmed by producers. It is now needed to consider specifying additional product categories from commercial machines and equipment which are currently covered only by 20 per cent, and newly prevailing high energy-consuming products. Regarding commercial machines and equipments, many products are exempted from the target candidates due to the lack of established objective and quantitative method to measure the energy consumption efficiency. Therefore, it is particularly required to examine the measuring method and strengthen the countermeasures for commercial sectors where energy consumption considerably increases.

Sources: Jaenicke, M. (2008) 'Ecological modernisation: new perspectives', *Journal of Cleaner Production*, 16, 557–565.
ECCJ (2008) 'The Top runner Program in Japan', Energy Conservation Center, Japan, http://www.eccj.or.jp/top_runner/index_contents_e.html, date accessed 14 November 2008.

reduce emissions with new technologies in order to reduce compliance costs. The firm has a double incentive to adopt more radical environmental technologies: on the one hand, a clean technology may reduce emission abatement costs. On the other, by controlling its emissions the company reduces its tax payments (or, in the case of permits, uses fewer permits to bridge the gap between its actual emissions and its allocated permits).[111]

Although some authors believe that empirical evidence is generally consistent with theoretical findings that market-based instruments for environmental protection are likely to have significantly greater impacts over time than command-and-control approaches on environmentally-friendly technologies,[112] others are particularly critical in this regard.[113] All in all, it is safe to say that the superiority of market-based instruments in pulling innovation still needs to be empirically demonstrated.[114]

4.4.1.3 Other environmental policy instruments

Finally, a third category would encompass those environmental policy measures which cannot be included in the previous categories. Of course, this means that instruments which are very different from one another are considered here. Some of these instruments could be deemed 'voluntary' and others 'informational'.

- *Environmental Management Systems* (EMS) provide a systemic instrument for firms to identify their environmental impacts. EMS may or may not be certified by an independent third party. In this latter case, there are two alternatives at an international level: ISO 14001 and EMAS. Both are voluntary standards and have been developed to help firms to meet the requirements of an EMS and establish management processes to control and improve their environmental performance and reduce their environmental impacts.[115] Although asking for EMAS or ISO certification may be expensive for a firm (this is one of the reasons that few SMEs have adopted them), it has additional advantages to those stemming from the adoption of a non-certified EMS: the environmental image of the firm could be reinforced vis a vis key stakeholders, including public authorities, purchasing firms, consumers, etc.

It is assumed that EMS would provide an incentive for firms to correct their environmental impacts through eco-innovation. However, as observed by Del Río,[116] the empirical literature does not provide definitive conclusions in this respect, with some studies claiming a positive impact of EMS implementation on clean technology adoption[117] and others the opposite.[118]

Their influence on the uptake of radical eco-innovations is particularly controversial. Könnölä and Unruh[119] argue that EMS can contribute to inertia in present production systems and that, together with other factors this inertia can inhibit dramatic shifts toward more sustainable technologies and systems. Indeed, there might be a chicken-and-egg problem here: does EMS encourage the adoption of cleaner technologies or does the pre-existence of cleaner technologies in the firm increase the propensity to implement an EMS?[120] Firms adopting clean technologies may be more likely to do so because they are usually proactive ones, and not because they have adopted an EMS. Thus, mandating or providing incentives for firms to adopt an EMS might not be effective in encouraging eco-innovation.

- *Voluntary agreements* (VAs) encompass a wide range of initiatives. One of the most relevant is an agreement between the regulator and the firms whereby the latter commit themselves to reducing the emissions or discharges of pollutants by a certain amount before a given date. The threat of a regulation which would be imposed in the event of non-compliance is usually behind this agreement and provides an incentive for firms to comply. They have the potential to introduce flexibility and smooth dialogue between the firm and the regulator, which are positive elements in the promotion of environmental technological change. Furthermore, they allow the planning of investments for the long-term without being threatened by short-term changes in environmental regulation. However, some empirical studies (in the Dutch context) show that VAs stimulated the diffusion of EOP technologies but they had a modest effect on the promotion of radical clean technologies.[121] The information asymmetry between the regulator and the regulated and the inherent incentive of the latter to be subject to lenient targets is behind the limited boost to eco-innovation provided by this instrument. Elsewhere,[122] we suggest that an enhanced learning process between authorities, industry and other stakeholders can help solve such shortcomings and, in particular, facilitate the generation of alternative technological pathways to escape techno-institutional lock-in (see also Box 4.3).
- *Information disclosure schemes*. These are instruments which oblige firms to inform their communities or the public in general

Box 4.3   Toward prospective voluntary agreements: reflections from a hydrogen foresight project

In Könnölä *et al*[123] we proposed an integrative policy tool, the prospective voluntary agreement (PVA), as a vehicle that can help synchronise environmental and innovation policyfields. The PVA combines the virtues of two existing policy approaches: foresight activities and environmental VAs. Foresight initiatives create improved understanding of entire innovation systems and common vision for future actions. Environmental VAs utilize multi-stakeholder negotiation techniques to arrive at mutually acceptable goals that may generate more efficient results than regulatory actions for the environment. PVA combines these two approaches to commit key-stakeholders into action to create desirable and even radically different futures.

In a subsequent paper[124] we applied and elaborated this approach in the context of the Nordic Hydrogen Energy Foresight project (Nordic Foresight).[125] Conducted between the years 2003 and 2005, this project is particularly interesting from the viewpoint of PVA, as it deals with the facilitation of the systemic transformation from present energy systems toward the H2 energy economy. The exercise was a collaborative effort between the Ministries of five Nordic countries including Denmark, Finland, Iceland, Norway and Sweden along with extensive and numerous research, industry and government stakeholders. It was a pilot foresight exercise at Nordic level with a total budget of 730,000 euros, co-funded by the Nordic Innovation Centre, Nordic Energy Research program and 16 Nordicpartner organizations. Fundamentally, it was designed to provide decision support for defining Nordic R&D priorities and making effective framework policies for the introduction of H2 energy in Nordic countries. The main steps of the project included a series of pre-structured interactive scenario, vision, roadmap and action workshops, which were supported by extensive preparatory work including systems analysis and modelling of alternative H2 systems. In our paper we posited that PVA can assist decision makers in facilitating the emergence of the H2 economy through a process that ultimately commits the key-stakeholders to future actions, and we recommended the creation of further research on PVA with application to other technology fields.

about their environmental output (emissions and discharges) and, hopefully, enhance the environmental awareness of firms and increase public pressure to reduce the environmental impacts of their production processes. They encompass community, right-to-know and pollution inventories. One of the most well-known examples is the Toxic Release Inventories (TRI) in the US. In her assessment of the TRI, Norberg-Bohm[126] argued that, by complying with this legislation, both firms and the public have developed greater knowledge of the sources, types and quantities of emissions which has enabled firms to identify opportunities to reduce emissions while saving money and enabled the public to exert pressure on firms to reduce emissions. The information generated within the firm can stimulate pollution prevention. The evidence suggests that these instruments work best in the context of large companies and environmentally aware communities[127] and, thus, provide a limited driver to eco-innovation in other contexts.

- *Product-related policies* encompass a diversity of instruments which aim to reduce the environmental impacts of products. Some do so by allowing firms to learn more about the environmental impacts of their products from cradle to grave (through a life-cycle analysis (LCA) of their products), others provide a tool to let consumers know which products have lower life-cycle environmental impacts (ecolabels), while others make the producer responsible for taking care of the environmental impacts of the product after the end of its useful life (producer product responsibility) and thus design the product in a way which minimizes those impacts. To motivate firms to eco-innovate to achieve better environmental performance, they must understand their environmental impacts and their current costs for managing those impacts.[128] Nevertheless, the effectiveness of these instruments at encouraging eco-innovation still needs to be demonstrated. All in all, they should always be combined with other instruments (that is, not applied in isolation).

4.4.2 Innovation policy measures

Again, this category is made up of different initiatives. The most relevant are the following:[129]

- *Government funding of RD&D*. These are subsidies granted by the government to public or private institutions in order to cover part of the RD&D costs of invention, development and the first commercial application of eco-innovations (for example, through the co-financing of pilot and demonstration projects).[130]

This is a crucial instrument for mitigating the double externality problem of eco-innovations and encouraging them in their initial stages, when they are immature, that is likely to be costly and of inferior quality compared to existing, competing technologies. In this regard, they have proven to be a very effective instrument.[131]

However, it might also have some drawbacks. One of these is that it requires governments to pick winners, which has been demonstrated to lead to technological failures sometimes. If it is combined with the conducting of technological foresight studies (see p. 80), this problem can be circumvented to a certain extent, however. Another problem, common to investment subsidies is that of additionality and windfall profits, that is, some eco-innovations would probably be developed in the absence of R&D support, because they are attractive from a private investor point of view.[132]

- *Technological assistance programs.* A major factor inhibiting the uptake of eco-innovations is the lack of technological capacity or competency within the firm. This can be enhanced in various ways, that is, by providing firms with information on new eco-innovations or by training the human resources within the firm in the new eco-innovations. For example, regulators in some countries and/or regions already provide information on environment-related technological capabilities. Indeed, such programs lower the cost of eco-innovation because firms do not have to devote resources to gathering the information provided by the regulator.[133] This provision by government of technical information and advice can be particularly important to SMEs lacking in-house technical specialists.[134] Information should be used as a complementary instrument to others, and not as a single instrument.[135]
- *Training in new technologies.* This is one type of technology assistance program. If one of the problems with the uptake of eco-innovations is the difficulty on the part of existing human resources within the firm to manipulate the eco-innovation, then an instrument which provides training on the new eco-innovations might be particularly effective. Therefore, improving the skills base of the firm through educating and training its operators, workers and managers could encourage eco-innovation.[136] This is already done in several countries. For example, the government in Taiwan periodically organizes sector-specific cleaner production training workshops for industry.[137]

- *Strategic Niche Management* involves the creation of protected niches to promote the development and diffusion of emerging, promising eco-innovations. Niche markets are created through subsidies (or other instruments). Eco-innovations at the development stage, but also those already fit to be commercialized, often suffer from higher costs and perceived or real lower quality and are unfamiliar to potential users. The niche channels financial support for the technology and allows unitary cost reductions, the participation of different stakeholders in the development of the technology and a reduction of the uncertainty usually involved in such a process. Close collaboration between the actors (firms, users, public administrations) is encouraged. In addition, the niche provides information to the decision maker (and to consumers) which raises their awareness of the economic costs, the technical feasibility and the social acceptance of the new technology.[138]
- *Foresight exercises* can play an important role by building common visions on future developments across the policy fields and industrial sectors as well as by identifying various drivers for and barriers to eco-innovation. Foresight exercises also support the priority setting that contributes to the efficient use of resources and sharing the risks of common action plans.[139] Foresight exercises strengthen existing networks and stimulate the generation of new partnerships among the different actors related to the eco-innovation, which is crucial to connect technological supply and demand and wire up the innovation system.[140] Furthermore, foresight activities can foster the development and adoption of eco-innovations by identifying and assessing innovation ideas,[141] The goal is to identify technologies (eco-innovations) that are still at a pre-competitive stage of development and which may merit public support, given their social benefits, their potential for cost reduction and the barriers to their development or deployment.

  A related instrument is Environmental Technology Assessment, which focuses on the preliminary assessment and evaluation of the environmental consequences of specific technology options. It is a qualitative multidisciplinary tool based on dialogue and whose aim is to aid the selection of the most suitable technology option at the start of its development.[142]
- *Creation of a network of actors involved in eco-innovation* (networking). Empirical studies show that technological change is a social and dynamic process taking place successfully in networks

characterized by continuous interactions between actors.[143] An instrument which has proven relatively effective at encouraging eco-innovation is to stimulate directly the creation of knowledge networks for sharing information and knowledge between firms with the government acting as a match-maker. This has been the case of the Danish Clean Technology Development Programme, in which the Danish Environmental Protection Agency has played an active role in selecting environmentally beneficial projects and in finding the right partner with whom to co-operate.[144] The program brought together firms with an environmental problem and firms and institutes that could provide solutions to these problems. Thus, it built a network of technology suppliers, users, and research institutes and, according to Kemp,[145] it was highly effective in encouraging innovation.

4.4.3 Other measures to facilitate eco-innovation

- *Public procurement*, which can be regarded as either an environmental or a technology policy instrument, tries to create a demand for eco-innovations that are not currently attractive to the private sector. Empirical evidence has shown significant positive effects of public procurement on eco-innovation, although the aforementioned problem of 'picking winners' remains.[146]
- *Instruments targeted at SMEs*. In Chapter 3 it was shown that there are several barriers to eco-innovation in SMEs, including scant financial resources, low technological capability and relatively lower levels of environmental awareness. Several studies show that, in order to reduce environmental impacts in these firms, a combination of policy elements is needed: well-conceived regulations, accessible environmental tools, education and environmental awareness-raising, on-the-ground inspections, specific information and exchange of good practices.[147] In order to promote eco-innovation in SMEs, instruments which increase their technological competency should be used. In addition, other useful instruments include the creation of information centers on environmental technologies, subsidizing the carrying out of eco-audits, implementation of EMS and the training of the staff on environmental issues and providing special financial conditions (that is soft loans or subsidies) for investment in eco-innovations, especially of the radical type.[148] All in all, it is necessary to carry out an analysis of the barriers to eco-innovation for SMEs in specific sectors.

The identification of those barriers will provide valuable input for proposing policy measures.

- *Establishing long-term visions.* Some approaches are based on the idea that establishing a guiding vision for the transformation of the economy in the mid- and long-term towards sustainable patterns of production and setting targets accordingly could become strong drivers for investing in new technologies, and in replacing old technologies by more sustainable ones.[149] Two of the most relevant in this regard are performance targets and transition management. According to Calleja and Delgado,[150] performance targets set a performance level, which should become a minimum level within a certain time and which can be revised and get tougher with time: 'This will increase the chance for the Performance Targets both to deliver an improved market for the environmental technologies that are already on the market or close to market, and to "guarantee" a market for the new innovative products, processes and services, that are to be developed in the near future.' 'Transition management', developed by Rotmans, Kemp and van Asselt[151] is about working towards a transition

Table 4.2   Instruments to encourage eco-innovations

Environmental policy instruments	• CAC instruments (technology standards, performance standards) • Market instruments (taxes, ETS, subsidies, deposit-refund schemes) • Other (EMS, ecolabels, life-cycle analysis and producer product responsibility, voluntary agreements, information disclosure)
Technology policy instruments	• Government funding of RD&D • Technological assistance programs • Training in new technologies • Strategic Niche Management • Technological foresight studies • Environmental technology awards • Innovation waivers • Creation of a network of actors involved in environmental technological change (networking)
Other instruments	• Public procurement • Instruments targeted at SMEs • Establish long-term visions

Source: Authors' own table.

that offers collective benefits in an open, exploratory manner. The goals, as well as the instruments of change, need to be regularly re-evaluated. The transition objective is in fact a basket of objectives informed by the visions of those participating. Both objectives and final visions are determined socially and not just by expert scientific knowledge.[152]

It should be mentioned that the successful promotion of eco-innovation probably requires a combination of the aforementioned instruments, because the barriers to eco-innovation are multifaceted and related to different factors and each instrument may be particularly effective at tackling just one barrier, as discussed in the next section.

4.5   WHAT MEASURES ARE MORE APPROPRIATE FOR TACKLING SPECIFIC BARRIERS TO ECO-INNOVATION?

Obviously, not all measures are equally effective at mitigating the influence of the barriers to eco-innovation which were mentioned in Chapter 3. This section provides a brief discussion of those instruments which are more likely to deactivate specific barriers to eco-innovation, taking into account the aforementioned classification of these obstacles.

4.5.1 Factors internal to the firm

Generally, measures in this area are aimed at encouraging eco-innovations by mitigating the negative influence of several barriers: financial constraints, lack of internal technological competency and a corporate strategy in which environmental protection maintains a low profile thanks to the attitude of managers. Finally, the impact of all these barriers tends to be felt with special intensity in SMEs and, thus, the development and adoption of eco-innovations in these firms is particularly difficult. Therefore, some instruments should specifically aim at tackling the obstacles to eco-innovation in these firms.

4.5.2 Factors external to the firm

Other instruments should aim either to stimulate or mitigate the external factors and actors that either drive or inhibit the uptake of eco-innovations. In this context, the role of public policy should be to combine carrots and sticks, that is, to activate the influence of social actors through provision of information flows, encouragement of collaboration and creation of actor networks and to use the coercive forces of environmental regulation (through traditional environmental command-and-control regulation or market-based instruments).

4.5.3 Techno-economic characteristics of the technologies

Finally, a set of instruments could be used to reduce the negative influence on eco-innovation of barriers related to the techno-economic characteristics of eco-innovations, such as their costs, their level of complexity and potential incompatibility with the existing production system. Again, depending on the problem, a particular combination of environmental policy, technology policy and other instruments can be recommended.

In line with the above discussion, Table 4.3 identifies the most effective measures to mitigate the aforementioned barriers and encourage the uptake of eco-innovations.

Table 4.3   Summary of the most-effective measures to tackle different barriers to eco-innovation

BARRIER/DRIVER	MEASURES
1. Factors internal to the firm Financial situation	• Information campaigns emphasising the existence of win-win eco-innovations (short pay-back periods) • Partial subsidies for up-front investments • Flexibility in target compliance • Instruments to distribute risk such as public and private venture capital funds
Size (SMEs)	• Provide training and information on environmental compliance and eco-innovations. • Provide financial support (direct subsidies, accelerated depreciation schemes, tax exemptions…) • Flexibility in target compliance • Enhance intra and inter-sectoral alliances and clusters
Characteristics of the sector	• Combine cross-sectoral with sector-specific measures • Sector VAs
Lack of technological competency (employees)	• Subsidize environmental and energy audits • Provide environmental training courses for employees • Training on new technologies • Technological assistance programs • Support R&D investments • Promote a networking approach, that is collaboration partnerships and information flows between the firm and other actors

(Continued)

Table 4.3   Continued

BARRIER/DRIVER	MEASURES
Attitude of managers towards change, environmental protection and innovation	• Support environmental training courses for managers • Support the implementation of environmental management systems in companies • Support the realization of an LCA of the company's products • Foresight exercises • Environmental technology awards • Information provision to firms • Establish long-term visions
2. Factors external to the firm Economic downturn	• Encourage the uptake of eco-innovations with short pay-back periods • Investment subsidies for the adoption of cleaner technologies
Lack of information	• Promote information dissemination to firms through industrial associations and Chambers of Commerce • Support R&D investments • Organize or support environmental training courses for employees. • Training on new technologies • Technological assistance programs • Support the implementation of environmental management systems in companies • Foresight exercises • Establish long-term visions
Suppliers	• Foresight exercises • Establish long-term visions • Creation of a network of actors involved in environmental technological change (networking) • Improve performance testing, verification and standardization of the innovations reaching the market
Final consumers/ industrial clients	• Increase the environmental information levels of the general population (consumer and purchaser awareness with environmental problems) • Implement information disclosure programs • Support the implementation of credible (standardized) ecolabels • Support the realization of life-cycle assessments of products along their entire value chain • Use public procurement as a driver to accelerate the uptake of environmental technologies

(Continued)

Table 4.3   Continued

BARRIER/DRIVER	MEASURES
Competitors	• Level the playing field and avoid treating otherwise similar firms unequally (avoid exemptions)
Industrial associations	• Use these organizations as a useful intermediary with companies (information dissemination and training courses)
Environmental NGOs and green parties	• Provide information on environmental problems and cooperate with firms • Promote engagement of business-NGOs partnerships in public problem solving
Civil society	• Increase public awareness of environmental problems • Support the realization of LCAs in firms • Support the implementation of standardised ecolabels
Research centers	• Promote links between research centers and firms (that is, when subsidizing R&D investments) • Creation of a network of actors involved in environmental technological change (networking) • Foresight exercises
Financial institutions	• Provide subsidies on interest rates • Implement instruments to distribute risk such as public and private venture capital funds
3. Techno-economic factors Costs and cost-savings	• Level the playing field through environmental policy measures (preferably economic instruments) which penalise conventional technologies and encourage eco-innovations (carrot and stick) • Strategic Niche Management • Public procurement (if long-term cost-reduction potential of the technology is identified) • Inform about likely win-win opportunities in the sector (energy-efficiency) • Encourage the adoption of EMS and the realization of energy and environmental audits (subsidies) • Investment subsidies for the adoption of cleaner technologies
Complexity of eco-innovations	• Support the organization of training courses on the use of the new technology for the existing workforce and/or provide fiscal advantages for the hiring of specialized, highly skilful human resources

(*Continued*)

Table 4.3   Continued

BARRIER/DRIVER	MEASURES
Compatibility with the existing system. Existence of an installed based. High up-front costs. Complementary innovations	• Technological assistance programs • Foresight exercises • Provide subsidies covering part of the necessary up-front investments (especially for SMEs) • Consider the capital cycle when proposing measures • Provide information (especially in the case of technologies with high up-front costs but short pay back periods) • Strategic Niche Management
Sectoral technological opportunities	• Consider the characteristics of the sector (including the sector's system of innovation) when proposing measures to encourage eco-innovation • Foresight exercises
Criteria to assess the new technologies	• Information dissemination on eco-innovations • Foresight exercises • Establish long-term visions

Source: Authors' own table.

4.6   WHAT MEASURES ARE MOST APPROPRIATE FOR PROMOTING SPECIFIC TYPES OF ECO-INNOVATION?

Different eco-innovation types may be more sensitive to the influence of certain instruments than others. A policy strategy to encourage eco-innovation should take these differences into account. This section discusses which measures are likely to be more suitable for promoting different eco-innovation types. In particular, it is discussed which measures are more effective at encouraging immature versus mature, process versus product and incremental versus radical eco-innovations.[153]

As argued in section 4.4, a combination of measures is needed to boost eco-innovations. This is even truer in the case of systemic radical eco-innovations. In other words, the higher we move up the eco-innovation hierarchy, the more likely it is that a combination of instruments will be needed to encourage the uptake of eco-innovations. This involves applying environmental and technology policy instruments, as well as 'other' measures which can be effective in particular settings. Given that the major aim of environmental policy instruments is to internalize the externalities, that is to reduce the pressures on the environment and do so at a reasonable social cost (which sometimes will involve the promotion of environmentally sound technological change), environmental policy will be implemented irrespective of the need to encourage eco-innovation. Thus, complementary instruments will be required.

4.6.1 Mature versus immature eco-innovations (related to the stage of the innovation cycle)

Immature eco-innovations are still at a pre-competitive or pre-commercial stage and need to improve their quality and/or reduce their costs in order to ultimately enjoy commercial success. Supply-push measures are particularly effective at achieving this aim:

- Supporting investments in R&D in the technology would help reduce those costs and improve its quality.
- Strategic Niche Management allows the technology to advance along its learning curve and reduce its costs and create a body of actors that become familiar with the new technology.
- Technological foresight studies enable an analysis of the technological and socio-economic feasibility of eco-innovations, providing information on technologically and economically feasible courses of action in eco-innovation and encouraging actors to follow them.
- Creation of actor networks also facilitates information flows between agents engaged in the innovation process and, thus, the realization of the necessary improvements in eco-innovations in order to make them attractive for further commercialisation.
- The creation of shared long-term visions may positively affect the development of eco-innovations by identifying likely scenarios and courses of action in which eco-innovations can play a relevant role and reducing the risks for potential investors in eco-innovations.
- Public procurement could be highly useful in this initial stage of the innovation process, because it generates a demand for technologies which otherwise would not exist (because of their high costs), effectively creating a market niche in which they can develop (that is, reduce their costs and improve their quality) without competing with much more mature technologies. Indeed, public procurement is likely to be part of the wider approach of Strategic Niche Management.

In contrast, the demand-pull provided by environmental policy instruments is more suitable for mature technologies, which have already reached the commercialisation stage and are ready for adoption and diffusion. Given their alleged (although contested) superiority, this demand-pull should preferably be based on market-based instruments (taxes, tradable permits). Ecolabelling schemes and providing information to consumers and firms may contribute to boosting the demand-pull required for these eco-innovations.

Insofar as up-front investment costs are a major barrier to their adoption and diffusion, information provision and investment subsidies for the adoption of cleaner technologies (covering part of the investment and limited in time) should also be granted. Furthermore, special attention should be paid to the adoption of mature eco-innovations by SMEs and instruments should be implemented accordingly. In this case, 'carrots' (in the form of investment subsidies and information campaigns) are likely to be more effective at stimulating the uptake of eco-innovations than 'sticks' in the form of taxes, ETS or CAC regulation), although this issue deserves to be the focus of further research.

Finally, technology-policy instruments such as training in new technologies, technological assistance programs and the creation of a network of actors involved in environmental technological change can be particularly effective at stimulating the adoption of mature eco-innovations since they favour their integration into the existing production process of the firms and/or increase firms' knowledge of their existence.

4.6.2 Process versus product eco-innovations

Although not too much research has been done on the different factors driving or inhibiting the development, adoption and diffusion of process or product eco-innovations, existing (though scant) literature has shown that they are likely to differ.[154] This means that the most effective instruments are also likely to be different between those two categories. While traditional environmental regulation (in the form of CAC such as performance-based standards or market-based instruments such as taxes or emissions trading schemes) or other instruments specifically aimed at process innovations (such as EMS) seem to be more effective for process eco-innovations, those instruments which are more directed towards enhancing the market-pull of eco-innovations (such as ecolabelling or providing information to consumers) or others particularly aimed at products (such as product bans or creation of niches for specific products) should rather tackle product eco-innovations. Nevertheless, most instruments considered in section 4.3 are probably equally effective at encouraging the uptake of product and process eco-innovations (for example, VAs and support for R&D investments). Furthermore, environmental policy instruments are needed to stimulate both types of eco-innovations.

4.6.3 Incremental versus radical eco-innovations

In general, the same type of instruments can be applied to both types of eco-innovations, but some are better targeted at radical eco-innovations than others. In general, radical eco-innovations are more disruptive and, thus, need a greater degree of support, more stringent regulations, targeted instruments and a wider array of measures which tackle different barriers (economic, technological, social and otherwise). Thus, a major factor encouraging these eco-innovations is not the choice of instruments but the style of regulation and some other aspects mentioned in section 4.2. Of these, probably the most relevant is the stringency of regulation: radical eco-innovations are unlikely to be adopted in the absence of ambitious environmental targets and/or high levels of support for these eco-innovations. In addition, these technologies will need the implementation of different types of technology policy instruments which reduce their costs, improve their quality or increase their degree of adaptability to the existing productive system. In this context, strategic niche management, subsidies to cover the initially high upfront costs, training in new technologies, technological assistance programs, technological foresight studies and the creation of a network of actors involved in environmental technological change can be considered effective at stimulating eco-innovations. Finally, other measures such as public procurement and the establishment of long-term visions may be particularly effective in this regard.

In contrast, incremental eco-innovations, which can be easily introduced into the production process without major disruptions and sometimes at a relatively low upfront cost, do not need this level of public policy commitment. Most incremental innovations are already mature and highly cost-effective, and their lack of adoption is probably related to informational problems regarding their existence and characteristics. This is why (in addition to environmental policy instruments) information-based instruments are particularly effective in this respect.

Table 4.4   Summary of the most effective measures to encourage specific types of eco-innovations

Immature eco-innovations
- Predominantly supply-push measures (technology policies)
- R&D investments
- Development of actor networks
- Strategic niche management
- Technology foresight studies
- Environmental technology awards
- Public procurement
- Establish long-term visions

Mature eco-innovations
- Predominantly demand-pull measures (environmental policies)
- Market-based instruments
- Information provision
- Training in new technologies
- Technological assistance programs
- Creation of a network of actors involved in environmental technological change (networking)
- Investment subsidies for the adoption of cleaner technologies

Process eco-innovations
- EMS
- Information disclosure
- Government funding of RD&D
- Training in new technologies
- Creation of a network of actors involved in environmental technological change (networking)
- Investment subsidies

Product eco-innovations
- Ecolabels, life-cycle analysis and producer product responsibility (information campaigns targeted at consumers)
- Government funding of RD&D
- Technological foresight studies
- Creation of a network of actors involved in environmental technological change (networking)
- Establish long-term visions
- Public procurement

Incremental
- Information dissemination to firms
- Creation of a network of actors involved in environmental technological change (networking)

Radical
- Design elements and style of regulation is key: stringency ...
- Government funding of RD&D
- Subsidies to cover the initially high upfront costs
- Training in new technologies
- Technological assistance programs
- Strategic Niche Management
- Technological foresight studies
- Creation of a network of actors involved in environmental technological change (networking)
- Public procurement
- Establish long-term visions

Source: Authors' own table.

CHAPTER 5

Business strategies for eco-innovation

5.1 INTRODUCTION

Since the publication of *Changing the Course*, the introductory book on eco-efficiency by the World Business Council for Sustainable Development's Steven Schmidheiny,[1] companies have increasingly sought win-win solutions that combine simultaneous improvement in corporate competitiveness and environmental performance. Theoretical work supports this approach[2] and argues that pollution is a sign of both environmental and economic inefficiency, and that many cost-effective environmental measures are inadequately exploited by managers. This divergence from neoclassical profit-maximization arises because managers are constrained by imperfect information, cognitive limitations and the existence of inappropriate organizational/incentive structures within companies.[3]

The general corporate response to these challenges has been to improve management controls through the implementation of formalistic and procedural Environmental Management Systems (EMS). A variety of European and inter-national EMS were introduced throughout the 1990s and now over 130,000 companies hold ISO 14001 certificates worldwide.[4] Beyond these official registrations, many more companies – and other organ-izations including universities and public agencies – have implemented uncertified environmental management systems. Thus EMS have seemingly become the pre-eminent approach to environmental management globally. EMS-driven incremental approaches to environmental management appear to account for 70–90 per cent of environmental technology expenditures, and have focused principally on waste management, energy use and water consumption.[5] In this chapter, we discuss environment management beyond the standardized EMS and explore ways in which the private sector can become proactive and differentiate between environmental management efforts and integrate eco-innovation into their corporate strategy.

Sooner or later, environmental damage will have a negative impact on the economic system that caused it, and, inevitably, the related cost must be paid. Here, eco-innovation makes it possible to reduce this cost and/or generate overall benefits that outweigh it. Eco-innovation has many social benefits: it helps society grow and prosper in a way that is environmentally sustainable; it helps create a more competitive, creative and innovative economy; it contributes to creating new markets, industries and jobs; and further afield, eco-innovation can become a company's trademark recognized by its customers and other interested parties. However, bringing about eco-innovation depends basically on the individual benefits received by the innovator. There is no doubt that the way companies organize their manufacturing processes and the characteristics of the products and services they launch have a critical impact on our environmental surroundings. Changing these decisions will depend on companies' assessment of their potential benefits and risks. Unfortunately, surveys often reveal that companies could conduct a more in-depth assessment of the costs or benefits of their environmental activities. Furthermore, regardless of their willingness to eco-innovate, the ability of companies to do so will be subject to the sectoral, national and international innovation systems they depend on.

Eco-innovation can help enhance a company's competitive edge in different ways:

1. improved operating and reductions in the costs caused by ineffective resource management
2. reduction in pollution control and waste management costs
3. reduced risk of breaching environmental regulations
4. marketing innovation itself and the creation of new markets or market segments
5. improved image and relationships with customers, suppliers, authorities and employees.

Generally speaking, the benefits of eco-innovation are not easily measured by companies or statistics agencies, which is undoubtedly in keeping with the traditional view that the environment is more of a burden than an asset. However, one of the interesting conclusions of a study of more than 1,500 companies in all the manufacturing and service industries of five European countries revealed that the uptake of the most beneficial environmental innovation had increased the sales of 16 per cent of the surveyed companies.[6] Another more recent survey of 40 global companies in Europe, US and Japan whose businesses rely heavily on technology, concluded that 95 per cent of the surveyed companies believe that eco-innovation has the potential to generate added value for business.[7] Amongst the companies which said they had already incorporated sustainability into their business, 60 per cent reported improvements in turnover and 43 per cent in their year-end results due to cost reduction. The companies which had not yet incorporated sustainability also regarded eco-innovation as a potential source of benefits in terms of market share, income and profit margins.

Indeed, eco-innovation is increasingly offered to businesses as a panacea to solve today's major sustainability and competitiveness challenges. However, ultimately, the success of the eco-innovation is dependent on diverse factors, of which not all are always in the hands of the company – as noted in Chapter 2. Therefore, the key question is what management can really do to take up an eco-innovation in its corporate strategy. In this chapter, we approach eco-innovation from the business perspective. Following the framework of the design, user, product/service and governance dimensions, we identify starting points and strategies to manage eco-innovation.

5.2   DESIGN DIMENSIONS OF ECO-INNOVATION

As described in Chapter 2, the design of environmentally benign products and services may be stimulated by exploring the opportunities offered by the three design dimensions: additional components, sub-system changes and system changes. Most businesses invest in additional components to secure their licence to operate but also in the development of components in search of competitive advantage. This is especially true in the case of seeking sub-system changes and eco-efficient solutions. However, it is less common to find companies being proactive proponents of system change leading to eco-effective management practices.

The design and development of a new eco-innovation is a complex and demanding process that requires taking into account the diverse dimensions of innovation management such as the management of research and development (R&D) projects, their financing and related intellectual property issues. In particular, the focus on the environmental and economic performance of the product or service means that careful examination of its anticipated environmental benefits and related present and future policy measures is crucial. However, this is not easy. As discussed in Chapter 2, a product once considered environmentally sound may subsequently be considered even harmful.

Therefore, environmental performance should also be assessed at the system level. Even if the component addition would be a real improvement for the environment, the system it is part of may be considered environmentally harmful. For example, as mentioned in Chapter 2, the use of catalytic converters in combustion engines reduces volatile organic compound emissions but increases CO_2 emissions due to lower fuel efficiency. Fundamentally, it supports the legitimacy and use of the combustion engine instead of exploring alternatives to it. In that case, the added component may be a part of a bigger problem. It is crucial that managers prioritize and define design efforts and their respective required resources, expertise and design tools.

One of the first steps to integrated design dimensions of eco-innovation in company practice is acquiring the necessary expertise. The successful integration of a new design of the component addition or sub-system change requires particular attention to engineering abilities – either in-house or in the form of external partnerships. Additionally, designing the system change may need the engagement of multidisciplinary teams and external partnerships with other companies and research institutes.

The managerial decisions to initiate eco-innovation projects can be supported by taking stock of the existing initiatives and tools for designing eco-innovations. Here, we provide brief descriptions of some of the most common and practical tools for the design and assessment of eco-innovation. Following the approach described in Chapter 2, we start with the discussion of the design tools for minimizing environmental impacts. The tools for eco-effective solutions to environmental challenges are dealt with later.

5.2.1 Design tools for minimizing environmental impacts

A number of design approaches which focus on minimizing environmental impacts of products and services are available, including life-cycle analysis, design for environment and eco-efficiency. They address environmental improvements mainly by means of additional components (end-of-pipe technologies) and sub-system changes (eco-efficient solutions). Commonly used life-cycle analysis (LCA) involves the evaluation of the environmental aspects of a product system through all stages of its life-cycle. Also called 'life-cycle assessment', 'life-cycle approach', 'cradle-to-grave analysis' or 'ecobalance', it represents a rapidly emerging family of tools and techniques designed to help environmental management. The LCA supports the design and production of new products and materials. It can also be used as a basis for eco-labelling requested by consumers, NGOs and international and national government agencies and as an instrument for industry, leading to cost-savings and competitive advantages. LCA can help to assess whether a company's choices are environmentally sound, be it in the design, manufacture or use of a product or system. Companies using LCA can discover important product improvements and new approaches to process optimization. For instance, Alcan – a global manufacturer of primary aluminium and related products based in Canada – used LCA when the company re-designed its aluminium foil packaging and reduced the mass by 50 per cent. LCA was used to help quantify the benefits (reduction in cardboard use, more efficient use of retail shelf space and more economical transportation).

The term 'life-cycle' refers to the assessment of raw material production, manufacture, distribution, use and disposal, including all required transportation steps. Together, these phases form the life-cycle of the product. Environmental impacts can be categorised in many ways. For instance, quite typical categories are global warming (greenhouse gases), smog, ozone layer depletion, acidification, eutrophication, eco-toxicological and human-toxicological pollutants, desertification, land use, as well as depletion of minerals and fossil fuels. In the LCA, such impacts generated along the life-cycle phases are inventoried, like emissions to air, water or soil, resources taken from the biosphere, or land uses (see also Table 5.1). It is thus possible to assess which processes in a product's life-cycle are important contributors to damages and which are the major determinants of environmental performance.

Each phase of the product's life-cycle consumes materials and energy (inputs) and releases wastes and emissions into the environment. Additionally, each stage in the product life-cycle has social impacts and involves economic flows. The above matrix of Table 5.1 can be used to provide an overview of the environmental inputs and outputs at each phase of the product life-cycle. It also gives some idea of where additional information is needed. It can help the environmental team make a quick qualitative assessment of the life-cycle. The columns correspond to the different product life-cycle phases and the rows concentrate on the relevant impacts on the environment. LCA procedures are gradually gaining ground as an important part of corporate environmental management systems. For instance, LCA forms part of ISO 14000 environmental management standards.

However, LCA efforts are typically focused on the environmental assessment of *existing* products. In this sense, most attention is paid to incremental improvements in *present* products. These efforts offer

Table 5.1   An example matrix for life-cycle analysis

	Raw material production	Manu-facture	Distribution	Usage	Disposal	Transportation	The whole life-cycle of the product
Greenhouse gases							
Acidification							
Smog							
Ozone layer depletion							
Eco-toxicological pollutants							
Eutrophication							
Human-toxicological pollutants							
Desertification							
Land use							
Depletion of minerals							
Fossil fuels							

significant progress in their short-term economic and environmental efficiency, but become less profitable in the long-term, leading only to limited improvements in environmental performance. Unlike LCA incremental improvements, far-reaching environmental improvements can be achieved through the implementation of more fundamental, strategic choices to support eco-innovation at the early stages of the product development process (as an example, see Box 5.1).

According to some estimates, 80 per cent of the products we buy today become waste within one year of purchase. Recycling is the collection of waste materials for re-processing into new marketable goods. Unfortunately, for most companies recycling their products at the end of their useful life is a difficult and complex task. There are many barriers to the successful collection and reprocessing of materials. Perhaps the most important is the fact that most companies have based their business on what is called a 'through-put model' of production. In this model material inputs are 'put through' production processes to create marketable goods and services. These products are sold to the company's customers and forgotten. When they

Box 5.1   STRETCH: A strategic tool in Phillips for environmental design

The STRETCH method was specifically designed by Phillips to go beyond conventional LCA and address strategic choices in design for environment. The method consists of five steps, which help identify the most promising environmental product opportunities:

1. the identification of the crucial driving forces that will influence the business strategy in general;
2. the design of a limited number of plausible scenarios that the company can adopt on the basis of step 1, leading to a list of potential product market strategies;
3. the specification of potential environmental opportunities and threats for each scenario on the basis of a checklist of environmental options;
4. the selection of environmental challenges per product leading to a substantial improvement of its environmental performance; and
5. the implementation of the environmental challenges ultimately selected.

Source: Cramer, J. and Stevels, A. (1997) 'STRETCH: Strategic Environmental Product Planning with Philips Sound and Vision', *Journal of Environmental Quality Management*, Autumn Issue, 91–101.

have served their purpose and come to the end of their useful life, customers do the normal thing and throw them in the garbage where they join millions of other tonnes of worn-out products in landfills. This results in a massive waste of resources and energy.

In the last few years, the concept of Design for Environment (DfE), or eco-design, has also become an integral part of management practices to minimize environmental impacts. While LCA is often used to analyze existing products and services, DfE focuses on the design of new products and services (see for example Box 5.2). Business may find it more efficient to design products for disassembly, modular upgradeability, and recyclability at the outset than to deal with disposal problems at the end of a product's life.

Design for environment can reduce reprocessing costs of products to market more quickly and economically. The economic and environmental benefits have crystallised into the concept of

Box 5.2   EcoDesign Pilot: Online tool for design for environment

The Institute for Engineering Design in Vienna has developed an eco-design tool. Starting with product development strategies enables the improvement of an existing product. In order to improve its environmental performance, each product requires specific measures depending on its environmental impact at different stages of its service life. Thus, different measures have to be taken for products whose main environmental impact takes place at the use stage (use-intensive) than for products whose main impact occurs during manufacture (manufacture-intensive). The tool includes the eco-design checklist of measures for the different types of products such as raw material-intensive, manufacture-intensive, transportation-intensive and disposal-intensive products.

Improvement objectives and strategies for raw material-intensive products:

- Use alternative materials, selecting the right materials
- Use less of a given type of material, reducing material inputs
- Make intensive use of resources, optimizing product use, optimizing product functionality, improving maintenance
- Use resources as long as possible, increasing product durability, improving reparability, reuse materials contained in the product, improving disassembly, reuse of product parts, recycling of materials.

Improvement objectives and strategies for manufacture-intensive product:

- Use less energy and material in the production process, reducing energy consumption in production process, optimizing type and amount of process materials
- More efficient use of materials used in the production process, avoiding waste in the production process, purchase of external materials/components, ecological procurement of external components
- Use the product as intensively as possible, optimizing product use, optimizing product functionality, improving maintenance, use the product for a longer period of time, increasing product durability, improving reparability

- Reuse components and/or the product, improving disassembly, reuse of product parts.

Improvement objectives and strategies for transportation-intensive product:

- Change packaging, reduction of packaging
- Change transportation, reduction of transportation.

Improvement objectives and strategies for disposal-intensive product:

- Use alternative materials, selecting the right materials
- Prolonged use of the product, increasing product durability, improving reparability
- Disassembly and recycling, improving disassembly, reuse of product parts, recycling of materials.

Source: EcoDesign (2008), http://www.ecodesign.at/index.en.html (home page), date accessed 14 November 2008.

eco-efficiency. WBCSD[8] defined the principles of eco-efficiency as follows:

- A reduction in the material intensity of goods or services;
- A reduction in the energy intensity of goods or services;
- Reduced dispersion of toxic materials;
- Improved recyclability;
- Maximum use of renewable resources;
- Greater durability of products;
- Increased service intensity of goods and services.

The practical tools developed for evaluating eco-efficiency include, for instance, the Eco-compass – developed by Dow Europe (see Box 5.3) – and the packaging scoreboard of Wal-Mart, developed to improve the performance of its suppliers (see Box 5.4). Since eco-efficiency includes economic issues as well, it creates links between environmental issues and the financial goals which management is trained to focus on. Indeed, financial evaluation must also be carried out in order to establish whether the proposed changes are economically valuable. In case

Box 5.3   ECO-COMPASS: A practical efficiency scorecard
developed by Dow Europe

The Eco-compass was developed by Dow Europe to provide a practical and simple tool for management decision-making. LCA is an important tool for gathering and analyzing data, but the final assessment often becomes so complex that it is difficult to base decisions on this method only. The Eco-compass is developed to overcome these disadvantages; was designed to condense environmental data into a simple model, which would assist in the integration of environmental issues into the business decision process.

The compass has six poles or 'axes', which are intended to represent all significant environmental issues: mass intensity, reducing human health and environmental risk, energy intensity, reuse and revalorisation of wastes, resource conservation and extending service and function. The Eco-compass is a comparative spider web diagram, which evaluates new options or designs against the original design or 'base case'. Each of the axes records a score from 0–5 for the new product. The base case always scores 2 in each dimension and the new option can score from 0 (environmental impact doubled) to 5 (environmental impact reduced by at least factor 4). All six dimensions are considered to ensure that every aspect of ecological and resources security is taken into account. The trade-offs between them are highlighted too. Eco-compass data is always expressed per specific unit and measures a delivery of a service to a customer.

Dow Europe's eco-compass has been used for several businesses, among them the well known Ranx Xerox case. Ranx Xerox was remanufacturing, reusing or recycling the 80,000 copiers it takes back each year. This is a typical win-win situation:

• Customers deliver their old machine and get a remanufactured machine for a cheaper price than a new one, but with the same quality
• Xerox saves money because reuse is cheaper than producing a new machine
• The impacts on the environment decrease because of less use of raw materials and energy and the decreased emissions

- The eco-compass for Xerox remanufactured copiers compared to an ordinary machine shows that:
  - Service extension has increased from score 2 to score 3 (more durable machines)
  - Revalorisation from score 2 to 4 (2/3 of the machines are recovered)
  - Energy from 2 to 3 (less use of processing virgin materials)
  - Mass (mass intensity reduced by 19 per cent through less use of virgin materials)
  - Health and environmental potential risk remain unchanged (score 2)
  - Resource conservation not changed.

Sources: Fussler, C. and James, P. (1996) *Driving Eco-Innovation: A Breakthrough Discipline for Innovation and Sustainability* (London: Pitman Publishing).
DPPEA (2008), North Carolina Division of Pollution Prevention and Environmental Assistance, http://www.p2pays.org/ (home page), date accessed 14 November 2008.

Box 5.4   Wal-Mart Packaging Scorecard to Suppliers

In November 2006, Wal-Mart Stores, Inc. launched a packaging scorecard for its suppliers in order to reduce packaging across its global supply chain. The packaging scorecard is a measurement tool that allows suppliers to evaluate themselves relative to other suppliers, based on specific metrics. The metrics in the scorecard evolved from a list of favourable attributes known as the '7 R's of Packaging': Remove, Reduce, Reuse, Recycle, Renew, Revenue, and Read. Wal-Mart outlines the following metrics for the packaging scorecard:

- 15 per cent will be based on GHG/CO_2 per ton of Production
- 15 per cent will be based on Material Value
- 15 per cent will be based on Product/Package Ratio
- 15 per cent will be based on Cube Utilisation
- 10 per cent will be based on Transportation
- 10 per cent will be based on Recycled Content
- 10 per cent will be based on Recovery Value
- 5 per cent will be based on Renewable Energy
- 5 per cent will be based on Innovation.

These criteria are valuable tools for suppliers to determine how their packaging innovations, environmental standards, energy-efficiencies and use of materials match up to those of their peers. Suppliers will receive an overall score relative to other suppliers, as well as relative scores in each category. For example, a supplier may find it is in the 50th percentile in the Cube Utilisation category for effectively using space in pallets and shipping containers, but that same supplier may only be in the 20th percentile in Recycled Content. This model gives suppliers the opportunity to focus on specific changes within the context of a fluid environment, driving constant change and improvement in the supply chain.

Wal-Mart shares the packaging scorecard with its global supply chain of more than 60,000 suppliers. Suppliers will be able to input, store and track data, learning and sharing their results. Wal-Mart uses the packaging scorecard to measure and recognize its entire supply chain based upon each company's ability to use less packaging, utilize more effective materials in packaging, and source these materials more efficiently relative to other suppliers.

Source: Walmart Stores, http://walmartstores.com/ (home page), date accessed 14 November 2008.

of the use of the Eco-compass, Fussler and James[9] define the objective for eco-innovation projects by using the five innovative moves:

- Accept the eco-efficiency challenge and assemble key data. You need environmental, product and marketing information to identify needs and ground ideas. You must also define your expectation of value and the criteria you will use to assess it
- Identify eco-efficiency opportunities for each compass dimension. The central question is always how environmental impacts can be reduced so that customer value is increased
- Organize the ideas emerging from stage two
- Harvest the value options that emerge at stage three to identify potential eco-efficiency winners
- Prepare and commit to the implementation of the most promising proposals.

5.2.2 Design tools for system change and eco-effective solutions

The idea of taking into consideration not only the negative but also positive impacts of human activities as a design criteria has been developed recently in connection with the concept of eco-effectiveness which addresses system-level changes.[10] This approach builds on the analogy between natural and socio-technical systems elaborated in industrial ecology,[11] how industrial systems should incorporate principles exhibited within natural ecosystems and shift from linear (open-loop) systems – in which resource and capital investments move through the system to become waste – to closed-loop systems where wastes become inputs for new processes.

Particularly, the identification of by-product synergies and the development of industrial parks have further expanded the design focus from individual products or companies to value networks and industrial clusters. An eco-industrial park is a community of manufacturing and service companies which improve their economic and environmental performance by collaborating in the management of environment and resource aspects including materials, energy, water, information and habitat. The principle underlying eco-industrial parks and by-product synergy is that one industry's waste stream can be used as a raw material (input or energy) by another. It is a simple idea, but one which has enormous potential for reducing waste volumes and toxic emissions to air and water, as well as cutting operating costs. In order to facilitate an exchange of materials and resources, businesses need to work together to determine what unwanted by-products exist, and what their potential applications are. The resources may be then be exchanged, sold, or passed free of charge between sites, creating a by-product synergy, when available (see for example Box 5.5).

The exploration of industrial synergies has created a positive process of identifying areas of improvement and efficient use of resources. However, to move towards biocompatible production practices and lifestyles it is crucial to examine the fundamentals of human activities. Towards this end, the Natural Step was developed in Sweden in 1989 by Karl-Henrik Robèrt, who used a consensus process involving the country's top scientists to define principles of a sustainable society. The principles look at the earth as a complex system of which humans are an integral part. The four systems conditions listed form the basis of the Natural Step:

1. Materials that humans take out of the earth such as lead and mercury cannot be allowed to accumulate in the environment. The environment and health-related issues due to lead and mercury are probably the most well known problems the first condition addresses.

> ### Box 5.5   Kalundborg Eco-industrial Park
>
> The most well known example of industrial parks is found in Kalundborg, Denmark. Kalundborg is an industrial port city of 20,000 people, approximately 110 Km west of Copenhagen and home to several large industries:
>
> - Asnaes Power Station – Denmark's largest coal-fired power station
> - Statoil – Denmark's largest refinery
> - Gyproc – alarge plasterboard factory
> - Novo Nordisk – an international biotechnology company manufacturing pharmaceuticals and industrial enzymes
> - City of Kalundborg – an industrial city of 20,000 people.
>
> Over two decades, these partners developed a series of material and waste exchanges that simply evolved and were not originally planned. A collection of one-on-one deals were struck among the various companies which made economic sense for each of the pairs of participants, and as it turned out, good sense for the environment.
>
> *Sources*: Alberta Environment (2008), http://www3.gov.ab.ca/env/waste/pprevention/indeco/parks.html, date accessed 14 November 2008.
> Industrial Symbiosis Exchange of Resources (2008), http://www.symbiosis.dk (home page), date accessed 14 November 2008.

2. Materials that are created by humans cannot build up faster than the ecosystem can break them down. Examples of this range from materials which are harmful in relatively small doses such as DDT, PCBs and ozone-depleting chemicals, to materials which are less harmful but are being produced in very large quantities, such as CO_2.
3. Human activity cannot destroy the ability of the earth to provide the services we need. Examples include farming practices that cause erosion or land use practices that destroy the flood-calming and water-filtering abilities of wetlands.
4. Resources need to be used equitably and efficiently. Equitable distribution means that poor people will not have to destroy their natural resources just to survive in the short-term.

The Natural Step process helps companies to understand the connections between their business and the earth's ecological processes. The Natural Step in many ways is a continuation of other efforts by business to improve its processes and reduce its impact on the world. These other efforts have included Total Quality Management, Total Quality Environmental Management, pollution prevention, toxics use reduction, design for the environment, ISO 9000, and ISO 14000. The Natural Step moves beyond these to focus on how businesses will work in a sustainable society.

Along similar lines, the active proponents of the eco-effective design approach, McDonough and Braungart[12] have launched the concept of cradle-to-cradle as opposed to the conventional cradle-to-grave LCA approach (see Box 5.6). The fundamental elements of cradle-to-cradle design are based on the principles that drive these systems in nature:

5.2.2.1 Waste equals food

- Design materials and products that are food for other systems. This means designing materials and products to be used over and over in either technical or biological systems
- Design materials and products that are safe. Design materials and products whose life-cycle leaves a beneficial legacy for human or ecological health
- Create and participate in systems to collect and recover the value of these materials and products.

5.2.2.2 Use current solar income

- The quality of energy matters. Use renewable energy
- Celebrate diversity
- Water is vital for humans and all other organisms. Manage water use to maximize quality and promote healthy ecosystems while remaining respectful of the local impacts of water use
- Use social responsibility to guide a company's operations and stakeholder relationships.

Within this concept, the systemic approach to environmental design leads to two alternative design perspectives:[13] 1) closed cycles referring to the design of the uptake of the products back to industrial production processes at the end of their useful life to produce products of equal or more value; and 2) open cycles referring to the design of

Box 5.6   Cradle-to-Cradle Design Certification

MBDC, a consulting firm of McDonough and Braungart, also offers cradle-to-cradle certification services that provide a company with a means to measure achievement in eco-design and help customers purchase products. This certification program includes requirements for:

- Product/Material transparency and human/environmental health characteristics of materials
- Product/Material reutilization
- Production energy
- Water use at manufacturing facility
- Social fairness/corporate ethics.

The assessed product is defined in relation to the appropriate cycle (that is technical or biological) and all components are defined as either biological or technical nutrients. If the product combines both technical and biological nutrients, they should be clearly marked and easily separable. Based on the interpretation of the data for all criteria, chemicals and materials are 'scored' for their impact on human and environmental health. A key factor in this evaluation is the risk posed by the component/chemical, which is a combined measure of identified hazards and routes of exposure for specific chemicals and materials, and their intended use in the finished product.

Source: MBDC Cradle to Cradle Certification (2008), http://www.c2ccertified. com (home page), date accessed 14 November 2008.

products that are biodegradable and become nutrients to new cycles within the ecosystem:

- According to the first perspective, the product materials, such as minerals or plastics, need not be minimized because they are used again and not thrown away as waste to provide landfill. Industry can make considerable savings by recovering valuable materials from used products and avoiding environmental sanctions
- According to the second perspective, products made of natural, safely biodegradable materials can be returned to nature to feed ecosystems instead of harming them. Thus, at the end of its useful

lifetime, the 'disposal' of the product can become easy and even valuable.

These two approaches need to be applied in an intelligent way, taking into consideration the impacts of the whole lifetime and life-cycles of products. For example, as an alternative to using only natural, biodegradable fibres like cotton for textile production (a pesticide-intensive agricultural process), it may be more environmentally friendly still to use non-toxic synthetic fibres designed for continuous recycling into new textile products. Examples include also the Ford Motor Company, which has developed a concept car called the Model U (following Ford's famous Model T) which offers all the convenience and functionality of a normal car, but has designed out many of the environmentally damaging aspects. As a design consultant on the project, William McDonough explains it this way:

> It's a vision for cars that are made entirely of materials with positive human and environmental impacts; biological and technical nutrients made and assembled so they can be separated when the car is disassembled, and returned to the soil or to industry; polymers and metals recovered and recycled at the same level of quality or better, for reuse in generation after generation of vehicles; engines running on energy that's derived from the sun, and producing no pollution.

Indeed, McDonough considers that eco-effectiveness can have profound implications for industries and end-users in relation to how they see their impacts on the environment. He even sees it presenting a challenge for maximizing positive impacts of human activities on the environment, 'driving your car can be a positive event on all counts' (see also, Box 2.2 in Chapter 2).

Effective recycling requires companies to rethink their business models and incorporate the recovery of their worn out products when they reach the end of their useful life. It requires 'closing the loop' and designing a reverse logistics model to capture a company's obsolete products. These companies should regard these materials not as waste, but as assets. Once a new model is in place, waste products become valuable resources that the company can use over and over again. This is already true for most steel and aluminium manufactures. By some estimates, 80 per cent of all aluminium ever produced is still in circulation. According to one aluminium executive, 'that aluminium is one of our valuable assets and we want it back!'.

Once the material is recovered, companies also need effective operations to reuse and recycle the materials. Unfortunately, most efforts are usually 'downcycling,' which means that the collected materials are used in 'lower' quality products. For example, a car tyre is melted down and used as road paving materials. While this is better than burying the tyres in a landfill, it still leads to resource exhaustion in the future. Innovative companies are looking to eliminate this waste by designing products that can be collected and their material recycled back into a new product. Shaw Industries, a textile manufacturing firm, has developed carpets and flooring materials that involve no downcycling (see EcoWorx case in Chapter 6). When the carpeting is worn out, it is collected and the material is 'upcycled' back into new and better carpet. This 'full circle' recycling represents the cutting edge in eco-intelligent innovation.

Another advanced approach to environmental design, taking into account different system levels, are the 'Twelve Principles of Green Engineering' developed by the American Chemical Society as a framework within which to examine existing products and guide their re-design as well as to evaluate new product designs. Green engineering is the development and commercialisation of industrial processes that are economically feasible and reduce the risk to human health and the environment.[14] The Twelve Principles have been applied, for instance, to the EcoWorx system, described in Chapter 6.

5.3   USER DIMENSIONS OF ECO-INNOVATION

Users can play a crucial role both in the development of new eco-innovations and in their application and wider diffusion. How the user community accepts the innovation and is willing to learn and participate in the development of the product or service often determines the success or failure of the whole innovation process. Separate corporate research laboratories seem to be disappearing and/or transforming into market-driven contract research entities.[15] This reflects the paradigmatic change in corporate R&D from basic science and technology push driven innovation processes to innovations that emerge close-to-the-market.[16] Main drivers for close-to-the-market innovation processes come from societal changes of modernisation and global competition that require faster and better RTD and business operations. At the same time, there are major long-term societal challenges, such as climate change and the social equity dilemma between the North and South. All this calls for a proactive role for corporate innovation activities to engage in close collaboration with other stakeholders to explore alternative futures and prepare common action plans for innovations and industrial renewal.

5.3.1 User perspectives in the development of eco-innovation

The heart-lung machine and the first automated drug pumps were not developed by firms manufacturing medical equipment[18], but by doctors at the leading edge of practice. In the same way, novel food categories like sports energy drinks and gels were developed by sports enthusiasts. Some companies are actively trying to take advantage of this process of user-centered innovation.[17] For the business interested in the renewal of their activities and generating new eco-innovations, it may be highly practical to work close to the user. The user-centered innovation process can be a sharp contrast to the traditional model, in which products and services are developed by manufacturers in a closed way, the manufacturers using patents, copyrights, and other protections to prevent imitators from free-riding on their innovation investments. In this traditional model, a user's only role is to have needs, which manufacturers then identify and fill by designing and producing new products. The manufacturer-centric model does fit some fields and conditions. However, users may be the first to develop many new industrial and consumer products. Furthermore, the contribution of users is growing steadily, largely as a result of ongoing advances in computer and communications capabilities.

Companies may receive the stimulus to eco-innovate in the form of a 'market pull' from their customers, who are other actors in the supply chain. This might be the case both from final consumers (if the company produces final demand products), as well as from industrial clients (if the firm manufactures intermediate products, that is products which are purchased by other firms). Customer pressure to eco-innovate is likely to increase in product market segments that are close to final consumers. However, low consumer and purchaser awareness of environmental problems may act as a significant barrier to eco-innovating. However, at least in Europe, the tendency seems to be towards growing environmental awareness, which can be an important driver in the future.

In order to involve users into the innovation process systematically, firms need a special ability to identify which users are capable of providing valuable inputs in innovation projects and how to engage them in innovation activities. The lead user methodology[18] aims to identify and involve progressive users in the idea generation and development phase (see also Box 5.7). Lead users differ from ordinary users in two

Box 5.7   Lead user method

According to Von Hippel, the implementation of lead user integration involves four major steps:

- Identification of trends
- Identification of lead users
- Development of lead user product concept
- Market testing.

Identification of trends: Before one can identify lead users in a given product category of interest, one must identify the underlying trends on which these users have a leading position. Methods used could range from intuitive judgments of experts ('Delphi method') to simple trend extrapolation and more complex econometric models. It seems easier to predict future trends for industrial goods than it does for consumer goods.

Identification of lead users: On the basis of the detected trends, the second step is to identify a sample of lead users. Lead users should be at the leading edge of the trend being studied and should display correlates of high expected benefit from solutions to related needs. The identification of lead users is certainly the most crucial step of this approach. According to the relevant literature, lead users can be identified by databank analyzes, surveys or personal interviews.

Development of lead user product concepts: The third step is to produce innovation oriented information on lead user needs and use contexts. The outcome of this step is one or more new product or service concepts judged by participants to be responsible for lead user needs. Methods in this step could range from standard market research to active involvement of lead users, for example by product development workshops.

Market testing: As the needs of today's lead users are not necessarily the same as the needs of future customers, the final step in the lead user method is to test whether concepts found valuable by lead users also will be valued by the more typical users in the target market.

Since the introduction of the method in 1986, lead user projects have been applied by a number of companies, including Hilti, 3M, Nortel Networks, Phillips, Pitney-Bowes, Nestle, Kellogg, Verizon, Siemens, and so on.

Sources:
von Hippel, E. (1988) *The Sources of Innovation* (Oxford University Press).
von Hippel, E. (2005) *Democratizing Innovation* (MIT Press).

respects. First, they are among the first ones to identify new needs. Second, they benefit significantly by obtaining a solution to those needs and, therefore, are highly motivated to engage in the new product development process.[19] The concept of the lead user method can be expanded on by focusing on sustainable lead users.

Furthermore, some industries, such as utilities, have developed specific approaches to include customers' needs and preferences in their approach to pollution prevention. Demand-side management focuses on understanding these needs and uses of products in a way that may lead to the discovery of new business opportunities. Demand-side management is based on three fundamental principles:

1. do not waste the product (electricity)
2. sell exactly what the customer demands, and
3. make the customer more efficient in the use of the product.

However, this approach has prompted criticism, as it may have been interpreted as unsuitable for conventional business concepts.

Taking into account the major challenges user innovation pose to manufacturers, Von Hippel[20] identifies three general possibilities for manufactures to (re)position their activities:

1. Produce user-developed innovations for general commercial sale and/or offer custom manufacturing to specific users.
2. Sell kits of product design tools and/or 'product platforms' to ease users' innovation-related tasks.
3. Sell products or services that are complementary to user-developed innovations.

Firms in fields where users are already very active in product design are experimenting with all these possibilities.

Furthermore, a systematic search for user innovations and the further development of innovation created by lead users can provide manufacturers with a better interface to the innovation process as it actually works, and so provide better performance.

Organized cooperation is also common, with users joining together in networks and communities that provide useful structures and tools for their interactions and for the distribution of innovations. Innovation communities can increase the speed and effectiveness with which users and also manufacturers can develop and test and diffuse their innovations. They also can greatly increase the ease with which innovators can build larger systems from inter-linkable modules created by community participants.

5.3.2 User competencies and new networks for eco-innovation

While the business can consider it practical to work together with users in order to develop new eco-innovations, it is likely to be as important for the management to see the company itself as a user of eco-innovations. However, making the most of the opportunities of eco-innovations is often conditioned by the expertise the company has available, especially in the case of high-technology applications. Even if the eco-innovation is not developed in-house, a trained workforce and expertise should also be present, in order to properly install and adapt the newly purchased equipment to the major techno-economic features of the company, but also in order to operate the new equipment and to maintain it. It has been found that plant managers are often unwilling to invest in clean technologies because they do not have the in-house technical capacity, skilled technicians or engineers to operate clean technologies. As observed by Montalvo,[21] insufficient availability of expertise in eco-design, current training and clean technology capacity building at sector level and insufficient understanding and experience in cleaner production project development and implementation play a role in the adoption of new cleaner production processes.

If the firm has previously invested in R&D, this would have a positive impact on the adoption of eco-innovations, because this investment increases the knowledge of the firm, which is key to engaging in information flows to be aware of the existence of potential eco-innovations relevant for the firm and to be able to implement it within its pre-existing production process (absorptive capacity). Some empirical studies have already shown the impact of a lack of technological competency on the development and adoption of eco-innovations, focusing on clean technologies. For example, lack of awareness/understanding of cleaner production principles was found to be a barrier to the uptake of cleaner production practices in South African industry.[22] Visser et al[23] also established empirically that education and training of potential adopters is essential. The Environmental Technologies Action Plan (ETAP) of the European Union illustrates this relevance with an example in the construction sector, where the diffusion of the most advanced energy saving technologies is dependent on small local fitters and repair companies.[24] In an analysis of the implementation of best available technologies (BATs) in the Italian galvanic industry, Cagno and Trucco[25] discovered that the technical and operational know-how of firms was one of the two critical elements for BAT implementation (the other being the profitability of those technologies).

Technological skills can be enhanced, according to Ashford[26] by both (1) increases in knowledge or information about cleaner opportunities, partly through formal Technology Options Analysis, and partly through serendipitous or intentional transfer of knowledge from suppliers, customers, trade associations, unions, workers, and other firms, as well as reading about environmental and safety issues (all leading to increased technological diffusion); and (2) improving the skills base of the firm through educating and training its operators, workers and managers, on both a formal and informal basis, leading to technological innovation.

A key aspect of the technological ability to eco-innovate (development and adoption) and use technological opportunities offered by the market depends on the creation of relationships and the formation of strategic alliances with actors across the production chain (customers or suppliers) and to use collaboration networks with research institutions in order to outsource the acquisition of knowledge needed for the innovation process.[27] Closely related to collaboration amongst firms is the notion of inter- and intra-trade across the supply chain and its inherent power relations. The capacity to engage with and influence suppliers of technology, materials and inputs has been reported as a strong determinant of innovation. This is especially the case in industrial sectors close to large retail chains.[28]

Relevant actors in this respect include both input suppliers and equipment suppliers, who are key sources of technical information. However, the role of equipment suppliers is much more relevant in this regard, especially in the event that the company decides to purchase an eco-innovation rather than to develop it in-house. In this case, the role of suppliers might not only be as a key informant, but also as an effective collaborator in the adaptation of the technology to the characteristics of the existing production process. Furthermore, some eco-innovations are even developed jointly between the firm and its equipment suppliers. Berkhout[29] distinguishes between 'abatement technologies' (what we have termed 'end-of-pipe'), which are usually bought in from specialist suppliers; process technologies, which are developed through partnerships between capital goods suppliers and leading producers; and product changes, which are managed in-house as a critical source of competitive advantage. Equipment suppliers are a key element of the supply side of eco-innovations.[30] This might be problematic if, as stressed by ETAP,[31] it may be difficult to disseminate them because distribution channels for new technologies are not as good as those for established technologies.

5.4   PRODUCT SERVICE DIMENSIONS IN ECO-INNOVATION

In Chapter 2, we considered two crucial product service dimensions. First, the change in product service deliverable and, second, the change in the value network processes. Both dimensions deal with the changes in the earning logic of the company and the added value delivered to the customer. Product service dimensions can play a crucial role in the process of redefining the purpose of product lines or even the corporate mission and of converting existing business practice towards sustainability. Ultimately, the exploration of product service dimensions of existing practices may lead to the identification of new customers and business partners. The business can identify new opportunities by revisiting what they offer to their customers and how well they meet customer needs with what they offer. Williams[32] categorises different kinds of deliverables of product service systems:

• Product-oriented services
• Use-oriented services
• Product renting or sharing
• Result-oriented services.

Product-oriented services include concepts that focus on selling product as well as supporting services needed during the stage of product use. This includes offering advice and consultancy, for instance, advising on the most efficient use of the product. For example,

Castrol, a North-American supplier of professional lubricants and associated services, offers lubricant service packages that provide the customer with more than just the product. These include needs assessment, site surveys, analysis of costs and productivity indicators, training and performance assessment for opportunities to reduce lubricant consumption. They develop profit from cost savings given to customer, rather than just the volume of chemicals they sell. Another example of combining product with services is the Xerox Corporation, which originally only produced photocopiers, but has developed into a document company. They now offer a range of services including document translation, software, consulting services and outsourcing services. They have also developed their asset management program, where products are sold or leased under contract, guaranteeing customer satisfaction through functioning machines at a fixed price per copy.

Use-oriented services cover the approaches that focus on leasing the product. The provider retains ownership of a product and is responsible for maintenance and repair. In this case the user pays a regular fee and has unlimited and individual access. In the US, the carpet manufacturers DuPont and Interface have introduced product-service solutions by leasing carpets to consumers. They also offer service packages for maintenance and carpet cleaning. They recycle old carpets through carpet reclamation schemes. Millicare, also in the US, started out as a cleaning system and developed an environmental services system for office carpets and business clients. They offer maintenance services for carpets for reconditioning and reinstalling old carpet in other areas.

Product renting or sharing refers to the provider retaining ownership of the product and its maintenance and repair. Hence, the user pays a regular fee but does not have unlimited and individual access. In this case, the same product can be used simultaneously by many users. In Switzerland, the Mobility company is an organization of 1,400 cars at 850 locations in 350 communities for 37,000 customers. Customers pay a membership fee to Mobility and in return have access to a range of different vehicles, from a large van or lorry down to a small car.

Result-oriented service is a concept in which case the customer pays per service unit. The customer buys output of a product only according to level of use or functional result. The provider and consumer may also agree on an end result without specifying how the result is delivered. For example, Dow Chemicals developed the Safetainer system in response to German regulations on the handling of chlori-nated solvents. Dow has developed a closed-loop system of delivery and take-back of the used solvents using Safetainers, to recycle the solvents back to customers.

The product service dimensions of eco-innovation also address how the added value to the customer is generated. This calls for particular consideration of the overall business strategy and logic, including the convergence of supply chains. In doing so, the focus on management and operations moves from short-sighted local optimization to the entire supply chain during the production, consumption, customer service and post-disposal disposition of products. This stresses the relevance of a supply chain and value network perspective in eco-innovation. It can be argued that the search for environmentally superior solutions, and their successful implementation, requires a broader view of innovation that goes beyond internal management systems and the factory gates of any single company. No single com-pany, or government for that matter, can define and implement com-prehensive environmental solutions alone. There is an increasing need to have business capabilities to orchestrate interactions between dif-ferent actors in the value chains and networks.

5.5   CORPORATE GOVERNANCE FOR ECO-INNOVATION

Environmental governance innovation refers to all new and applied institutional solutions for resolving conflicts over environmental resources. From the view point of a company, the governance dimen-sion challenges management to look at the corporate functions and their roles as a part of society. It challenges management to renew its relation-ships with other stakeholders, particularly with government. This may be especially important in the search for environmental solutions, which often require system level changes and active engagement of the govern-ment and the business to jointly explore new ways to do things. In this section, we look at the governance challenges for the private sector from the viewpoint of corporate governance and management systems, as well as from the viewpoint of collaboration with the public sector and other stakeholders to overcome major barriers to eco-innovate.

Environmental issues are gradually entering the corporate routine, mainly thanks to the adoption of environmental management systems (EMS). Wagner[33] interprets the existence of EMS certification as a sign of competencies within the firm (that is environmental strategy related

to competency). This author considers ten dimensions of EMS implementation, including written environmental policy, procedure for
identification and evaluation of legal requirements, initial environmental review, definition of measurable environmental goals, program to
attain measurable environmental goals, clearly defined responsibilities,
environmental training program, environmental goals as part of a continuous improvement process, separate environmental/health/safety
report or environmental statement, and audit system to check environmental programs. In addition to EMS, other relevant organizational
factors have been identified in the literature: whether firms inform
consumers about environmental effects of product and production
processes, whether market research on the potential of green products
is carried out, whether firms use eco-labelling or carry out product
recycling, whether firms have implemented life-cycle assessment and
whether firms carry out benchmarking activities.[34]

Eco-innovation often requires a corporate culture which is
favourable to change in general and particularly proactive with
regard to environmental protection and innovation. This is so because
eco-innovation is at times a risky practice. Therefore, changes in corporate culture often come from external sources, which is also the
case in the energy sector, dealing with climate change issues (see
Box 5.8).

**Box 5.8   External pressures and the shift in the climate
policy of energy companies**

Like most of its fellow oil companies and a number of industry
associations, BP was formerly a member of the Global Climate
Coalition (GCC): The coalition has lobbied governments heavily
and has mounted persuasive advertising campaigns in the US to
turn public opinion against concrete action on greenhouse gas
emissions. The so called 'carbon club' leads the way in undermin-
ing public support for action to curb climate change. BP, attempt-
ing to brand itself as progressive, was one of the first to withdraw
from the GCC in 1997. In 1998, Shell followed BP and left the
coalition and, by early 2000, Texaco and others were joining the
movement away from the GCC.

Source: Corporate Watch (2008), http://www.corporatewatch.org.uk/, date
accessed 14 November 2008.

A necessary internal condition is a proactive stance on the environment. In other words, a corporate management commitment to environmental issues would contribute to engagement in eco-innovation practices. A proactive environmental strategy has to be adopted, environmental goals have to be established (including a written environmental policy) and an organizational structure with clear environmental responsibilities has to be implemented. This is a challenge for the firm. When these preconditions are absent then environmental responsibilities are not defined and adoption of eco-innovations is not likely to be considered.[35] Visser et al[36] empirically found that company strategy and the vision of the CEO and the management team were decisive to engaging in eco-innovations. Further to internal environmental management, companies are increasingly joining forces not only with other companies, but also governmental, nongovernmental and international organizations. For instance, the UN Global Compact initiative has enhanced cooperation among stakeholders around the world (see Box 5.9).

Especially incumbent companies tend to focus on *exploitation* activities through the optimization of existing production systems. While this can lead to improvements in environmental performance, it can also turn management efforts away from *exploration* activities that can lead to new, superior production and business models. EMS can exacerbate this tendency by focusing environmental innovation on incremental pollution reduction and away from new environmentally superior approaches. The concern is that EMS lock-in may foster a lock-out of initiatives for exploring discontinuity changes. It could be argued that over time this limitation may be overcome with the saturation of opportunities for incremental EMS improvements. Exhaustion of opportunities can occur because the first environmental improvements are typically the most economically viable, but as the low-hanging fruit[37] is harvested, it becomes harder and harder to find similar kinds of incremental efficiency improvements. As incremental improvements become exhausted, management attention can turn towards exploration activities. From the viewpoint of environmental protection, however, it makes a clear difference if the company pursues incremental improvements as long as possible or if it fosters radical changes by exploring new opportunities for discontinuous improvement early on.[38] While obviously not the only important factor, EMS is part of the overall innovation regime. If indeed, public and private policy makers wish to foster discontinuous environmental improvements then both

Box 5.9   UN Global Compact: Ecological Building Partnership

The Global Compact provides engagement opportunities for companies to contribute to the mission of the United Nations. Participating companies are encouraged to undertake partnerships with United Nations Agencies, other companies, governments, and Non-Governmental Organizations (NGOs) in order to help address significant global issues. The Global Compact has adopted a three-pronged model for describing the types of partnerships that companies can undertake. These include:

- Core business partnerships in which companies seek to use their own business operations
- Strategic Social Investment/Philanthropy in which companies provide funds or in-kind donations to support United Nations projects
- Advocacy partnerships in which companies collaborate with the United Nations to develop principles or guidelines in support of broad United Nations goals.

One example of advocacy partnerships is the Sustainable Building and Construction Initiative, which Lafarge initiated together with the United Nations Environment Programme (UNEP) and industry leaders to develop more sustainable practices for the buildings sector. As an industry leader, Lafarge is committed to influencing business partners and stakeholders to create more sustainable buildings. The company clearly recognizes that these goals are best achieved via a platform where the construction industry as a whole can develop and present its position. With a mandate to foster the identification and implementation of solutions to global environmental problems, the UNEP was ideally positioned to convene such a platform. Within a year, membership of the partnerships doubled to reach 30 companies from the original 15, representing all the different stakeholder groups along the life span of buildings.

Industrials, construction companies, real estate developers, financers, architects and local authorities are working with the UNEP to increase energy efficiency and reduce CO_2 emissions of buildings as well as develop benchmarks for sustainable building. In 2006, the initiative focused on three significant issues:

1. Establishment of a specialized think tank to analyze the sustainability performance of the building sector.
2. Identification of concrete proposals to include positive incentives for sustainable building in an agreement following the current Kyoto protocol, which ends in 2012.
3. Identification of policies and tools to promote life-cycle analysis and energy efficiency in buildings.

In March 2007, SBCI published the report 'Buildings and Climate Change: Status, Challenges and Opportunities'. It highlights the significant role that buildings play in climate change and points to solutions for improving their environmental impact. With the building sector producing some 40 per cent of waste and CO_2 emissions in developing countries, this joint effort on the part of private and public actors from across the globe can play an integral role in combating global climate change. Through the partnership, Lafarge has the opportunity to build and share information with a broad range of other key actors in the areas of construction and sustainable development.

Sources:
UN Global Compact (2008), http://www.unglobalcompact.org/, date accessed 14 November 2008.
UN Global Compact (2007) 'Joining forces for change: demonstrating innovation and impact through un-business partnerships', http://www.unglobalcompact.org/docs/news_events/8.1/Joining_forces_for_change.pdf, date accessed 14 November 2008.

businesses and governments need to consider the implications of broad EMS adoption.

Business organizations need to balance two conflicting needs to survive in the long-term. *Exploiting* existing production systems and product lines to maximize shareholder returns is clearly important in the short-term. However, limiting managerial attention to this role can threaten the long-term viability of an organization in the face of discontinuous change that alters the basis of competition in an industry.[39] For long-term survival, companies also need to pursue *exploration*, or the search for discontinuous innovations and market opportunities. To meet this demand, Tushman and O'Reilly have developed the concept of *ambidextrous organizations* as an organizational design that can balance these conflicting needs. This is equally true for environmental management innovations. Companies therefore need to develop alternative management activities and actively explore for discontinuous product and service innovations that eliminate environmental degradation at the design stage.[40] They need to be ambidextrous in their search for environmental improvements, something that over-reliance on EMS may hinder.

The generation of radically new environmentally benign options requires a redefinition of stakeholder roles and institutional structures in addition to actual changes in the production systems under management control. This means that managers must engage in an extended view of production systems to include, not only suppliers and customers, but also government and civil society stakeholders as partners in the innovation process. This participatory approach does not only relate to companies, but also to public policy-makers. Both policy-makers and other stakeholders tend to shape institutional context through their strategic actions of creating and claiming value[41] and can help create new social networks and agreements which can open up possibilities for lock-in breaking innovations. Governmental environmental policy-makers also need to be ambidextrous. In addition to providing incentives for the implementation of EMS standards, policy must also spur variations and the emergence of competing coalitions through support for the development of their widely different architectures, configurations, features and standards.[42] Furthermore, the exploration of new opportunities to eco-innovate is likely to lead to collaborative networks towards other industries, the government and academia (see, an example on the European Technology Platform, Box 5.10).

Box 5.10 Forest Industry led European Technology Platform

Since 2003, the Commission has encouraged industrial stakeholders to set up European Technology Platforms which the European Council has also promoted as one of the coordination tools to set up European R&D priorities, action plans and timeframes (European Commission, 2005). Among over 30 parallel initiatives, the planning of the Technology Platform for the Forest-Based Sector (FTP) was started in autumn 2003 by the European

Confederation of Woodworking Industries, the Confederation of European Forest Owners and the Confederation of European Paper Industries. In keeping with the general Commission guidelines (European Commission, 2005), the development of FTP consisted of a three-stage process:

1. Emergence and setting up, which was achieved by producing a vision document explaining the strategic importance of the FTP activity and its desired development objectives
2. Definition of a Strategic Research Agenda (SRA) consisting of agreed research priorities, including measures for enhancing networking and clustering of the RTD capacity and resources in Europe, and
3. Implementation of the SRA through the establishment of a new Technology Initiative or the application of Community research programs (that is, FP7), other sources of European funding, national RTD programs, industry funding and private finance.

Source: Forest-based Sector Technology Platform (2008), http://www.forestplatform.org/ (home page), date accessed 14 November 2008.

5.6   CONCLUSIONS

This chapter has addressed the issue of what managers can do to take up eco-innovation in their corporate strategy. Following the approach proposed in Chapter 2, we answered the question by addressing the main dimensions on the dashboard of eco-innovation from the point of view of corporate management.

From the design dimensions, first we pinpointed the need to acquire required internal competencies, but also to build strategic partnerships with other companies. Second, we considered it crucial to apply and develop dedicated design tools to systemize and ensure a proactive approach to environmental design. The design issue needs to be addressed at all levels: individual products and services as well as production processes and value chains which are likely to require different tools.

The user dimension of innovation has emerged particularly in user driven sectors, such as software or sports equipment. However, the user plays an ever more important role in other industries and hence is likely to make a difference in eco-innovation too. Specific tools already exist to engage users in product and service development.

Furthermore, the user dimension may also provide an appropriate starting point for management to address the company itself as an innovating user of eco-innovations.

Product service dimension touches the core of a business strategy, for example what is the earning logic of the company and how the company creates value added to its customers. Eco-innovation opportunities can be identified by linking the products with services or even moving away from selling products to offering service that fulfil the needs of the customers. Here, the evidence on different business models in practice can be practical and extendable to another business, even from one sector to another. Furthermore, the product service definition also seems to offer fresh opportunities to create new profitable partnerships.

Last, we addressed the governance of eco-innovation as a crucial dimension to enhance the use of available resources and skills in favour of the development and application of eco-innovations. Towards this end, the company needs to support the uptake of environmental issues in the management of internal and external processes, together with their stakeholders. Environmental management systems are relevant – often the first step to integrating environmental issues into the operations. However, even more important benefits can be obtained by integrating environmental objectives and eco-innovation into the corporate strategy and R&D targets. Furthermore, the governance innovation challenges management to renew its relationships with other stakeholders, including working together with government agencies and building public-private partnerships. This may be especially important in the search for environmental solutions, which often require system level changes. Industry can take an active role in envisioning alternative future routes together with its stakeholders and proactively designing sustainable production systems that look beyond individual products or production plants. This participatory approach is needed at both a public and private decision-making level.

In practice, eco-innovation is often a combination of the dimensions of the design, user, product/service or governance innovations. Hence, the major challenge for management is how to coordinate linkages among these dimensions; how to establish fruitful communication between different stakeholders and proactively manage their engagement in the development of eco-innovations and to benefit from the synergies in order to avoid negative surprises, for instance in terms of user acceptance or lack of government support.

CHAPTER 6

Eco-innovations in practice

6.1 INTRODUCTION

The earlier chapters provided background and some practical guidance on how the eco-innovation can be dealt with. However, there are many kinds of eco-innovations and in practice various factors influencing on the innovation process are likely to intertwine in many ways. This led us to an important conclusion. Really understanding eco-innovation and its management and policy require research on individual cases of eco-innovation; learning from the experience. We strongly believe that the effective management and policy of eco-innovation depend much on the understanding of the specific conditions of the innovation. The use of a case study approach is particularly suitable for this purpose, as it is ideal for generating theoretical and pragmatic insights from empirical observations when little is known about a phenomenon and when there is disagreement within the literature.[1] More specifically, we decided to conduct multiple cases, since multiple cases can increase the external validity, and, ultimately, the generalizability, of research findings.[2]

In Chapter 6, we will provide the reader a set of detailed case studies of eco-innovation that can be considered to be successful in terms of having positive impacts both to competitiveness and sustainability. The cases have been chosen mainly to describe the diversity of eco-innovations and related different management and policy efforts rather than as cases of best practice. The main common nominator of the cases may be in the ability of their proponents to address different dimensions in a combined manner.

In Table 6.1 the analyzed cases of eco-innovations are listed, followed by their respective sectors, short descriptions and characterizations within the Eco-innovation Dashboard.

Table 6.1   Cases of eco-innovations in view of industrial sectors and the typology of eco-innovations

CASE	DASHBOARD OF ECO-INNOVATION

ECOCEMENT/Construction

The innovation process of Ecocement is characterized by sub-system change, user development, product-service process and governance innovation. This case can be also characterized as a multidimensional innovation process in which different factors interacted in a favourable way leading to a successful innovation. This eco-innovation offered an efficient and safe, but partial, solution for resource management and, simultaneously allowed the eco-innovator to explore the commercial opportunities of using urban waste for cement production.

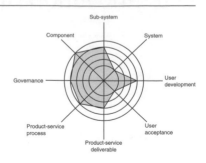

AUTOMATED VACUUM WASTE COLLECTION/Resources management

This case shows an innovation process characterized, in particular, by radical changes at sub-system design level and in the product service-related process innovation. This eco-innovation seems to have clearly identifiable benefits as regards both competitiveness and sustainability. The case also provides a relevant insight into how to introduce and develop radically different kinds of solutions. In this process a new type of value networks were developed building on proactive in-house R&D and continuous work on building partnerships with both private and public sector stakeholders.

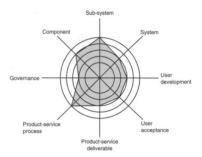

HIGH SPEED TRAIN SYSTEM/Transport

The innovation process of the high speed train system is characterized by the changes in sub-system level and product-service process. Coming about with this eco-innovation required new expertise and often new partnerships, thus creation major changes in the value chain. This leads to important management challenges to deal with organizational changes and establishment of new partnerships. Also local and national governments played crucial role promoting the uptake of the systems in terms of financing, policy and regulation.

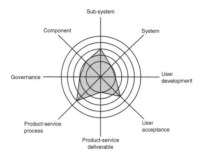

(*Continued*)

Table 6.1 Continued

CASE	DASHBOARD OF ECO-INNOVATION

ECOWORX/Industrial processes

EcoWorx can be characterized as an eco-innovation with radical changes particularly in the design and product-service dimensions, which have led to a new more environmentally friendly product system with closed-loop solutions. The re-design of the product value chain and the building up of the reverse logistics system have been radical changes in the product-service process. The creation of the new product meant radical changes in product-service deliverable. The success of EcoWorx has led the eco-innovator to take environmental issues to the heart of the company strategy.

CARBON CAPTURE AND STORAGE/Energy

The innovation process of the carbon capture and storage (CSS) technique is characterized, in particular, by component and governance change. This case study shows that an end-of-pipe technology such as CCS can be a cost-effective alternative for tackling the climate change problem in the future, complementary to other more radical options, within a wide technology basket.

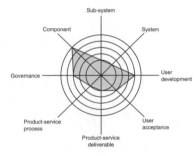

HYBRID SYNERGY DRIVE/Transport

The Hybrid Synergy Drive innovation, characterized by component, sub-system and governance change, seems to be a partial solution to the conflict between protecting the environment and driving. While it does not represent a system change but rather a drop-in innovation, it is a step in the right direction, which should be complemented with other measures to achieve sustainable mobility systems.

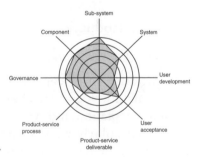

THE GREEN HOTEL PROJECT/Services

The innovation process of the Green Hotel Project is characterized, in particular, by design of component addition. This eco-innovation can be characterized as purely technological, and focused on the rational use of energy. It is mostly a component addition, 'drop-in' eco-innovation, which requires both little changes in the way the hotel business is run and even less in the behaviour of end-users (guests).

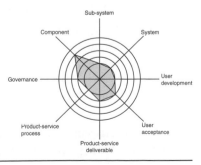

6.2   CASE STUDY 1: ECOCEMENT

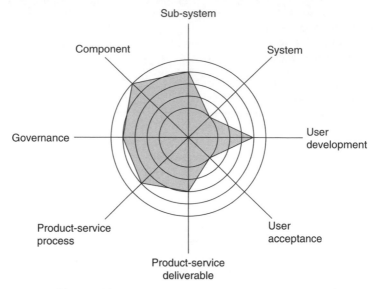

Figure 6.1   Dashboard of Eco-innovation: The innovation process of Ecocement is characterized, in particular, by sub-system change, user development, product-service process and governance innovation
Source: Authors' own figure.

6.2.1   Introduction

6.2.1.1   Background

The production of cement involves a wide range of sustainability issues, including climate change, emissions to air and water, natural resource depletion and worker health and safety.[1] The cement industry is particularly energy intensive (between 60–130 kg of fuel per tonne of cement), accounting for 2 per cent of global energy consumption and 5 per cent of total industrial consumption. The predominant energy source of the global cement industry is petroleum coke (a by-product of the oil refinery process), consuming up to 70 per cent of the total amount of coke produced, predominantly in North and South America. Technological improvements have gradually reduced the level of energy intensity from 4.7 kJ/tonne of clinker in 1973 to 3.6 kJ/tonne in 2004.[2] Concrete is responsible for 5–10 per cent of CO_2 emissions worldwide, making it the major climate change culprit after transportation and electricity generation.

On the other hand, in the last few years waste management has become a key environmental problem, particularly in rich countries. Some are encountering major difficulties in meeting this challenge, due to their specific singularities. Japan's resource-intensive consumer culture, together with its physical and sociological limitations as regards establishing new landfill sites, has increasingly led to the need to burn solid waste. The outstanding incineration rate is 75 per cent, with only residues being sent to landfills. This has significantly saved the volume of waste sent to Japanese landfill, but as it is generally known, this has also led to increasing risks of dioxins emissions or heavy metal escaping from incineration ash buried in landfills.[3]

6.2.1.2   *The innovator*

Ecocement was developed by Taiheiyo Cement Corporation as a way to address the problems of waste in Japan and, simultaneously, to explore the commercial opportunities of using urban waste for cement production. Taiheiyo, one of the leading Japanese companies in the cement industry today, was established in 1998 as a result of a merger between Chichibu Onoda Cement Corporation and Nihon Cement Co. Taiheiyo states that its mission is to contribute to social infrastructure development by providing solutions that are environmentally efficient, enhance its competitive position and bring value to their stakeholders. Ecocement innovation was clearly aligned with Taiheiyo's mission.

As a result of a National Project on behalf of the Ministry of International Trade and Industry (MITI), Taiheiyo focused on the possibilities of using a variety of wastes as alternative raw materials and fuels in the cement manufacturing process and established an environmental management business division. This public-private venture aimed to prolong the life of landfill sites in areas suffering wastes disposal problems, providing at the same time a new, cheaper, input into cement production and a new product for the company to market. Previously, the Japanese cement industry had used industrial waste as an energy source and to make mixed and ordinary Portland cement, but urban waste and incinerated ash had not yet been utilized for cement production.

In May 1999, together with Mitsui & Co., Taiheiyo Cement Corporation established Ichihara Ecocement Corporation, which engaged in the production and sale of Ecocement made from waste products, in particular incinerator ash. Operations began at Ichihara Ecocement in April 2001[4] as the world's first manufacturer of Ecocement from municipal waste incineration ash, proceeding from

26 cities and municipalities. The Ichihara plant, was built at a cost of
Y12.6 billion (US$10 million), with almost half the cost being subsid-
ized by central and local governments. The plant had a maximum
output of Ecocement of around 110,000 t/y. This meant 51,700 t/y of
incinerated ash that can be disposed of in Ecocement. In other words,
the amount of garbage and trash disposed of in the incineration facility in the Ichihara area could reach around 500,000 t/y, since the
amount of ash coming from incinerator is around one tenth of the
garbage.[5]

Until that time, incinerator ash was being used for land reclamation, with the municipalities paying some Y40,000 (US$325) per
tonne to dispose of it. The plant, whose managing costs were paid by
the local government, was expected to reduce the financial burden of
disposal to about Y25,000 per tonne due to the new destination to
produce ecocement. In addition to cost savings, the municipalities
were running out of places to dump ash, and recycling the ash into
cement was expected to reduce the filling rate of landfills significantly,
extending their lifespan.[6]

Ichiara Ecocement was recognized as making an effective contribution to using and recycling resources and received a Global 100 Eco-
Tech Award at Expo 2005 Aichi Japan on September 1 2005, and the
METI Minister's Award at the Fiscal 2005 Resource Recycling
Technology & System Awards on October 72005. Because it uses
large volumes of waste effectively, Ecocement has been acclaimed as a
twenty-first century environmental technology. Ecocement is also
attracting attention outside Japan.

6.2.1.3   The eco-innovation

The Japanese case of Ecocement innovation can be characterized
mainly as a sub-system change in the industrial ecology of resource
management. Ecocement is a type of hydraulic cement[7] produced
from incinerator ashes. This new type of cement was designed to use
municipal waste incinerator ashes in amounts of up to half of the raw
materials. In other words, it uses the waste from other processes as a
raw material in the cement production process, thereby providing a
double environmental benefit: a reduction of the extraction of
resources and a reduction in the amount of wastes which reach the
environment.

The concept of Ecocement offers a safe and efficient, but partial,
solution for resource management. Even if the waste is used as an

energy source and the ashes used for the production of Ecocement, it does not address the problem of waste generation. Additionally, the burning of waste materials may be regarded as 'downcycling', because these materials are not being reused for the same, or better, purposes.

Another key characteristic of Ecocement innovation is the important role of the user, the cement company taking the proactive role of extending its activity to providing waste management solutions. Furthermore, the governance innovation also played a crucial role by engaging in public-private partnership to initiate the development and demonstration pilot project and to establish the required changes of industrial standards to allow the application of Ecocement with different specifications than ordinary Portland cement.

6.2.2   Dimensions of eco-innovation

6.2.2.1   Design dimensions of Ecocement

The Ecocement design process arose from the opportunity to benefit from the synergies between waste disposal problems and the raw material requirements of cement production. To make this sub-system design approach operational, a series of incremental component changes were required in different phases of the process.

The manufacturing process of Ecocement is almost the same as ordinary Portland cement (OPC).[8] During the Ecocement process, porcelain fragments contained in the incineration ash are used and metal wastes are extracted and recycled when appropriate. Raw materials to produce 1 tonne of Ecocement can consist of, for example, 0.6 tonnes of municipal incineration ash (generated from 6.0 tonnes of municipal solid waste) and 0.8 tonnes of supplementary natural resources (limestone, and so on).[9]

Incineration ash is a suitable material for cement production, because its primary contents are the essential chemical components of cement clinker. The problem is that chlorine and heavy metals accompanying the primary components cause operational problems and deterioration in the quality and material safety of the cement. The key technology is not only to extract chlorine and heavy metals from the process but to recycle them as ore to be processed in refineries as valuable metals generating no additional wastes,[10] contributing both to energy conservation and CO_2 reduction.

Two new-type hydraulic cements, high early strength type Ecocement (HEC) and normal type Ecocement (NEC), were developed. The first type of Ecocement produced was designed to take advantage of chlorides in the incinerator ashes to make rapid-hardening cement. During the sintering process, chloride combines with calcium aluminate to form calcium chloroaluminate in place of tri-calcium aluminate. If an incinerator is situated near a cement plant, there are some methods to dispose of incineration ash. Bottom ash, which has a lower chlorine content, can be utilized as raw material of cement through a simple treatment system. On the other hand, chlorine rich fly-ash can be used as raw material if a bypass system or chlorine washing system is installed.[11]

Concrete is a composite of 'aggregate' material (rocks, sand, gravel) held together by Portland cement glue, and producing Portland cement means heating limestone and clay up to 1,300–1,600°C. Today, some industrial and urban wastes such as fly-ash, slag, silica fume, and rice hull ash, are used as cement-replacements having the dual benefit of replacing partly energy-intensive Portland cement, and of using material that would otherwise be landfilled. However, urban wastes consist also of harmful heavy metals and chlorine that may form dioxins or chlorides and cause adhesion trouble in the process of cement production. Also, their varying chemical compositions fluctuate daily, making it difficult to use urban waste as a raw material of cement. Industrial wastes, on the other hand, have clear origins and definite chemical compositions.

Ecocement can be considered fairly safe because the incineration process, which occurs at temperatures above 1,300°C, converts hazardous substances found in incineration ash, such as dioxins, into harmless substances, as well as allowing for the recovery of hazardous metals. However, today, the construction and production costs of an Ecocement plant are relatively high in comparison to a traditional cement plant, mainly due to (a lack of) economies of scale.

By adjusting the balance of chlorine from incineration ash and post-added alkalis, two types of Ecocement are produced, as mentioned above. Ordinary type (NEC), with maximum chlorine removal, has a chlorine content of 500 ppm or lower. This type does not rust reinforcing bars and has similar strength development to OPC. It is used in various fields including ready-mixed concrete where improved workability is needed. Rapid hardening type Ecocement (HEC), in turn, is produced without the addition of alkali and part of the chlorine is fixed as an essential component of clinker minerals. This chlorine results in rapid strength development comparable to high early strength cement at the early stage, while the late stage strength development is similar to OPC, and is expected to be used mainly in the fields of pre-cast concrete where enhanced productivity is needed.[12]

In comparison with standard cement manufacturing, the partial substitution of calcium carbonate (limestone) with calcium oxide (incineration ash), significantly reduces CO_2 emissions/tonne cement. Thereat, the Public Research Institute of the Japanese Ministry of Construction estimated that, for Ecocement production, CO_2 emissions will be cut by 50 per cent and energy consumption by 11 per cent.[13]

6.2.2.2 User dimensions of Ecocement innovation

- *User development* of Ecocement production process
  In Ecocement innovation, the Taiheiyo cement company played the key role of initiating the exploration of the potential use of waste ashes as raw materials in cement production. The pilot plant test was conducted by a consortium made up of Taiheiyo and three other companies. The early exploratory phases of designing Ecocement were undertaken by a Productivity and Technical Committee, who were supported by academics, MITI, the Ministry of Construction and the Ministry of Welfare. This detailed research phase sought to explore manufacturing technology options, addressing issues of harmful emissions and the safety of the product. A selected manufacturing technology was confirmed in 1997.[14]

- *User acceptance* of Ecocement innovation
  Ecocement provided benefits for municipal waste management as well as the development company, providing new eco-efficient product and production processes. At the time of the Ecocement launch, during the late 1990s, initial demand for Ecocement was estimated to be about 6 million t/y in Japan (over 80 million t/y of ordinary cement), if it were used for non-reinforced concrete, ground improving material, and breakwater blocks in construction of ports and harbours and marine structures as well as general civil engineering.[15] Hence, there seemed to be potentially major markets for Ecocement.
  In the last few years, similar kinds of processes have also been developed in Europe[16] and the US. However, despite the increasing

application of the Ecocement concept in the cement industry, Portland cement manufacturing technology still enjoys the dominant design position that is difficult to overcome with new technologies. The cement production sector typically enjoys good demand that does not require major changes in product strategy. The existing production routines and practices have a long history and an established position. Furthermore, since it is not a final consumer product, demand pull based on its superior environmental characteristics is unlikely to result in a mature market characterized by a fierce price competition, being only likely to supply small niches.

6.2.2.3   Product service dimensions in eco-innovation

*   Change in *product-service process* of Ecocement innovation
    In 2001, Taiheiyo Cement collected several hundred kinds of waste materials from 190 companies in 22 different industries, to a total of 6.2 million tonnes a year, and recycled them to produce Ecocement. Taiheiyo Cement developed an information network on waste materials on the Internet, connecting it with other companies. The network enabled the simultaneous sharing of information on kinds of waste materials and their makeup, amounts and processing methods, constituting an industrial ecological system with the cement industry at its center.[17]
*   Change in *product-service deliverable* of Ecocement innovation
    For the cement company, taking up the Ecocement project meant extending the scope of business beyond offering cement to its customers. In parallel to the production of a new type of cement, the company was to provide a solution to a major waste disposal problem. Hence the spectrum of customers was widened from the construction business to clients with waste disposal problems and potential new customers interested in other raw materials separated from the waste but not suitable for cement production.

6.2.2.4   Governance dimension of eco-innovation

Ecocement was developed through the cooperation of both public and private Japanese institutions. After extensive talks with various stakeholders during 1991–1992, the pilot plant development started, as stated above, under a national project funded by the MITI.

Several Japanese cement companies found that Japanese Industrial Standards restricted the use of cements containing wastes and worked with government officials to change the standards. In Japanese Construction Standard Law, any construction materials such as cement should comply with the relevant JIS (Japanese Industrial Standard). Ecocement, however, was outside the cement standard specification. Therefore, the industry asked the authorities to include Ecocement in the cement standard specification. This process involved considerable consultation with various stakeholders such as competitors, academia and government officers. On 20 July 2002, the Ministry of Economy, Trade and Industry established a JIS for Ecocement, which consists primarily of ash from incinerated municipal waste, and also officially announced a TR (Technical Report) on Melted Slag Aggregate, which consists of melted and solidified household waste, sewage sludge, etc. Ecocement has also been recognized as 'Type A Energy Efficient Cement' by the Japanese Institute of Civil Construction, Ministry of Construction.[18]

6.2.3   Dashboard of Eco-Innovation and impacts on competitiveness and sustainability

Building on the above discussion, Table 6.2 summarizes the case of Ecocement innovation within the dimensions of the dashboard developed in Chapter 2. Scores are also provided to reflect how radical the change occurred in these dimensions was.

The impacts of Ecocement innovation on competitiveness and environmental sustainability can be summarized as follows in Table 6.3.

6.2.4   Conclusions

Ecocement innovation can be characterized as a multidimensional innovation process in which different factors interacted in a favourable way leading to a successful innovation. Increasingly strong legislative and stakeholder pressure on the sustainability of the Japanese cement industry, together with the country's limited land area and objections from local residents to new landfill sites, provided the contextual basis for the public-private venture that developed Ecocement. This eco-innovation offered an efficient and safe, but partial, solution for resource management and, simultaneously, was aligned with Taiheiyo's mission to contribute to social and economic development, allowing the company to explore the commercial opportunities of using urban waste for cement production.

Table 6.2   Characterization of Ecocement eco-innovation

Dimensions of eco-innovation	Score (1–5)	Ecocement
1 *Design of component addition*	5	The manufacturing process of Ecocement is almost the same as OPC. The incineration and the use of incineration ashes in cement production are new components in the cement production and waste management.
2 *Design of sub-system change*	4	The inclusion of incineration ashes in the cement production leads to efficient improvements both in cement production and waste management systems. In comparison with standard cement manufacturing, this new technology reduces CO_2 emissions/tonne cement. Simultaneously, not only extracts chlorine and heavy metals from the process but also recycles them as ore to be processed in refineries as valuable metals generating no additional wastes.
3 *Design of system change*	1	Efficient and safe, but partial, solution for resource management. The burning of organic waste material is 'downcycling', because the waste materials can not be reused for the same or better purposes.
4 *User development*	4	Taiheiyo Cement corporation takes an active and prime key role in the development of Ecocement, together with academia and the public sector.
5 *User acceptance*	1	The cement industry relies strongly on the established Portland cement manufacturing technology, which enjoys a dominant design position that is difficult to overcome with new technologies. Existing production routines and practices have a long history and an established position. Demand generation for Ecocement seem to be one of the main barriers for the diffusion of this eco-innovation.
6 *Change in product service deliverable*	3	In parallel to the production of a new type of cement, Ecocement provides a solution to a major waste disposal problem. However, the innovation does not consist of service dimensions.
7 *Change in product service process*	4	Compared to Portland cement, the new value chain includes waste collection and incineration, separation of incineration waste, and so on.
8 *Governance change*	4	The Japanese authorities developed the technology together with private companies and included Ecocement into the cement standard specification via a process of considerable consultation with various stakeholders.

Source: Authors' own table.

Table 6.3 Impacts of Ecocement innovation to competitiveness and environmental sustainability

Dimensions of eco-innovation	Impacts on competitiveness	Impacts on environmental sustainability
Design dimensions	• Today, the construction and production costs of an Ecocement plant are relatively high in comparison to a traditional cement plant, mainly due to economies of scale (although, due to its social interest, costs may be partially subsidized).	• Partial solution to waste problem, though down cycling. • Ecocement can be considered fairly safe because the incineration process converts hazardous substances found in incineration ash, such as dioxins, into harmless substances, as well as allowing for the recovery of hazardous metals. • In comparison with standard cement manufacturing, for Ecocement production CO_2 emissions will be cut by 50 per cent and energy consumption by 11 per cent.
User dimensions	• Lowering inputs and energy costs is one of the main ways of improving competitiveness in the cement industry. • Since it is not a final consumer product, demand pull based on its superior environmental characteristics is unlikely to result in a mature market characterized by fierce price competition, being only likely to supply small niches. • Ecocement may have limitations in its use due to its different quality.	• Creates demand for waste incineration, down cycling the waste materials.
Product service dimensions	• The Ecocement project widened the spectrum of customers beyond offering cement to the construction business to provide a solution to new clients with waste disposal problems and potential new customers interested in other raw materials separated from the waste.	• The project aimed to constitute an industrial ecological system with the cement industry at its center.
Governance dimension	• Governance plays a key role to enable the application.	• The cement industry is becoming an essential part of the international waste management policy.

Source: Authors' own table.

6.3   CASE STUDY 2: AUTOMATED VACUUM SYSTEM FOR WASTE COLLECTION

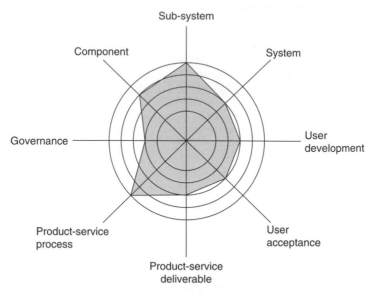

Figure 6.2   Dashboard of Eco-innovation: The innovation process of the automated vacuum system for waste collection is characterized, in particular, by radical changes at sub-system design level and in the product service-related process innovation
Source: Author's own figure.

6.3.1   Introduction

6.3.1.1   *The eco-innovation*

The automated vacuum collection system, also called 'pneumatic refuse collection', transports waste at high speed through underground tunnels to a collector where it is compacted, sealed in containers and then carried away. The system is based on pneumatics (from the Greek *pneumatikos*, coming from the wind), which means the use of pressurized gas to do the desired work. The system replaces traditional non-pneumatic waste collection, with waste containers and waste-collection vehicles.

Hence, this eco-innovation can be categorised especially as a radical sub-system change as it provides a new but partial solution to waste management. Even if automated vacuum waste collection does not resolve the problem of the generation of waste, it supports its environmentally sound and safe collection, separation and reuse. Thus, systems can play a crucial role in the design of feasible closed-loops in the product life-cycle by providing a systemic solution for producers to retrieve their products for 'up-cycling'. It offers outstanding opportunities to develop the efficient uptake of waste further, which could finally allow reintroducing the waste back into industrial or natural cycles in line with the system level design principles addressed in Chapter 2. Furthermore, radical changes occur in the product service process as this innovation builds on radically different technologies, expertise and partners throughout the value chain when compared to vehicle-based waste collection.

6.3.1.2 Background and innovators

Pneumatics was first documented by Hero of Alexandria in 60AD, though knowledge of the subject was not new. In modern times, pneumatic transfer systems are employed in many industries, but only recently have they been applied to waste collection to move municipal and commercial solid wastes. The leader in the development of such systems has been the Swedish company Envac Centralsug, which developed its first pilot projects in the 1960s. Thanks to ongoing R&D, Envac Centralsug has received several patents that have enabled it to achieve prime position in the market.[1]

In the 1960s, the Envac Centralsug group began to develop an automated collection system designed to enable refuse to be sucked along pipes from the place of origin to the final disposal point. Many technical problems had to be resolved during the development stage. The use of air to move homogeneous granules was a well-known technique but the behaviour of completely heterogeneous material moving along pipes sufficiently large for any type of refuse was totally unknown. New methods had to be developed to separate the means of transport (air) from the refuse, how the refuse had to enter the system, and so on.

The Envac system was first introduced at a hospital in Sweden in 1961, and the company has now completed some 600 installations worldwide in over 30 countries. Constant annual growth meant the company's revenue almost doubled between 1999 and 2002,[2] Only recently have other companies such as Oppent,[3] in the healthcare sector, and PneuLogix[4] developed similar types of systems for waste collection. The waste collection solution offered by Oppent is completely automated through electronic monitoring systems that control and set all operations. The system can be arranged to encourage sorting, whereby the user is provided with different hatches for different waste types. Oppent is currently focusing on the healthcare sector, but the company expects this technology to be adopted more widely in cities in the future.[5] Pneulogix systems are, in turn, designed to collect trash in residential areas, hospitals, office buildings and shopping malls.[6] Once the dimensions of change of the different vacuum waste collection systems are identified, together they explain the factors of success or failure.

6.3.2 Dimensions of eco-innovation

The automated waste collection system involves an innovation process that touches upon various dimensions of eco-innovation. The design dimensions deal with the development of a system that offers a radically different way of sorting and collecting municipal and industrial waste. The user dimensions particularly address how end users, often households, have to change their way of dealing with waste. The product service dimensions consider the added value of the system to the users and the necessary new partnerships and expertise to be acquired by the service providers. Finally, the governance dimension addresses the important role of local governments in enabling and fostering the uptake of waste collection systems as well as the required organizational changes in the service provider organizations.

6.3.2.1 Design dimensions of vacuum waste collection

The waste is sucked to a centrally located waste transfer station. To achieve this, an underground network of pipes is required, reaching distances of up to 1.5 km. Resources can be collected from a variety of drop-off points throughout a single building or even a residential development area, including restaurants and shopping complexes.[7] Working on the principle of under-pressure suction, the system comprises several collection points that are linked together by steel piping to a central collection station. Refuse is deposited, either indoors or outdoors, into an inlet and temporarily stored in a chute on top of a discharge valve. When full, the inlets are emptied one by one using a computer control system that switches on the fans – an air inlet valve is also opened to allow transport air to enter the system. The bags fall by force of gravity into the network of pipes and are sucked to the collection stations at a speed varying between 20–25 m/s, depending on the density of the waste. The refuse enters the station via a cyclone, whereby the transport air passes through dust and deodorant filters before it is released, and the refuse falls into a compactor that packs it into a sealed container.[8]

Basically, an automated refuse collection system consists of the following components:[9]

- Drop-off points, disposal portals on the street or disposal hatches inside buildings where users can deposit refuse at any time of day.
- A general network of underground pipes linking the disposal hatches or boxes to the collection station. The refuse inside the network is swept along to the collection station at set intervals by airflows at speeds of 60–70 km/hr.
- A central collection station where the transport air is separated from the refuse. The air enters a filter room for treatment before being released, completely clean, back into the atmosphere and the refuse is deposited in sealed containers which are then taken to treatment plants or the final destination. The collection station is usually located outside the area where the refuse is collected to avoid refuse lorry traffic on collection runs. One collection station can handle the waste of 7,000–8,000 homes, that is, about 25,000 kg/day of urban refuse.

Furthermore, vacuum collection systems can support waste separation at source. The process can cater for recycling, as there can be separate inlets for each fraction of waste, be it paper, organic waste, or plastic. Once pre-sorted and deposited in the inlets by individuals, all fractions are transported in the same pipes. However, to avoid any mix up, only waste from full inlets of the same fraction is emptied and transported at any one time, before moving on to another category of refuse. The control system directs a diverter valve to convey each category of waste into the correct container.

The vacuum system companies have came up with different advanced solutions to sorting waste. Envac has developed the waste bag identification system that enables households to use different bags (with different colours) for different kinds of wastes. In the collection station the bags are sorted automatically. In the case of Oppent,[10] a simple system for differentiated waste collection in multi-storey buildings has been developed to ease sorting and collection of waste. A waste chute crosses all the building floors. After having indicated the type of waste they have to throw away using a button or a key, users introduce it into the system by means of a hatch. At the bottom of the refuse chute, the different types of refuse are directed into different containers either through an automated carousel or thanks to the movement of the refuse chute end itself. The system can collect up to four types of refuse and can be fitted with a compactor that, by means of a photocell detecting refuse quantities, intervenes to reduce their size.

Nevertheless, one of the existing drawbacks of automated vacuum waste collection systems is that only very small amounts of glass can be processed due to its abrasive property. This means that it is often necessary to install a separate collection scheme for this material. Consequently, blockages occur occasionally in the vacuum systems, which are identified and cleared by the control system by opening and closing the discharge valves or restarting the fans. Also, service inspections are made to insure the quality of the service.[11]

Material and energy use remains a major challenge in vacuum waste collection systems. The environmental loads associated with the manufacture and installation of pipes, and energy consumption for pneumatic transport incur considerable environmental impacts. In order to reduce the environmental impacts of the vacuum waste collection system at an urban level, particular attention should be paid to the following aspects: improvements in energy (diesel/electricity/gas, etc.) consumption for pneumatic transport, use of the pneumatic system in its static variant (pipe network connected to a central station of electric pneumatic units), and changes of pipe materials.[12]

6.3.2.2   User dimensions of vacuum waste collection

The development of the system benefited from the close collaboration with the first customers. After fitting an initial, small pneumatic collection system in Solleftea Hospital (Sweden) in 1961, Envac started up the world's first large system in 1967 in Sundbyberg, a residential district in Stockholm. This installation, to which 600 homes were connected originally, has been enlarged in different phases and now deals with more than 2,000 homes, that is, some 7,000 residents. The experience of this first network, which has worked non-stop since then and collected more than 25,000 tonnes (or a quarter of a million cubic metres) of refuse, has been positive.[13]

Today, underground collection systems and transfer stations have been installed in historic city centers where space is at a premium, in new higher-density urban areas, stores, shopping centers and office towers, hospitals, hotels, industrial kitchens and airports around the world.

User acceptance has played a relevant role in the application of the system. This is particularly the case when sorting of waste is required. In the case of the bag sorting system of Envac and in the case of the simple sorting system of Oppent, households have the responsibility to sort their waste. This has been particularly demanding for households that are not used to sorting and recycling their waste. Using the system for the disposal of large and heavy pieces such as furniture has also caused occasional problems.

Flexibility appears to be a key feature of the technology, with each installation varying from the next. The collection station, however, is usually located away from the city, preventing the disruption caused by truckloads of rubbish being transported through polluted and congested urban areas. Business parks, warehouses and factories usually have larger inlets for their increased volumes of waste. These are normally only possible to open with the use of a key, transponder or card. The technology saves valuable space inside or outside buildings, that otherwise would be occupied by bins, transport paths/access roads and turning points. This also makes the technology economically attractive for the developers.

Over the following six years, some 25 automated pneumatic systems were installed around the globe. In Stockholm, some 20,000 homes on nine new housing estates were fitted with pneumatic refuse collection facilities, plus 5,500 homes in the new Olympic Villa in Munich (Germany); 7,500 homes in the Parque Central residential district (Venezuela); Walt Disney World in Florida (USA), etc.[14]

6.3.2.3 *Product service dimensions in eco-innovation*

Vacuum waste collection requires a radically different way of organizing the sorting and waste collection service compared to container and vehicle-based waste collection. Furthermore, the vacuum system builds on radically different technologies, expertise and partners throughout the value chain compared to vehicle-based waste collection.

The main advantages of the service in comparison with traditional refuse collection are that the automated vacuum waste collection system:

• Eliminates the drawbacks of traditional refuse collection systems: noise, odours, traffic problems, etc. The installation of a system leads to a drastic reduction in the road transportation of waste, improved hygiene and enhanced occupational health and safety standards. In contrast, traditional methods are often non-hygienic due to bags stockpiling on pavements and the unavoidable scattering of small quantities of refuse during collection.

- Integrates perfectly into the urban environment of cities and frees land for other types of facilities.
- Provides users with a 24/7 service in or near their home.
- Enables refuse separation at source, which facilitates recycling.
- Takes refuse to the lorries rather than lorries having to travel to the refuse. Traditional vehicle-based collection is noisy and polluting because of the presence of heavy vehicles dealing with refuse disposal.
- Is a hygienic, effective solution that reduces the environmental problems inherent in collecting solid urban waste.
- Avoids or reduces the occupational hazards inherent in traditional collection systems.
- Dignifies refuse collection work and operations.
- Is flexible, long-term, reliable and can be adapted to collect different types of waste separately.
- The maintenance costs less than the traditional refuse collection system. Traditional methods are especially expensive because of the use of a lot of labor, often during night hours.

However, the capital investments required are considerable when the system infrastructure is built and installed. The investments differ depending on whether it is a new construction or in an existing built-up area. The cost of establishing the system depends on the density of buildings in the zone, although it varies from 900 to 1,500 euros per home, in high-density areas, and from 2,000 to 2,500 euros in low-density areas. These are, therefore, very competitive prices even in the case of subsidized housing. After the initial 10-year-period, containers are normally replaced. The steel piping usually lasts for over 30 years. According to Envac, the capital investments are offset by the reduction of manual collection costs by about 30–40 per cent (residential) and 60–80 per cent (commercial).

Perhaps the potential is far greater for new urban developments than for existing urban areas, not simply because of cost, but also the inconvenience of overhauling a city's infrastructure. According to Envac, undertaking construction alongside other roadworks or the installation of gas and water pipes might be a solution. With regards to disadvantages, mention must be made of the following:

- Since this is an investment in infrastructure, the execution phases are long and the implementation level is complex.
- In established areas, pipe-laying may inconvenience end users, but only for a short time and in a specific area.

- The initial costs are high but are paid off in the medium-term, and operating costs are lower than the traditional collection system. Therefore the final cost per home is lower.
- Glass cannot be collected because of its high abrasiveness which would shorten the useful life of the facilities (30 years) considerably.
- The collection of paper and cardboard is not recommended because of their high density.

With a view to the product service process, the vacuum system builds on radically different technologies, expertise and partners throughout the value chain compared to vehicle-based waste collection. Hence, the installation and maintenance of the system means radically different competences in the organization of sorting and the waste collection service.

6.3.2.4 *Governance dimension of eco-innovation*

In the case of Envac, the municipal governments in Sweden played a particularly important role in the development phase of the innovation. Collaboration with the municipalities offered authentic conditions to apply the developed system and identify its strengths and weaknesses. With a view to the installation of new automated vacuum waste-collection systems, governments often play an important role as the articulator of the demand as well as financing the required investments. Such activities do not, however, necessarily require radical changes in governance practices or structures. From the viewpoint of the waste collection service provider, the governance of the change from conventional waste collection to vacuum systems requires proactive change management.

6.3.3 Dashboard of eco-innovation and impacts on competitiveness and sustainability

On the basis of the discussed dimensions of the automated vacuum waste collection system development and its application in different conditions around the world, it is possible to characterize this eco-innovation on the Eco-innovation Dashboard. In Table 6.4, the dimensions of eco-innovation are listed on the left, followed by the respective given scores and detailed descriptions of the vacuum waste collection system innovation.

Table 6.4   Assessment of vacuum waste collection system with the Eco-innovation Dashboard

Dimensions of eco-innovation	Score (1–5)	Description
1 *Design of component addition*	4	New patented components enable the development of the vacuum system for sorting and collecting waste.
2 *Design of sub-system change*	5	Vacuum systems have been used in many fields. However, the vacuum waste collection system is a radically new approach in waste collection compared to conventional waste collection.
3 *Design of system change*	3	Vacuum systems radically change the way the waste is sorted and collected, hence, they also provide partial solutions to sorting, reusing and recycling waste.
4 *User development*	3	The development of the system has been done through active piloting in the municipalities to offer a radically different system of waste collection.
5 *User acceptance*	3	Households and industrial users have to change the way they sort and dispose of waste.
6 *Change in product service deliverable*	3	Vacuum waste collection requires a different way of organizing the sorting and collection of waste, which improves the local environment in terms of the reduction of noise, odours and visual pollution.
7 *Change in product service process*	5	The vacuum system builds on radically different technologies, expertise and partners throughout the value chain compared to conventional waste collection.
8 *Governance change*	2	Requires some changes in the waste management practices of the client. Local governments often play a decisive role in demand articulation and permissions and financing the required capital investments.

Source: Authors' own table.

The impacts of automated vacuum waste collection innovation on competitiveness and environmental sustainability can be summarized as follows in Table 6.5.

6.3.4   Conclusions

The automated vacuum waste collection system can be categorised as a sub-system change as it provides a partial solution to waste management. Furthermore, radical changes occur in the product service process as this innovation builds on radically different technologies,

Table 6.5 The impacts of automated vacuum waste collection innovation on competitiveness and environmental sustainability

Dimensions of eco-innovation	Impacts on competitiveness	Impacts on environmental sustainability
Design dimension	• The vacuum system provides a cost-efficient and user-friendly alternative to conventional vehicle and container-based collection of waste. • The installation of the system requires high investments which are offset by lower maintenance costs.	• Considerable improvements in hygiene and noise management in the living environment. The system installation and maintenance require considerable material and energy resources. • Only a partial solution to ecologically sound system change. It reduces transport and corresponding emissions. Supports – but does not in itself create – eco-effective management.
User dimensions	• The value added and the maintenance costs of the vacuum system largely depend on the way it is used, that is, if the waste is sorted correctly and forbidden materials do not enter the system.	• The functioning of the system and its respective impacts on the environment largely depends on the users.
Product service dimensions	• Improved service for the end-users. When compared to vehicle-based waste collection, it is difficult to capture new clients but easy to maintain the client base. There is little competition between the vacuum system providers.	• The environmental benefits depend on the delivery of the system and its maintenance. This relies on the created new value network.
Governance dimension	• The business relies heavily on collaboration with the public sector, especially with the municipalities.	• The application and further diffusion of the vacuum system and, hence, positive environmental impacts are strongly influenced by the response of the public sector clients (public provision).

Source: Authors' own table.

expertise and partners throughout the value chain compared to vehicle-based waste collection. This eco-innovation seems to have clearly identifiable benefits as regards both competitiveness and sustainability. The case also provides a relevant insight into how to introduce and develop radically different kinds of solutions. In this process a new type of value networks were developed building on proactive in-house R&D and continuous work on building partnerships with both private and public sector stakeholders.

6.4   CASE STUDY 3: HIGH-SPEED TRAIN SYSTEM

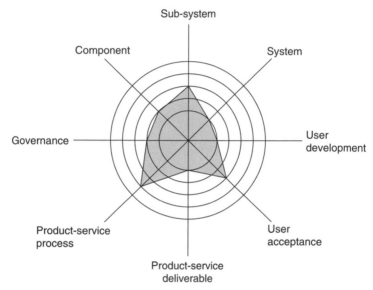

Figure 6.3   Dashboard of Eco-innovation: The innovation process of a high-speed train system is characterized, in particular, by changes at sub-system level and in the product-service process
Source: Author's own figure.

6.4.1   Introduction

6.4.1.1   *Background*

Railways can be considered the earliest form of mass transportation. Until the development of the motor car in the early twentieth century, they had an effective monopoly on land transport. Railway companies in Europe and the US have used streamlined trains since 1933 for high-speed services with an average speed of up to 130 km/h and a top speed of more than 160 km/h, thus enabling them to compete with the rise of the aeroplane. In Europe and Japan, the emphasis was on rebuilding the railways after World War II. In the US, emphasis was placed on building a huge national interstate highway system and airports.[1] Railways in the US have been less competitive partly because the government has tended to favour road and air transportation more than in Japan and European countries, and partly because of the long distances between the east and west coasts. Furthermore, with the exception of the east and west coasts, low population density in the US may have been a significant obstacle to the introduction of rail systems. Population density has always been a key factor in the success of European and Japanese rail transport, especially in countries such as the Netherlands, Belgium, Germany and Switzerland.[2] Upgrading rail networks requires large fixed investments and thus requires internalizing the negative environmental and social externalities of road transport, including the large number of fatalities occurring each year (42,953 fatalities in 2006 in the EU 27[3]), or high population densities to compete with planes and automobiles.[4]

6.4.1.2   The eco-innovation

Incremental improvements in conventional rail systems have made high-speed trains possible and competitive in the face of other forms of transport such as air and road traffic, which are more harmful to the environment. This is especially true over competing technologies, in particular, conventional railways, air travel and road transport.

There is no single definition of the term, rather a combination of elements – new or upgraded track, rolling stock, operating practices – lead to high-speed rail operations. According to the International Union of Railways (UIC), 'high-speed train' is a train that travels faster than 250 km/h on dedicated tracks, or 200 km/h on upgraded conventional tracks. Typically, high-speed trains travel at top service speeds of between 250 km/h and 300 km/h. The world speed record for a conventional wheeled train was set by a French TGV that reached a speed of 553 km/h (343 mph) in 2007. A Japanese magnetic levitation train (maglev) in development has reached 581 km/h (361 mph). Currently, however, the only maglev train in commercial service is operating in Shanghai, China. This case study does not cover maglev trains.

Generally speaking, trains can be considered an energy efficient and environmentally friendly way to move people and cargo, despite some negative impacts on the environment such as land use and barriers to animals moving freely through the countryside. Much of the technology behind high-speed rail is an improved application of existing train technologies (from the 1950s). Hence, a high-speed train system can be considered an incremental improvement to existing train systems.

By building a new rail infrastructure with twentiethcentury engineering, including the elimination of constrictions such as roadway at-grade (level) crossings, frequent stops, successions of curves and reverse curves, and sharing the right of way with freight or slower passenger trains, higher speeds are maintained. Recent advances in wheeled trains in the last few decades have pushed back the boundaries, tilting trainsets and air-brakes being among the advances. Features of a high-speed train system include, for example, no level crossings, barrier fences, concrete foundations, wide spacing between lines, curves with a radius less than 5 km are avoided and are tilted, more gradients than on conventional railway line, through stations are constructed with four tracks, tunnels are avoided.[5]

6.4.2   Dimensions of eco-innovation

In the case of a high-speed train system, it can be said that as an extension of the existing train system the high-speed train can largely be characterized as an incremental eco-innovation. Still, it is highly important to examine different dimensions of change in the innovation process in more detail in order to arrive at a comprehensive understanding of this eco-innovation and its management and governance. Fundamentally, just like any innovation, in the case of a high-speed train system too the dimensions of change can be identified, which together explain its factors of success or failure.

6.4.2.1   Design dimensions of the high-speed train system

High-speed trains in themselves are more environmentally friendly than air or road travel. This is due to:[6]

- lower energy consumption per passenger kilometre
- reduced land usage for a given capacity compared to motorways, and
- displaced usage from more environmentally damaging modes of transport.

Owing to current infrastructure designs in many nations, there are constraints on the growth of motorway and air travel systems. Some key factors promoting high-speed train systems is that airports and motorways have no room to expand, and have often reached saturation point. High-speed rail has the potential for high capacity on its fixed corridors, and has the potential to relieve congestion on the other systems.

Travel by rail becomes more competitive in areas of higher population density or where fuel is expensive, because conventional trains are more fuel efficient than cars (though sometimes less fuel efficient than buses). Very few high-speed trains use diesel or other fossil fuels but the power stations that provide electric trains with power do consume fuel, usually natural gas or coal. However, in Japan and France, a large proportion of the electricity comes from nuclear power. Even using electricity generated from coal or oil, trains are more fuel efficient per passenger per kilometre traveled than the typical automobile.[7] Due to the use of electricity and high efficiency, for instance in Spain, the high-speed trains on average appear to consume less energy and produce fewer emissions than any of their main alternatives.[8] In Spain the high-speed trains (AVE) recover almost 100 per cent of the stored kinetic energy. They have regenerative brakes and work in AC. They can return the energy to the national grid.

High-speed trains are far more environmentally efficient than aircraft, as trains consume less energy per passenger kilometre. This results in fewer CO_2 emissions, thus reducing the greenhouse effect responsible for global warming. From the point of view of required traffic control systems and infrastructure, high-speed rail has the added advantage of being much simpler to control due to its predictable nature, even at very high passenger loads. Compared to car travel, journeys by train incur much lower environmental costs, as well as being less stressful, more productive and more reliable than car journeys. In addition, the link between efficient and competitive public transport (such as high-speed rail) and sustainable urban planning has been noted by numerous studies over the past 50 years. High-speed railways have by far the highest capacity per unit of land they use. High-speed rail needs only a double track railway, one rail for trains in each direction. These have a capacity for 16 trains per hour, each train with a capacity of 800 passengers. This means high-speed rail has a maximum capacity of 12,800 passengers per hour. This is different to motorways, which take up a very large amount of space and often cannot satisfy demand fully at peak times.

High-speed lines may be considered if railways have reached saturation point and no extra services can be timetabled in. Train lines frequently do not go directly to a distant destination, often because they go to other towns in between. Building a new line for high-speed trains provides the option of building a direct straight line between cities, resulting in a shorter running distance. However, tilting mechanisms allow curves on existing railways to be negotiated with at up to 30 per cent more speed, which reduces the interest in building dedicated lines.

6.4.2.2   *User dimensions of the high-speed train system*

Shifting from other forms of transport to high-speed travel and the related acceptance of this eco-innovation needs to be examined in view of the other transport forms. For instance, the shift from conventional to high-speed trains could be characterized in most cases as incremental behavioural changes especially when the high-speed train complements conventional train routes. However, behavioural shifts can be considered rather radical. Behavioural changes may occur when car and air transport is substituted by the faster and more comfortable transport service provided by the high-speed train system.

A recent study in Spain concludes that train traffic seems to obtain 75 per cent of plane passengers when the journey time is reduced by two to three hours in a journey of 500 to 600 kilometres. In the same study, it was estimated that if the train's speed increases from 300 to 350 km/h it can gain eight minutes between Madrid and Barcelona, which may lead to 66,000 new train passengers a year.[9]

In some cases, radical changes may be required, particularly among users of the conventional train system, if the reduction of local train services and higher costs of the high-speed train service are to be accepted. In addition the local impacts on the environment in terms of land use, noise and impacts on nearby buildings may lead to local opposition to high-speed train systems.

From the viewpoint of the company providing the service, a high-speed train system can be considered quite a radical change as it usually means the construction of additional rail systems and the adoption of train technology that is different to conventional train systems.

However, the role of service providers as user innovators typically seems to be limited to outsourcing and some level of joint development activities. For instance, in Spain, the service provider, Renfe, has acquired the key technologies of high-speed train systems from France (Alstom) and Germany (Siemens).

6.4.2.3 Product service dimensions in eco-innovation

From the viewpoint of the service delivered to the passengers, a high-speed train system is mainly about improving the existing service, developing new connections, making connections faster and transport more comfortable. The goal is to improve competitiveness compared to other forms of transport, but essentially the business logic remains the same. Hence changes in the service provided are mainly incremental. However, providing the improved service means that the service providers need to acquire new skills in order to develop a new rail and train system. The company is likely to initiate new partnerships with technology providers, the construction sector and other industries.

6.4.2.4 Governance dimension of eco-innovation

In Europe, national governments have already committed huge amounts of funds to the development of their high-speed network in the coming decades. The European Commission also has an explicit strategy for 'revitalising the railways' as a means of shifting the balance between modes of transport in the face of the current dominance of roads.

However, until recently governments have been reluctant to use market instruments such as carbon taxes on air traffic and shipments to favour rail transport. In Spain, the high-speed trains (AVE) recover almost 100 per cent of the stored kinetic energy. They have regenerative brakes used today in many high-speed trains, which can return the energy to the national grid. However, no one pays for this returned energy, which leaves room for future governance innovation. Correct compensation might enhance the introduction of this technology and, hence, improve energy efficiency in general.

From a service provider's standpoint, high-speed train systems often lead to an upgrading of total quality management and environmental management systems in order to meet the required high maintenance standards of high-speed train systems. For instance, in Spain, Renfe has certified its high-speed trains with quality management standards.

6.4.3 Dashboard of Eco-Innovation and impacts on competitiveness and sustainability

On the basis of the discussed dimensions of high-speed train system development and its application in different circumstances around the world, it is possible to attempt to characterize this eco-innovation within the Eco-innovation Dashboard. In Table 6.6, the dimensions of eco-innovation are listed on the left-hand side of the table followed by their respective given scores and detailed descriptions.

The impacts of high-speed train innovation on competitiveness and environmental sustainability are multiple. While, technologically speaking, this eco-innovation is largely incremental, it requires considerable investments and natural resources to build the new system.

Table 6.6   Assessment of a high-speed train system with the Eco-innovation Dashboard

Dimensions of eco-innovation	Score (1–5)	Description
1 *Design of component addition*	2	The system requires new components that are mainly incremental improvements.
2 *Design of sub-system change*	3	Building a new system for high-speed trains provides the option of building modern and direct straight lines between cities.
3 *Design of system change*	1	Fundamentally, the system is an incremental improvement to existing rail networks. Despite the shorter travel times, most of the shortcomings of the rail system remain.
4 *User development*	1	Service providers typically outsource the technology solutions.
5 *User acceptance*	3	Changes in travel choices from road and air traffic to rail require radical changes in user behaviour. However, when passengers move from conventional trains to high-speed, behavioural changes are incremental in nature.
6 *Change in product service deliverable*	1	With the exception of faster and more comfortable travel, the service provided to the passenger is almost the same as with conventional trains.
7 *Change in product service process*	4	The installation of the new system requires new expertise and often new partnerships, thus creating major changes in the value chain.
8 *Governance change*	2	Service providers face organizational changes and the establishment of new partnerships. Local and national governments play a crucial role in promoting the uptake of the systems in terms of financing, policy and regulation.

Source: Authors' own table

Once the system is in place, it improves connectivity between urban centers and thus has a positive effect on economic development. The maintenance of the system is also energy and resource efficient compare to road and air traffic, leading to improvements in the environmental performance of the transport system as a whole. In Table 6.7, the impacts of the system on competitiveness and environmental sustainability are summarized in view of the dimensions of eco-innovation.

Table 6.7 Impacts of the system on competitiveness and environmental sustainability

Dimensions of eco-innovation	Impacts on competitiveness	Impacts on environmental sustainability
Design dimension	• Major market opportunities for technology development companies.	• Low energy consumption and emission levels. • Electric compulsion is an alternative to petrol and kerosene. • New infrastructure and operations have also created negative environmental impacts.
User dimensions	• User acceptance has led to a larger market share. • User innovation has led to better competitiveness.	• User acceptance and user innovation have led to the development of high-speed train systems with better environmental performance than their main alternative modes of transport.
Product service dimensions	• Incremental service improvements have led to larger market segments. • High-speed train systems have required high capital investments and new partnerships.	• Incremental service improvements have led to the substitution of other transport modes that are more harmful to the environment.
Governance dimension	• Governments have been the main investors in the high-speed train systems to improve connectivity between urban centers. It could be argued that the investments at that level could have been even more beneficial had they been used for other purposes.	• The government supported expansion of high-speed rail networks has required considerable natural resources but enhanced the rail systems to compete better with other more polluting modes of transport.

Source: Authors' own table.

6.4.4   Conclusions

The innovation process of the high-speed train system is character-ized, in particular, by the changes at sub-system level and in prod-uct service processes. The system requires new components that are mainly incremental improvements; though building a new system for high-speed trains provides the option of building modern and direct straight lines between cities. However, the system is an incre-mental improvement on existing rail networks. While the service provided to the passenger is almost the same as with conventional trains (despite the speed), the success of high-speed train systems is linked to important changes in travel choices from road and air traf-fic to rail. Coming up with this eco-innovation requires new expert-ise and often new partnerships, thus creating major changes in the value chain. This leads to important management challenges to deal with organizational changes and the establishment of new partner-ships. Local and national governments also play a crucial role in promoting the uptake of the systems in terms of financing, policy and regulation.

6.5   CASE STUDY 4: ECOWORX™, CARPET BACKING

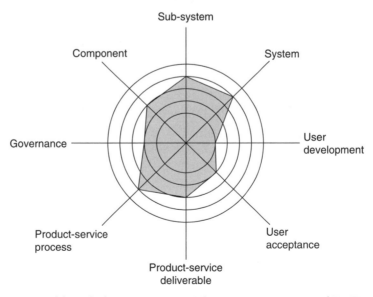

Figure 6.4   Dashboard of Eco-innovation: The innovation process of EcoWorx™ is particularly characterized by design and product-service changes
Source: Author's own figure.

6.5.1   Introduction[1]

EcoWorx backing technology was introduced in 1999 as a replacement for traditional carpet tile backing made from PVC. With over 500 million square feet in use around the world, EcoWorx is a high-performance backing that is completely recyclable into more EcoWorx numerous times. EcoWorx can be characterized as an eco-innovation with radical changes particularly in the design and product-service dimensions, which have led to a new more environmentally friendly product system with closed-loop solutions.

6.5.1.1   Background

The carpet industry appeared in mass production at the end of the eighteenth century. Carpets have been produced for centuries. The first weaving mill started producing carpets in Philadelphia. In the early years of the industry, new technologies lay the foundations of increased productivity. At the beginning of the twentieth century, new evolutions led to machine-made rug woven carpets simulating oriental handmade ones. It was only around 1950 that alternatives to cotton, the only fibre used in tufted products until then, were introduced into the industry. One of those fibres was nylon, which would dominate the market from then on thanks to its durable and cost-efficient properties. At that time, tufted products only accounted for 10 per cent of the carpet market. The development of new tufting production methods throughout the century eventually resulted in a 90 per cent market penetration of tufted carpet in today's industry. After half a century of growth, the carpet industry has become a mature market, whose capital-intensive characteristics of manufacturing have forced all market players to generate economies of scale.

Only in the last ten years has the carpet industry had to face a challenge at a different level: the environment. With growing concern about the long-term impact of current lifestyles on health and natural resources, customers – influenced by opinion leaders – might start changing their buying habits.

6.5.1.2   The innovator

The Shaw story began in 1946 when Clarence Shaw and his two sons R.E. (Bob) Shaw and J.C. (Bud) Shaw bought the Star Dye Company, a small business dealing in dyed tufted scatter rugs. In 1958, Bob became CEO and turned the fast-growing company into a carpet finishing business (Star Finishing Company). In 1967, the company made its first move into carpet manufacturing before going public under the name Shaw Industries Inc. in 1971.

For more than 30 years R.E. Shaw, the current chairman and CEO, led the company on a successful journey through an ever changing economic environment. Shaw Industries went through three distinct phases during that period after the boom years in the 1960s: a transitional decade until the early-1980s, a consolidation phase until the early 1990s and a 'new economy' in the mid- to late-1990s. While the market forces were different in each phase, Shaw's strategy of vertical integration was sustained by its management. Although there were less successful ventures as a consequence of this strategy, Shaw managed to control all outside forces that could affect its bottom line. More recent examples of this integration strategy were its fibre-manufacturing plants. They were a result of redefining the core business of Shaw Industries in the late 1990s after selling its retail business. From then on, Shaw identified itself mainly as a carpet manufacturer rather than a full floor service provider.

6.5.1.3 *The eco-innovation*

In 1995, Shaw took the initiative to make carpet sustainable and to become one of the most sustainable enterprises in the industry. Modular soft-surfaced floorings seemed to be most suitable to support the early recycling initiatives. Hence Shaw realized that environmental innovation should be focused on the carpet tile product line in order to limit the constraints of recycling and the implementation of change in general. Given that these 'new' products generated major market growth in the commercial carpet segment, Shaw can rightfully assume it has reconciled an innovative strategy with the product's image.

Shaw's new business model was based on the concept of eco-effectiveness (described in Chapter 2). As a result of its new strategy, Shaw Commercial was able to introduce EcoWorx™, a revolutionary new design for carpet backing, into the market in June 1999. Consequently, eco-effectiveness became Shaw's framework for developing existing initiatives further and taking them to a more revolutionary level without breaking the system. Today, Shaw claims that more than 70 per cent of its carpet tiles have an EcoWorx backing. This makes it an eco-innovation with a major impact on the carpet industry, considering the scale of implementation. The EcoWorx system represents a recyclable carpet tile product that is assessed using the 12 Principles of Green Engineering and cradle-to-cradle design principles to evaluate environmental, qualitative, and economic performance as compared to existing Shaw carpet tile products (see Chapter 5).

6.5.2 Dimensions of eco-innovation

EcoWorx is an eco-innovation with radical changes in multiple dimensions. In Shaw Industries, the efforts particularly in the design dimensions and product-service advances have led to a new more environmentally friendly product system and a closed-loop solution. Furthermore, user and governance changes have supported this industrial transformation process.

6.5.2.1 Design dimensions of EcoWorx innovation

Early environmental changes in the company (waste reduction and resource conservation) were followed by initiatives in changing the material matrix of carpet. During this process, which concentrated on product development, it was crucial that the use of alternative materials should result in products of equal or improved characteristics.

While the product's characteristics are the result of satisfying customer demand as regards quality and performance (related to the durability of the product), tufted carpet proves to be highly environmentally unfriendly. Not only does it require the use of vast quantities of fossil fuels as raw materials, the production process also demands a considerable energy and chemicals input for dyeing the fibres. PVC is a substance that has always been widely used in carpets and it is seen as one of the most problematic materials from an ecological point of view. The carpet industry's toxic and solid waste in its many forms (emissions, water and end-of-cycle product) leaves a devastating footprint on the environment. The process of change began within the company's R&D department and was based on Shaw's ideas and knowledge.

In contrast with the face fibre of carpets, making an environmentally friendly backing requires a radical re-design. There are two categories of backings: thermoset backings and thermoplastic backings. Although both have an equal level of performance, the first cannot be melted by being heated, because it will just burn. Thus thermoset backing can only be burnt after its useful life, making it more suitable for waste-to-energy than for recycling. Given today's technology, thermoset backings are dead-ends. EcoWorx belongs to the second category of backings and is a 100 per cent PVC-free recyclable backing system made from thermoplastic polyolefin compound with a fibre-glass reinforcing layer (stability). Thanks to hot-melt extrusion technology it is 100 per cent recyclable into new EcoWorx at the end of its useful life. EcoWorx is a cradle-to-cradle product that contains 40 per cent recycled content. Because of the sustainable benefits of EcoWorx, Shaw gave up PVC production completely in 2004. Other product characteristics are:

- No chlorine off-gas in a fire
- The same or better performance as PVC
- Lower embodied energy use during the production process
- 40 per cent lighter, allowing cost savings and lower CO_2 emissions from transport
- Contains a minimum of 40 per cent recycled compounds
- Class 1 fire rate (higher smoke rate than PVC)
- Used in combination with Fly-Ash filling, allowing full recovery of the Fly-Ash during the extrusion process and reusing it in new backing
- Compatibility with Nylon 6 in the depolymerisation process.

6.5.2.2 User dimensions of EcoWorx innovation

Drivers of environmental change in this industry are not only found in the applicability of design concepts to guarantee environmental sustainability, but also involve market acceptance and user dimensions. As mentioned above, the carpet industry is a mature market, whose products are regarded as commodities. The commercial building industry seems to have taken to EcoWorx tile, which pushed EcoWorx to the forefront when it was first introduced in 1999. Within five years, customers – mainly in the commercial building industry – had self-selected the new backing technology, which accounted for 70 per cent of Shaw's total carpet tile production by the end of 2003.[2] This shift in the commercial building industry has also been largely based on the fact that customers have considered that EcoWorx performs well not only in terms of its environmental impacts but also in terms of its functionality and quality. However, this customer sector has had little impact on the innovative phases of the eco-innovation. The design changes and the building up of the reverse logistics system have been initiated and mastered mainly by Shaw Industries and the carpet industry in general, rather than by the users of the carpets.

6.5.2.3 *Product service dimensions in eco-innovation*

Product service dimensions have played a key role in the eco-innovation process of EcoWorx. The re-designing of the product value chain and the building up of the reverse logistics system have been critical changes in the product-service process. Furthermore, the creation of the new product required promoting major changes in the product-service deliverable.

Change in product-service process of EcoWorx innovation   Through its environmental guarantee, Shaw commits to collecting all EcoWorx products for recycling into more EcoWorx at no charge. As a result, the company had to set up a new reverse logistics system which would allow it to manage the highly variable return flows of carpets. Unlike forward logistics, reverse logistics operations are complex and prone to a high degree of uncertainty, affecting collection rates, the availability of recycled production inputs, and capacities in the reverse channel. Setting up reverse logistics means dealing with major changes in the life-cycle of the carpets. Differences include the supply chain composition and structure, in particular (new parties may be involved and new roles assumed by existing parties, and the forward network may be different from the reverse logistics network), additional government constraints, rapid timing and uncertainty in the environment.[3]

In order to achieve this, Shaw came to develop a nationwide collection network, which meant collaborating with businesses across the US in establishing recycling centers for post-consumer carpet.[4] The Evergreen Nylon Recycling facility, the backbone of Shaw's recycling network, is currently designed to operate at a recycling rate of 100 million pounds of post-consumer Nylon 6 carpet annually. Carpet contractors and demolition companies look for one-stop disposal of all their post-consumer carpet uplifts. To get the Nylon 6 carpet for Evergreen, the network must find markets for the other carpet fibre types. It is estimated that the 100 million pounds of Nylon 6 post-consumer carpet required by Evergreen anchors up to 250 million pounds of landfill diversion of carpets of all types.[5]

The EcoWorx Recovery Technology Facility separates carpet made with EcoWorx into two recycling streams, one containing EcoWorx backing and the other containing Eco Solution Q face fibre. The latter goes off to the Evergreen Nylon Recycling Facility to complete its cradle-to-cradle cycle. What is not Eco Solution Q face fibre is down-cycled to make a material of a lesser value, such as carpet pad.

For EcoWorx tile, the process is called elutriation. It consists of grinding the carpet into a coarse mixture, then separating the elements based on their weight using air flow and gravity.[6]

Change in product-service deliverable   The major change in the product-service deliverable occurred in the shift from selling carpets to providing carpet solutions. As mentioned above, Shaw does not only sell the carpet, it also takes responsibility for picking up all EcoWorx products. This is a major change in the product-service both in view of the deliverable to the customer as well as in view of the management of the carpet and its raw materials. Furthermore, because of the sustainable benefits of EcoWorx, Shaw gave up PVC production completely in 2004. However, unlike some other carpet companies – for instance Interface – Shaw has not considered leasing or other more advanced service concepts to create stronger ties with its customers and reduce material flows. Even though Shaw commits to taking back the used carpets and reusing them, it is still selling the carpets instead of the functionality of the carpet.

6.5.2.4   *Governance dimension of eco-innovation*

Shaw's concern about the environment has been demonstrated by eco-efficiency programs since 1992. Shaw's commitment to the environment is expressed by the publication of Shaw's environmental policy written by the CEO R.E. Shaw.[7] It confirms the senior management's engagement in the differentiating area of environmental sustainability. Nevertheless, within the current market structure such investments would only pay off if the new process and products were economically viable. Shaw's clear vision and alignment of its strategy with the characteristics of the industry have proven to be of excellent guidance in this process of change and environmental commitment.

Shaw Specified Commercial (S|C) is an example of Shaw management's commitment to move forward on the economic and environmental sustainability agenda rather than to rest on its laurels. In this division Shaw anticipates the real issues in the business, such as treating the disposal of old carpets made out of non-biodegradable materials as a serious waste management issue. The program is reactive on the flattening demand curve by developing new product and process innovations.

Shaw industries also participate actively in the development of the industry's environmental practices. For instance, US carpet manufacturers, including Shaw, and other players need to know how best to structure the taking back of carpets (reverse logistics systems) and what operational difficulties they will face.[8] The Carpet America Recovery Effort (CARE), which is a joint industry-government initiative to promote carpet recycling, tackles reuse and waste reduction of post-consumer carpet.[9]

EcoWorx has also benefited from government initiatives to reduce non-toxic solid waste. In the US, the main environmental driver for reducing the level of non-toxic solid waste has been the need to reduce the amount of material going into landfills. Local governments have tried to reduce landfill use and have put pressure on manufacturers to take steps towards source reduction. Federal, state/provincial and municipal governments in North America have started implementing energy management programs, in which they promote the purchase of carpet with at least 25 per cent recycled content. Partly as a result of this government pressure, US carpet manufacturers signed a memorandum of agreement in 2002, targeting a 40 per cent diversion of carpet waste flows from landfills by 2012. Between 20 per cent and 25 per cent of all used carpet is to be recycled. However, it still remains to be seen whether the US carpet industry as a whole will be able to meet its 2012 goals.[10]

Major governance support for EcoWorx has also been the number of awards it has received, which have helped to boost the uptake of the product among customers. In 1999, EcoWorx won the NeoCon Best of Show 'Most innovative' award in Chicago as well as the Governor's Award for Pollution Prevention in the State of Georgia, and in 2003 the Presidential Green Chemistry Award from the Environmental Protection Agency. This recyclable backing has less embodied energy than traditional PVC carpet tiles, while maintaining equal or greater performance. Shaw is one of few manufacturers to ever receive this distinction. EcoWorx is a cradle-to-cradle product that contains 40 per cent recycled content and has been assessed by the MBDC Design Protocol as safe for human health and the environment. EcoWorx backing is also recognized with Cradle to Cradle Silver Certification, giving Shaw the only carpet products to earn this designation that contributes to USGBC's LEED® Green Building Rating System™.

6.5.3   Dashboard of Eco-Innovation and impacts on competitiveness and sustainability

Building on the discussion above, in Table 6.8, the changes in the EcoWorx innovation process are summarized within the dimensions

Table 6.8　Characterization of EcoWorx eco-innovation

Dimensions of eco-innovation	Score (1–5)	EcoWorx
1 *Design of component addition*	3	The tile consists of new components such as thermoplastic polyolefin compounds with a fibreglass reinforcing layer.
2 *Design of sub-system change*	4	EcoWorx eco-innovation contributes to the environmental performance improvement of the backing. Thanks to the hot-melt extrusion technology it is 100 per cent recyclable into new EcoWorx at the end of its useful life.
3 *Design of system change*	4	In comparison with standard carpet backing, EcoWorx constitutes a re-design as a 100 per cent PVC-free and 100 per cent recyclable backing into new EcoWorx at the end of its useful life, being a cradle-to-cradle product that contains at least 40 per cent recycled content. EcoWorx is also compatible with Nylon 6 in the depolymerisation process making reuse of the components easier.
4 *User development*	1	The commercial building industry has had little impact on the innovative phases of the development of EcoWorx, the design changes and building up the reverse logistics system.
5 *User acceptance*	2	The fast uptake of EcoWorx in the commercial building industry has largely been based on the fact that the customers have considered EcoWorx performs well not only in terms of its environmental impacts but also in terms of its functionality and quality.
6 *Change in product service deliverable*	3	The creation of the new product meant radical changes in product-service deliverable.
7 *Change in product service process*	4	The re-design of the product value chain and the building up of the reverse logistics system have been radical changes in the product-service process.
8 *Governance change*	2	Legislative support and industrial initiatives have supported the establishment of a reverse logistics system. Government and industry supported awards have promoted the adoption of EcoWorx. Taking up environmental issues in the Shaw corporate strategy has also played an important role in the success of EcoWorx.

Source: Authors' own table.

of the dashboard developed in Chapter 2. Scores are provided to characterize how radical the change occurred in these dimensions has been.

EcoWorx can be seen to have played a major role in the renewal of Shaw industries. The success of EcoWorx has led the company to abandon the use of PVC in its production lines and to take environmental issues to the core of the company's strategy. This has likely impacts on the whole carpet industry as well as its main customer sector, e.g. the building industry. The impacts of EcoWorx innovation on competitiveness and environmental sustainability can be summarized as follows in Table 6.9.

Table 6.9 Impacts of EcoWorx innovation on competitiveness and environmental sustainability

Dimensions of eco-innovation	Impacts on competitiveness	Impacts on environmental sustainability
Design dimensions	• The new product enabling the replacement of PVC created competitive advantage.	• EcoWorx replaced harmful PVC in Shaw production lines. Take-back and reuse of EcoWorx tile is an important step toward closed material cycles.
User dimensions	• The building industry has adopted the new product.	• The building industry adopted the product quickly, which led to environmental performance improvements.
Product service dimensions	• Reverse logistics create added costs, but enhance customer relation and loyalty. It also supports stability in resource management.	• Reverse logistics and reuse of EcoWorx tile represents innovative value chain management that has led to environmental performance improvements.
Governance dimension	• Legislative and industrial initiatives have favoured the uptake of EcoWorx and the establishment of reverse logistics systems.	• Legislative support, industrial collaboration and the recognition of EcoWorx environmental benefits have supported the adoption of the product and improvements in environmental performance.

Source: Authors' own table.

6.5.4 Conclusions

EcoWorx can be characterized as an eco-innovation with radical changes particularly in the design and product-service dimensions, which have led to a new more environmentally friendly product system with closed-loop solutions. In comparison with standard carpet backing, EcoWorx constitutes a re-design as it is 100 per cent PVC-free and 100 per cent recyclable, becoming new EcoWorx at the end of its useful life. The re-design of the product value chain and the building up of the reverse logistics system have been radical changes in the product-service process. The creation of the new product meant radical changes in product-service deliverable. Taking up the environmental issues in the Shaw corporate strategy has also played an important role in the success of EcoWorx. The success of EcoWorx has led the company to take environmental issues to the heart of the company's strategy.

6.6 CASE STUDY 5: CARBON CAPTURE AND STORAGE (CCS)

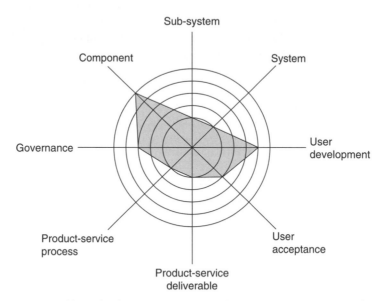

Figure 6.5 Dashboard of Eco-innovation: The innovation process of CCS is characterized as user driven component addition innovation of which adoption depends strongly on the governance efforts
Source: Authors' own figure.

6.6.1 Introduction

6.6.1.1 Background

The emissions of greenhouse gases associated to energy-production activities, which are expected to cause significant global climate change, comprise one of the main environmental concerns today. The most important anthropogenic greenhouse gas is CO_2, which arises mainly from the use of fossil fuels. Fossil fuels currently provide about 85 per cent of the world's commercial energy needs.

The combustion of fossil fuels to produce electricity is a major source of those emissions and, thus, the electricity generation sector has been identified as one that should be addressed in this regard, as shown by several regulations in the EU and US. Some eco-innovations, such as improved energy efficiency and use of alternative energy sources, will help to reduce emissions but some argue that a rapid departure from fossil fuels, if that is possible, may cause serious disruption to the global economy, as energy supply infrastructure has a long lifespan.

Capturing CO_2 for storage in deep geological formations (carbon capture and storage, CCS) is regarded as a technique that could make the continued use of fossil fuels compatible with large reductions in greenhouse gas emissions, especially in power generation and large energy-consuming industries.[1] For example, the European Commission[2] argues that 'we cannot reduce EU or world CO_2 emissions by 50 per cent in 2050 if we do not also use the possibility to capture CO_2 from industrial installations and store it in geological formations.'

If a 50 per cent reduction is needed worldwide by 2050 in order to meet the 2°C target and this requires a 30 per cent emissions reduction in the developed world by 2020, rising to 60–80 per cent by 2050,[3] then it is clear that all mitigation options are needed to achieve this reduction, including CCS.[4] This is a consensus of virtually all models and studies carried out thus far.[5]

The role that CCS could play in the portfolio of climate change mitigation options, alongside other alternatives, depends on how costs decline with increasing experience, and the extent to which public and political opinion will allow the development of a supportive policy and regulatory environment.[6]

CCS can be thus characterized as an end-of-pipe innovation which allows continued use of fossil fuels while at the same time reducing the environmental impacts in terms of GHG emissions related to such use. It is expected to promote innovation and position companies and countries in a new technology market.[7]

This 'add-on', drop-in characteristic is worth emphasising. Compared to other alternatives, significant reductions might be achieved in existing and new power plants with a low impact on energy infrastructures, which would allow extending the use of fossil energy in a carbon-constrained world.[8] Indeed, its compatibility with the existing techno-economic complex is regarded by some authors (and potential users) as its most attractive feature. This means compatibility of CCS with today's electric power infrastructure, but also with other aspects of the techno-economic system, including the accumulated knowledge on fossil fuel technologies and existing skills, adapted to a fossil fuel regime. As highlighted by Johnson and Keith,[9] as new CCS plants were built around familiar technologies, they could make use of existing construction techniques, managerial training, and equipment suppliers. This 'drop-in' feature is likely to facilitate the uptake of this technology, despite its costs and other potential barriers which will be discussed below.[10]

6.6.1.2   The eco-innovation

According to the Intergovernmental Panel on Climate Change (IPCC),[11] 'CCS involves the use of technology, first to collect and concentrate the CO_2 produced in industrial and energy related sources, transport it to a suitable storage location, and then store it away from the atmosphere for a long period of time'. CCS is thus a broad term used to describe a set of technologies aimed at capturing CO_2 before it enters the atmosphere, compressing it, and injecting it deep underground, ensuring it remains stored there indefinitely.[12] The major application for CCS and the focus of this case study is the reduction of CO_2 emissions from power generation by fossil fuels, principally coal and gas, but it can also be applied to CO_2-intensive industries such as cement, refineries, iron and steel, petrochemicals, oil and gas processing and others.[13]

All three processes of CCS (capturing CO_2 from the gas steams emitted during electricity production, transporting the captured CO_2 and storing it underground) have been used for decades, albeit not with the purpose of storing CO_2. Regarding the CO_2 capture stage, CO_2 can be captured either before or after combustion using a range of existing and emerging technologies. In conventional processes, CO_2 is captured from the flue gases produced during combustion (post-combustion capture). It is also possible to convert the hydrocarbon fuel into CO_2

and hydrogen, remove the CO_2 from the fuel gas and combust the hydrogen (pre-combustion capture).[14] With regard to the storage phase of the CCS process, there are four main mechanisms that trap CO_2 in well-chosen geological formations. The first is structural trapping, which is the presence of an impermeable cap-rock which prevents CO_2 escaping from the outset. The second is called residual CO_2 trapping, where CO_2 is trapped by capillary forces in the interstices of the rock formation, which develops about ten years after injection. The third issolubility trapping, where the CO_2 dissolves in the water found in the geological formation and sinks because CO_2 dissolved in water is heavier than normal water. Finally, mineral trapping happens when dissolved CO_2 chemically reacts with the formation rock to produce minerals.[15]

CCS is currently not deployed on a commercial scale and it is generally considered an immature technology. However, rather than seeing CCS as a technology itself, it should be regarded as a value chain of different components. These components are at different stages of technological maturity.[16] For example, enhanced coal-bed methane recovery was considered by the IPCC[17] to be in the demonstration phase, whereas another storage option, enhanced oil recovery (EOR), is characterised as a mature market technology. As observed by Groenenberg and de Coninck,[18] oxyfuel combustion is in the research phase, while pre- and post-combustion capture of CO_2 are 'economically feasible under specific conditions'.[19]

6.6.2 Dimensions of eco-innovation

6.6.2.1 Design dimensions

Design of components. The add-on nature of CCS technology does not involve a change in the existing components of the electricity generation process, but rather the addition of a new component at the end of the value chain. In other words, the basic production process is left untouched, but its impact on GHG emissions is taken care of through CCS.

Design of sub-system change. Significant GHG emissions reductions might be attained with CCS, compared to the functioning of power generation plants without CCS. Thus, it entails an optimization of sub-systems leading to lower emissions of global pollutants. However, it does not lead to a significant change in the configuration of the sub-system.

Design of system change.   As argued above, CCS is an EOP technology that can be added to existing electricity generation processes, although it is cheaper if these are previously adapted to have this technology implemented. In other words, it is more expensive to retrofit existing coal installations with CCS than to build new coal units with CCS incorporated.[20] Therefore, the impact of CCS on systems change is negligible but it could even be detrimental if it leads to delays in the adoption of radical energy technologies and, thus, to systemic lock-in. Indeed, although this could be regarded as a positive state of affairs from a short-term perspective, it might not be if a longer-term perspective is assumed. Many authors argue that, in the long-term, radical changes in the way we produce and consume energy are required in order to tackle the climate change problem and that we need more than mere technological fine-tuning, which extend the existing fossil-fuel based technological system. However, even if CCS really proves to be a cost-effective alternative for mitigation, it would not be enough to displace renewable energy totally, rather only the most expensive renewables, it thus reduces the overall cost of achieving a given CO_2 target.[21]

6.6.2.2   User dimensions

User development.   Most components of CCS technology are still not mature, although quite advanced in demonstration.[22] Further R&D investments and demonstration projects are needed to make the technology attractive to potential users. This also applies in the other direction as well: user development and involvement is expected to be key to demonstrating the feasibility of the technology and to generating further improvements through public-private partnerships. Indeed, the European Commission has put forward the need to build up CCS demonstration projects in order to fully assess the operation of the technology as well as its real mitigation costs.

User acceptance.   From the point of view of potential users, the technology has a major plus: the 'drop-in' characteristic, which allows the continuation of the traditional activity of fossil-fuel electricity generation (see 6.6.1.1). However, there are also perceived drawbacks of this eco-innovation from an adopter perspective, the most relevant being costs and an uncertain policy promotion framework. The total costs of CCS includes the cost of CO_2 capture and compression, the cost of CO_2 transport (typically via a pipeline) and the cost of CO_2 storage.[23] The IPCC[24] identifies the ranges of costs of CCS in the literature for three different types of new electric power plants with and without CCS: a natural gas combined cycle (NGCC), pulverised coal (PC) and integrated gasification combined cycle (IGCC).[25] IPCC data shows that the increase in the costs of electricity (COE) of a power plant with CCS is in the range of \$12/MWh to \$34/MWh. This means that, in the absence of a public policy to support CCS, this technology is unlikely to be adopted.

Rubin et al[26] update those estimates, using the Integrated Environmental Control Model (IECM). Without CO_2 capture, the PC plant has the lowest levelized COE at \$53.0/MWh, while the NGCC plant is highest at \$60.3/MWh. This result contrasts with the studies reported in the previous table, which showed NGCC to be the lowest-cost system based on lower natural gas prices of approximately \$2-4/GJ (versus \$6/GJ here). However, the costs of both PC and NGCC with CCS would still be higher than the costs of PC and NGCC without CCS (in the ranges of \$43-52/MWh and \$31-50/MWh, respectively).[27] Davison[28] calculates the costs of emission avoidance by comparing the cost and emissions of a plant with capture and those of a baseline plant without capture. A PC plant without capture was chosen as the baseline coal-fired plant. The baseline gas fired plant is a combined-cycle plant without capture. CO_2 avoided costs of CCS range between \$27 and \$39/tCO_2 for the coal plant and \$48 and \$102/tCO_2 for the gas plant (these greater costs for the gas plant are explained by the lower CO_2 emissions avoided per kWh of electricity generated).[29] These are middle-to-upper range CO_2 mitigation costs and fall slightly above or much above current and expected CO_2 allowance price ranges in the European Union Greenhouse Gas Emission Trading Scheme (EU ETS).[30]

It is important to acknowledge that the so-called 'energy penalty' of CCS (increases in specific fuel consumption for CCS systems compared to a plant without CCS) has a significant negative impact on plant-level consumption of fuel and emissions.[31] This leads to additional power plant capacity needed to operate the CCS system resulting in a greater capital costs (\$/kW) and a greater COE (\$/MWh).[32]

In contrast to the 'energy penalty', benefits (negative sequestration costs) may arise if CO_2 can be used for CO_2-enhanced oil and gas recovery.[33] To sum up, the costs of CCS deployment are relatively high, which is a barrier to its diffusion. CCS projects are large and therefore capital-intensive. This requires appropriate policy frameworks and measures. This will be dealt with in section 6.6.2.4 below.

In addition to costs and supportive policies, the deployment of CCS is likely to be affected by acceptance problems – on the part of the general public. This issue has two interrelated aspects. One is the perceived risks of the technology and another is the lack of information about it. Regarding the perceived risks to local health and safety, it has to be ensured that the CO_2 captured and stored remains isolated from the atmosphere and biosphere, and is thus environmentally secure and effective as a climate change mitigation option. Indeed, in the EU, stakeholders seem to be most concerned about ensuring that stored CO_2 remains underground (as well as about the potential diversion of effort away from energy efficiency and renewables).[34] Related to the perceived risk of the technology is the lack of accessible information. This technology is still largely unknown to the general public, but it could have potential acceptability problems. In general, there is relatively little information on CCS expressly aimed at the general public. Research has shown that focus groups become more supportive of the technology once they have received basic information and understand the context better.[35] Information instruments are needed to tackle this problem – an issue to which we shall return in section 6.6.2.4.

6.6.2.3. *Product service dimensions in eco-innovation*

Change in product-service deliverable.   CCS does not involve major changes in the product service delivered and is unlikely to change the perception of the customer relation (unless a system of guarantee of origin from CCS is implemented). If, in order to be radical, product service (or business model) innovation requires a redefinition of the product service concept and how it is provided to the customer,[36] then CCS can not be considered a radical innovation.

Change in product-service process (supply chain).   CCS involves no great change as regards the value chain, rather only an addition to it at the end of the process, not related to the production of electricity itself, rather to one of its negative environmental externalities, that is, GHG emissions. Of course, this leads to the emergence of a new business, the manufacturing of CCS technology, its application in existing plants and the design of new plants integrating CCS. However, the electricity supply chain is largely unaffected (that is, production, consumption, customer service and post-disposal disposition of products), except for the so-called 'energy penalty' resulting in additional fuel consumption of a power plant with CCS compared to one without (see p. 171).

6.6.2.4. *Governance dimension of eco-innovation*

Two key aspects already discussed are particularly relevant in this respect:

1. The need for the technology to be accepted by the general public, which calls for the dissemination of information on climate change and on CCS in particular.
2. The high costs of CCS for potential adopters, which calls for public policies that internalize the negative environmental externalities of CO_2 emissions and allow cost reductions in the technology. This means that climate policies (leading to a carbon price) and technology policies (support for R&D investments and demonstration projects) should be combined.

According to Wright et al,[37] 'The concept of injecting and storing pressurised gas underground is not something people embrace without a degree of understanding. Awareness of, or familiarity with not just CCS but the whole issue of climate change seems to be an important factor in shaping public perceptions of CCS'. In an empirical analysis of stakeholders' attitudes towards CCS, the authors found that public appreciation of the need for CCS increased when people are informed of the need to have a mix of mitigation technologies and policies to tackle the climate change problem, whereas, in the absence of a strong link to climate change, the general response to CCS was ambivalence. They also found that engaging the public on the topic of energy technologies, when set in the context of climate change, generally improves stakeholder attitudes towards CCS and results in increased support for demonstration projects. Therefore, government and project developers need to devote resources to informing the public about CCS. In addition, an informed media will help to educate the general public about CCS.[38]

An important issue regarding governance is cooperation between actors. The cooperation between different stakeholders (public and private research centers and electric utilities), in the form of public-private partnerships through demonstration projects, seems to have been key to the development of the technology and is considered to be crucial for further cost reductions and improvements in the technology.

Regarding public policies, as a largely immature technology which has not been deployed on a large scale, its high costs require the combination of two types of measures: a climate policy instrument (for example, in the form of an emissions trading scheme or a carbon tax) and technology policy instruments (in the form of support for R&D investments and demonstration projects). One of these instruments used in isolation is unlikely to result in substantial adoption of the technology and, thus, in major costs reductions.[39] Each is a necessary albeit insufficient condition for large-scale deployment of CCS. The gap between the costs of CCS and likely prices in the EU ETS (see p. 171), combined with the volatility of the carbon price, make it unlikely that including CCS in the EU ETS would be enough to encourage the uptake of this technology (although it will be enough for some CCS options) and make it likely that additional incentives policies will be needed to ensure large-scale deployment of CCS.[40]

6.6.3 Dashboard of Eco-Innovation and impacts on competitiveness and sustainability

Table 6.10 summarizes the discussion in the previous section on CCS eco-innovation within the dimensions of the dashboard developed in Chapter 2. Scores are also provided to characterize how radical the change is in the considered dimensions.

The impacts of CCS on competitiveness and environmental sustainability can be summarized as follows in Table 6.11.

6.6.4 Conclusions

EOP technologies are usually spurned in the eco-innovation and environmental technological change literature, because they use a corrective approach and do not result in systemic changes with long-term effects. In contrast, this case study has shown that an EOP such as CCS can be a cost-effective alternative for tackling the climate change problem in the future, complementary to other more radical options, within a wide technology basket. Nonetheless, some authors have shown concern that this could delay systemic changes towards a less carbon-intensive energy system based on renewables.

However, even if CCS really proves to be a cost-effective alternative for mitigation, it is unlikely to be enough to displace renewable energy totally, rather only the most expensive renewables, reducing the overall cost of achieving a given CO_2 target. The implication is that some EOP technologies allow us to 'gain time' and reduce overall costs when long-term but ambitious environmental targets have to be attained. It also suggests that some environmental problems require a shrewd combination of complementary measures, some of the EOP type, others that are more incremental and yet others that are more radical (system change).

Table 6.10 Characterization of CCS eco-innovation

Dimensions of eco-innovation	Score (1–5)	Description
1 *Design of component addition*	5	CCS is a radically new component at the end of the traditional thermal electricity generation process.
2 *Design of sub-system change*	1	Reductions of GHG emissions by the plants adopting this technology are achieved compared to power plants without CCS. However, it requires additional fuel consumption compared to an electricity plant without CCS (although the net effect is positive from a CO_2 perspective).
3 *Design of system change*	1	CCS is an EOP innovation and does not involve a radical system change. For some authors, it could even be detrimental in this regard (see text). All in all, it is a partial solution to climate change mitigation, but a cost-efficient measure within a basket of mitigation technologies.
4 *User development*	4	The electricity utilities are actively engaged in the development of CCS. Technology adoption depends on further demonstration, improvements and costs reductions as a result of learning effects and R&D investments.
5 *User acceptance*	2	Its add-on character is an attractive feature for potential adopters. However, user acceptance will depend on several aspects, the most important being the costs and improvements in the technology and policy measures (existence of a carbon price). High economic (cost) and regulatory uncertainties. Public knowledge and social acceptance is a relevant parameter for its diffusion.
6 *Change in product service deliverable*	1	Reduced CO_2 emissions of provided electricity to customers is an improvement that may or may not be perceived by the customer. Hence, no changes needed in the delivered product service, nor in the perception of the customer relation.
7 *Change in product service process*	1	No major changes in the value chain – only a final addition to it regarding its environmental impacts. However, the 'energy penalty' affects the efficiency of the whole process.
8 *Governance change*	3	Requires public policies of various sorts to be adopted. Technological cooperation in the form of public-private partnerships through demonstration projects will prove crucial for further cost reductions and improvements in the technology (EU approach).

Source: Author's own table.

Table 6.11   Impacts of CCS eco-innovation on competitiveness and environmental sustainability

Dimensions of eco-innovation	Impacts on competitiveness	Impacts on environmental sustainability
Design dimensions	• The costs of CCS at present are relatively high. However, since these costs are expected to fall (through technology policy measures in the form of R&D and demonstration projects) and carbon prices are expected to rise in the future (due to more stringent targets), CCS is expected to be cost-efficient within a wider basket of mitigation options.	• All climate mitigation simulations and models predict an important role for CCS in reducing CO_2 emissions. In spite of the 'energy penalty', the whole CO_2 emissions balance is favourable.
User dimensions	• CCS avoids the scrapping of not fully depreciated power plants (at a cost). It can be integrated into the design of new power plants. It is more expensive to retrofit existing coal installations with CCS than to build new coal units with CCS incorporated.	• No specific demand for electricity from CCS (that is, the product is not differentiated).
Product service dimensions	• For the power plant, CCS involves compliance with regulations in a more cost-effective manner (that is, it saves buying emission permits). But carbon prices have to be above CCS mitigation costs. No impact on the quality of the final product (electricity) although there is an impact on its costs (price).	• No specific demand for electricity from CCS plants (no easy product differentiation).
Governance dimension	• Governance (in the form of promotion policies) is crucial to the uptake of CCS. Public acceptance is also considered important in this regard.	• CCS is considered to be an additional important technology for climate change mitigation from a medium- and long-term perspective. Therefore, it is a target of national and international policies in this realm.

Source: Authors' own table.

6.7   CASE STUDY 6: HYBRID SYNERGY DRIVE

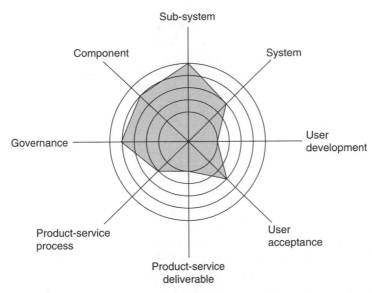

Figure 6.6   Dashboard of eco-innovation: The innovation process of the Hybrid Synergy Drive is particularly characterized by component, sub-system and governance changes.

6.7.1   Introduction

Cars are a key element of our mobility and, thus, in this sense, they contribute to societal well-being. However, they are also a source of social and environmental problems, including traffic accidents, traffic congestion, noise, local pollution (NO_x and CO, among others) and emissions of greenhouse gases (for example CO_2).

Indeed, environmental protection and car use are largely conflicting activities and so it is difficult to find a compromise between the two. However, in order to respond to social and political pressures regarding global climate protection, the automotive industry has been seeking a new channel of automobile technology developments – including hybrid, electric, and fuel cell vehicles. Toyota was the first to develop and market a petrol engine-electric motor hybrid vehicle – the Prius – which is the focus of this chapter.

Toyota Prius is the market leader in hybrid vehicles. Toyota patented the Hybrid Synergy Drive system and introduced the Prius in 1997 in Japan and launched an improved version into the US and European markets in 2000.[1] There was further improvement in the 2004 model, considered the third-generation Toyota Prius, which is regarded as larger, more powerful and more practical than its predecessors.[2]

On the other hand, it is necessary to bring down costs through economies of scale, which translates into the need for greater sale volumes. The costs of making hybrids are still higher than those of regular petrol vehicles. That usually means a higher retail price, which can outweigh short-term fuel-efficiency savings, or result in lower margins for manufacturers, or both. Toyota's strategy is to sell one million Prius units by 2010, up from 281,265 in 2007.[3]

6.7.2   Dimensions of eco-innovation

6.7.2.1   Design dimensions

The hybrid system of Prius uses a combination of petrol engine and electric motor depending on the driving conditions.[4] Under urban conditions, only the motor drives the vehicle to save energy and reduce emissions. When the vehicle is on the motorway, the petrol engine is started to power the vehicle and charge the battery for the motor. Therefore, environmental improvements come from regenerative braking (and from) shutting off the internal combustion engine (ICE) when the car is stopped, allowing a smaller, more efficient engine which is not required to follow the driving cycle closely.

Design of components.   The Prius combines a conventional engine and an electric component. Thus, some elements in the manufacturing of the Prius are different to other, more conventional cars, requiring new components with respect to those alternatives. This is the case of the battery component or the dash. However, other elements do not change much, precisely to meet user requirements regarding performance, which continues to be perceived in the traditional manner. This is, for example, the case of the tyres (which are identical to other cars).

Design of sub-system change.   Significant energy efficiency gains are attained with the Prius, especially in stop-and-go, urban traffic conditions, that is, it contributes to the environmental performance improvement of the sub-system to reduce negative impacts on the environment. The hybrid system offers 100 per cent improvement in fuel efficiency and 50 per cent reduction in CO_2 emissions. Hybrids attain their greatest efficiency advantage – potentially greater than

100 per cent – over conventional vehicles in slow, stop-and-go traffic, whereas much of their efficiency benefits are lost in long-distance, constant high-speed driving.[5]

Testing the Toyota Prius under a variety of driving conditions in Japan, Ishitani et al[6] found that the hybrid electric design gave 40–50 per cent better fuel economy at average speeds above 40 km/h, 70–90 per cent better in city driving at average speeds between 15 and 30 km/h and 100–140 per cent better fuel economy under highly congested conditions with average speeds below ten km/h.[7]

According to data from Toyota, well-to-tank fuel efficiency is the same for a petrol vehicle and for a Prius (88 per cent). In contrast, the tank-to-wheel vehicle efficiency is 16 per cent for a petrol vehicle and 37 per cent for a Prius. This makes the overall efficiency (well-to-wheel) of a Prius higher (32 per cent) than a conventional petrol vehicle (14 per cent).[8] Carbon monoxide (CO) and nitrogen oxides (NO_x) emissions are also drastically reduced to one-tenth of the previous level.[9]

There have been further improvements since the introduction of the first version of the Prius. For example, higher voltage in the 2004 Prius allows higher motor power with reduced electrical losses and a new braking-by-wire system maximizes recapture of braking energy. The 1998 Prius compact sedan attained 42 mpg on the US CAFE[10] cycle; the 2004 version attains 55 mpg, in spite of being larger (medium size).[11] Another example concerns the batteries. The power density of Prius' nickel metal hydride batteries has improved from 600 W/kg1 in 1998 to 1250 W/kg1 in 2004 – a 108 per cent improvement. Similarly, the batteries' specific energy has increased 37 per cent during the same period.[12]

However, more improvements are needed, particularly regarding two key aspects: cheaper and better batteries and reduction of overall costs through economies of scale. Batteries account for about half the hybrid premium. But cheaper lithium ion cells won't appear for several years. On the other hand, batteries have not advanced technologically at the rate the internal combustion engine has since their invention.[13] It seems that a major challenge lies in the manufacturing of low-cost, high-power lithium ion batteries for hybrids. Notwithstanding, this eco-innovation entails an eco-efficient solution and the optimization of sub-systems leading to lower emissions of global and local pollutants and less noise.

Design of system change.   The Prius brings about an incremental change regarding the way mobility is provided, that is, it can not be considered a radical system change in this regard, because people still drive an individual automobile, partly based on oil as a fuel, although a much more efficient one. Although the emphasis has been on the better fuel economy of the Prius and its associated advantages in terms of CO_2 emissions, other environmental impacts should be considered, that is, a life-cycle analysis is deemed necessary.[14] Despite future plans to provide a new functionality to plug in and charge Prius when parked in order to reduce fuel consumption, it does not involve a reconfiguration of the existing system, that is, in terms of system change, the Prius should be regarded as a drop-in innovation. Radical change concerns the design of the car, but does not affect the wider issue of mobility and its major problem: car dependence. In order to have system change, the changes in the design of the automobile with respect to conventional cars (that is, the combination of conventional and electric engines) should be combined with a reduction in overall transport mobility and a change to more energy-efficient modes (rail).

6.7.2.2   User dimensions

User development.   The development of the system was carried out by Toyota through a very ambitious R&D plan, followed by a strong marketing campaign. We only have anecdotal evidence of user engagement in the development of the eco-innovation, that is, users seem to have had a very limited role in the initial development, although probably much more so in later versions. One of these improvements may not concern the technology itself, rather the design of the car. For example, Smith[15] observes that the 1997 Prius had 'appearance problems', 'looking oddly stretched and tubular, as if the innovation in the engineering needs to find some expression in the bodywork'. This has been corrected in later designs. Later technological improvements are probably the result of R&D trying to adapt to the preferences of the users. Feedback from users may have led to some improvements. Toyota may have adjusted the features of the car as the company learned from consumer feedback.[16]

User acceptance.   It is well known that users take some time to adapt to new innovations and, thus, their initial diffusion is slow. Hybrid vehicles are still quite new, and awareness of the technology, its benefits, and comparable performance to a petrol engine remains fairly low. Nevertheless, since its introduction, hybrid sales have expanded considerably. Worldwide hybrid sales were about 541,000 in 2005.[17] Toyota delivered the one millionth hybrid in June of 2007, with over half (541,210) delivered in the US.[18] By 2010, Toyota aims to sell one million hybrids per year, but that will still only be around 10 per cent of its total sales.[19] Persuading the buying public that hybrids are a mainstream option continues to be a challenge even for Toyota. Indeed, earlier in 2007 Toyota had to start offering sales incentives on the Prius for the first time ever, to boost sales of the second-generation model. One reason is the cost of the hybrid systems for larger vehicles.[20]

It was probably lack of knowledge and distrust of the functionality properties of the Prius which made its initial adoption very slow (as with any technology). In addition, a low score seems to be given by purchasers to the 'environmental attributes of the car'. A market-research survey carried out by Toyota in 2002 on the main attributes valued by purchasers of cars showed that environmental protection ranked in thirteenth position behind 'good quality and reliability, well styled cars, good performance, comfortable cars, technically advanced cars, personality and character, innovative company, fun to drive, good after-sales service, concern for safety, recently launched interesting models, prestige make and extensive dealer network'.[21] Adaptations concern the design of the car itself (that is, its appearance), as well as its performance. In contrast to earlier versions of the car and to other hybrids, the car looks much like a 'normal' car, while at the same time being 'different'.[22] Although 'being different' can be a barrier, it is also what makes the Prius attractive to potential buyers.[23]

The Prius requires some changes on the part of the user, for example, regarding some aspects of driving behaviour. Commonly, hybrid engines require time and patience to gather speed, and some even argue that it is not 'such an exciting car to drive'.[24] It is also much more silent than petrol cars.[25] Adaptation also concerns some of the electronics of the car (starting the car, for example), which need training and acclimatization.[26]

However, two elements make this eco-innovation attractive in this regard. On the one hand, some aspects of the Prius involve a continuation of current mobility and driving patterns, that is, drivers do not need substantial additional training, which certainly contribute to its attractiveness. The technological improvements are highly compatible with the traditional way of driving a car.[27] On the other hand, some of the benefits from this eco-innovation are not only social, but can be privately appropriated, leading to a private as well as a social benefit. The comparatively greater fuel efficiency and, thus, lower energy consumption means lower costs for drivers. This benefit should be compared to the higher initial costs of the car. According to the European Environmental Agency, the Prius will add about US$4,000 to the price of a medium sized sedan.[28]

Therefore, the relevant questions are: do the fuel economy benefits outweigh the higher initial costs? And, if this is not the case, are people willing to pay for this (expensive) innovation? Are they buying it? If so, why?

Whether or not fuel economy benefits offset the higher initial costs of the car depends on several variables, including the number of kilometres driven by the car, the share of these distances driven under stop-and-go conditions (urban trips), fuel costs and whether there is some type of public policy incentive for hybrids (see 6.7.2.4 for details on policy schemes currently implemented to promote this technology). For example, a UK driver would benefit from a reduced vehicle excise duty of £70 and in London a 100 per cent discount on the £1,000 congestion charge is applied to drivers of hybrid cars. In addition, for those driving 15,000 miles a year, savings of £477 in petrol costs can be attained. The overall costs can be up to £1,547 a year compared to users of cars with petrol, which suggests that the greater initial costs would be offset in two years.[29] However, analysis done in the US market, where petrol costs are lower, are not so favorable for the Prius. For example, with petrol prices at $2.50 a gallon, it would take 10 years to recoup the extra $3,000 cost of the Honda Accord hybrid (not the Prius).[30]

Indeed, sales of the Prius are very sensitive to changes in public support and gasoline prices.[31] Lave et al[32] already showed that, for the Prius to be attractive to US consumers, the price of gasoline would have to be more than three times greater than at present, that is, $1.35/litre would be required.[33]

The implication for hybrids in general and Toyota in particular is that more efforts should be made to cut the costs of the car or increase its fuel economy. Hybrids are inherently more expensive to manufacture.[34] As awareness and demand grows, the initial cost is likely to decrease due to economies of scale. R&D, learning effects and economies of scale over the last 100 years have improved conventional internal combustion engine (ICE) vehicles to the best contemporary examples. Hybrid systems have received only a tiny fraction of the attention given to the conventional ICE vehicle.[35]

However, even if the Prius is not cost-effective for drivers, its environmental advantages may lead environmentally conscious drivers to be willing to pay a premium for these cars. Indeed, in its marketing campaigns, Toyota highlights three major attributes of the Prius: fuel economy (fuel-efficient vehicles), driving performance and environmental performance. The initial marketing strategy was based on environmental protection. Indeed, the marketing strategy has been changing from an emphasis on environmental protection in the first-generation Prius (1997) to four marketing pillars in the second-generation Prius: consumption (4.3 litres every 100 km), performance (acceleration between 0 and 100 km/h in 10.9 seconds), eight-year guarantee and environmental protection (104 g CO_2/km, 4.3 litres/100 km, 90 per cent recyclable).[36]

Probably, one of the drivers of its adoption is customers' feeling that they are being responsible towards the environment when they buy a car like this.[37] The increase in sales, which has led to a significant niche for Prius (although quite far from mass-diffusion), as well as anecdotal evidence, suggests that many people are willing to pay this premium. Indeed, one of the alleged failures of the most important competitor of the Prius, the Honda Accord Hybrid was a lack of 'green' recognition, which was said to be a factor behind its poor sales.[38] However, the lower sales performance of the Honda may also be related to the lower fuel economy of the Honda compared to the Prius.[39]

Something highly attractive for potential customers was that the private (fuel efficiency) and social (lower environmental pollution) benefits did not come at the expense of quality, comfort, functionality or safety. This does not seem to have been the case in the hybrid cars of competing manufacturers (like the Honda Insight).[40] Making the environmental choice often means compromising on performance. But the new Toyota Prius rewrites this rule.[41]

6.7.2.3. *Product service dimensions in eco-innovation*

Change in product-service deliverable.   Largely because of the reasons already mentioned in the previous section, the Prius does not involve major changes in the product service delivered and does not change the perception of the customer relation. If, to be radical, product service (or business model) innovation requires a redefinition of the product service concept and how it is provided to the customer,[42] then the Prius can not be considered to be a radical change in this regard.

Change in product-service process (supply chain).   The Prius involves some changes regarding the value chain. For example, a new business with respect to battery provision has emerged. In addition, mainten-ance services of the Prius are likely to be provided at non-Toyota garages if there is a widespread diffusion of the Prius and, thus, a mar-ket opportunity emerges for car mechanics to meet this demand. However, the focus of management and operations remains on local optimization of the energy efficiency of the car during driving, but does not shift to the entire supply chain (that is, production, consumption, customer service and post-disposal disposition of products).

6.7.2.4.   *Governance dimension of eco-innovation*

The Prius case suggests that Toyota gained competitive advantage through this environmental innovation. It also suggests that high degrees of top management commitment were necessary in order to get the project off the ground, especially in the initial stages, when the prospects of technological and market success were unclear. This is so because significant levels of R&D investments were required and because the Prius involved a willingness on the part of customers to pay a premium price for a car with a high novelty.

A major motivation for this commitment on the part of managers to develop the Prius may have been the 'early mover advantage'.[43] The company wanted to be sure that if alternatives to the petrol-based internal combustion engine started to gain traction, they would be driving the change, not being driven by it. This bet was a long-term one, that is, one not expected to lead to short-term market benefits. Its origins can be traced back to 1992, when Toyota announced the 'Earth Charter', a document outlining goals to develop and market vehicles with the lowest emissions possible.[44] In 1993, following the lead of Honorary Chairman Eiji Toyoda, Toyota R&D Executive Vice President Yoshiro Kimbara created G21, a committee to research cars for the twenty-first century, leading a year later to the 'Prius'.[45]

The Prius is regarded by Toyota as an effective means of improving the brand image of the company in the sense that people perceive it as a 'greener' business, on the three-point scale of 'environment, security and comfort'. Indeed, this seems to have been the problem with other hybrids, which were not recognized as being 'green'.[46] However, the brand benefits of the Prius for Toyota might not only (or even chiefly) be related to the environmental aspect. Instead, the Prius may have allowed Toyota to exploit a reputation as a technologically-advanced car manufacturer, able to develop a car with a twenty-first century, reliable technology.

The economics of the Prius suggests that, given its high initial cost, long driving distances would be necessary in order for fuel economy benefits to offset those costs. In the absence of a generalized willingness to pay for its environmental protection advantages, the widespread adoption of the Prius is likely to be slow. The environmental externalities avoided with the Prius and its higher private costs compared to other cars justify the implementation of public support for this technology which either increase the attractiveness of purchasing a Prius or of using it.

An additional rationale for supporting this technology is related to the learning effects and economies of scale taking place during diffusion. If hybrids have a large potential for cost reductions and quality improvements as a result of diffusion, which will lead to making it competitive with ICE vehicles, then subsidizing the technology is justified.[47]

Among the instruments to support hybrids in general, the following have been applied in Europe, the US or elsewhere and could also be applied in the future:[48]

- Reduced annual road tax rates or tax rebates for individual drivers.[49]
- Tax rebates for company car drivers.
- Tax breaks for manufacturers.[50]
- Fuel efficiency standards (like the CAFE standards in the US). It requires manufacturers to reduce the fuel consumption of new cars sold. Since the Prius has a greater fuel economy, their production helps manufacturers achieve the targets.
- CO_2 emissions standards (like the ACEA, KAMA and JAMA agreements in the EU), which require European, Japanese and Korean manufacturers to reduce their CO_2 emissions per km to $130 \, g \, CO_2$ in 2012.
- Parking fee exemptions or rebates.[51]
- Access fee exemptions or rebates.[52]
- Exemptions from access restrictions to city centers. For example, some cities restrict high-occupancy lines to vehicles with more than two passengers. Hybrids could be exempted from this requirement.[53]
- Grants on the acquisition of hybrids could be provided for purchasers.[54]

On the other hand, it should be mentioned that, although the Prius could be expected to have benefited from the technological cooperation between different types of actors (including private or public research centers), there is no evidence that this has happened.

6.7.3 Dashboard of Eco-Innovation and impacts on competitiveness and sustainability

Table 6.12 summarizes the discussion in the previous section on the Toyota Prius eco-innovation within the dimensions of the dashboard developed in Chapter 2. Scores are also provided to indicate how radical the change is in these dimensions.

The impacts of Prius innovation on competitiveness and environmental sustainability can be summarized as follows in Table 6.13.

Table 6.12 Characterization of the Prius eco-innovation

Dimensions of eco-innovation	Score (1–5)	Description
1 *Design of component addition*	4	Some key new components are required with respect to a conventional car. The combination of conventional and electric parts replaces the totally conventional engine.
2 *Design of sub-system change*	5	Significant energy efficiency gains are achieved, especially in urban traffic conditions.
3 *Design of system change*	3	The Prius changes some aspects regarding the way mobility is provided, but it does not involve a radical system change (drop-in innovation).
4 *User development*	1	The development of the system has been carried out by Toyota through a very ambitious R&D plan. Limited role of users in its first initial development, although to some extent in later versions.
5 *User acceptance*	3	Some changes are required by the user (possibly driving behaviour), but some of the benefits from this eco-innovation are privately appropriated (that is, lower energy consumption). Other aspects represent a continuation of current mobility and driving patterns.
6 *Change in product service deliverable*	1	No changes in the product service delivered and no changes in the perception of the customer relation.
7 *Change in product service process*	2	Some changes regarding the value chain (that is, battery provision, maintenance services at non-Toyota garages).
8 *Governance change*	4	Requires the adoption of public policies of various sorts. No evidence of technological cooperation between different types of actors.

Source: Author's own table.

Table 6.13   Impacts of Prius eco-innovation on competitiveness and environmental sustainability

Dimensions of eco-innovation	Impacts on competitiveness	Impacts on environmental sustainability
Design dimensions	• The higher initial costs are partially or totally offset by lower fuel costs.	• Lower energy consumption and its associated environmental advantages: lower CO_2 emissions, lower emissions of local pollutants, lower noise.
User dimensions	• Prius is more competitive in stop-and-go driving conditions (urban centers) and for long driving distances. The user relies fully on the Toyota garage for the maintenance of Prius.	• Once the Prius is bought and driven, the functioning of the system and its respective impacts on the environment does not depend much on the users.
Product service dimensions	• Improved service for the end-users. Some changes in driving performance with respect to 'normal' cars. The inclusion of hybrid synergy drive system requires modifications both in the production and maintenance of the car.	• The production and to some extent the maintenance of the hybrid system cause additional environmental impacts. The eco-innovation supports road traffic rather than other alternative forms of moving with possibly lower environmental impacts.
Governance dimension	• The business case for Prius depends on several variables, including the number of kilometres driven by the car, the share of these distances driven under stop-and-go conditions, the costs of petrol and whether there is some type of public policy incentive for hybrids.	• The adoption of the Prius and, thus, its environmental advantages, depends on the willingness to pay of drivers for environmental protection. Failing this, public policies are strongly needed.

Source: Authors' own table.

6.7.4   Conclusions

The Prius seems to be a partial solution to the conflict between protecting the environment and driving. While it does not represent a system change, rather a drop-in innovation, it is a step in the right direction, which should be complemented with other measures to achieve sustainable mobility systems. Furthermore, future plans to provide a new functionality to plug in and charge Prius when parked in order to reduce fuel consumption indicate that in the long-term Prius may truly function as a bridge in the transformation process from petrol to electric vehicles.

The Prius case clearly shows that eco-innovations can have both positive environmental and competitiveness impacts for manufacturers and users. However, in spite of clear economic and performance advantages of the eco-innovation, the inertia characteristic of technological systems makes its initial adoption difficult. This calls for several (temporary) measures aimed at breaking the lock-out on cleaner alternatives.

6.8   CASE STUDY 7: GREEN HOTEL PROJECT

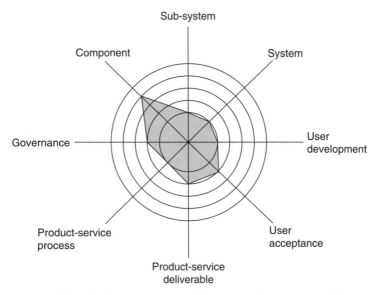

Figure 6.7   Dashboard of eco-innovation: The innovation process of the NH Green Hotel Project is particularly characterized by design of component addition

6.8.1   Introduction[1]

6.8.1.1   *Background*

Given the overall (and increasing) scale of the hotel business worldwide, tackling the environmental impacts caused by this service activity should receive special attention from a sustainability perspective.

Environmental impacts are mostly related to energy consumption, water use and waste discharged.[2] Therefore, measures aimed at enhancing the environmental sustainability of the hotel business should be directed towards tackling those impacts. A more sustainable operation of the hotel business by managers includes aspects related to policy and framework (top-down commitment), staff training and awareness, environmental management, purchasing and supply chain policy[3] and people communities (being sensitive to the needs, culture and interests of local communities).[4]

This case study uses the dashboard of eco-innovation developed in Chapter 2 to analyze a project tackling one of the dimensions of environmental impacts (reduction in energy consumption). Energy consumption in a hotel accounts for between 3 per cent and 6 per cent of total running costs,[5] so there is much to gain from measures which strike a suitable balance between comfort and consumption of energy.[6] In hotels, the main energy consuming systems are: heating, air conditioning and ventilation, hot water production, lighting, electricity (lifts, etc.) and cooking.[7]

Space conditioning, water heating, and lighting together account for almost 80 per cent of all energy consumed in a typical hotel (data for the US).[8] The remaining energy is consumed by cooking, office equipment, refrigeration, and other miscellaneous uses. The above data suggests that, in addition to reducing environmental impacts, a reduction in energy consumption can have a significant impact on the bottom line.

6.8.1.2 *The innovator*

NH Hotels stands at number three in the European ranking of business hotels. NH Hotels has 344 hotels with 50,171 rooms in 22 countries in Europe, America and Africa. NH Hotels currently has 16 projects for new hotels under construction, which shall add almost 3,000 new rooms.[9]

According to the NH 2007 Corporate Responsibility Report, an ecological approach based on sustainability occupies center stage throughout its entire business cycle, ranging from hotel planning, design and construction to their daily running and the services they provide to clients. The key elements of NH corporate strategy regarding environmental protection and competitiveness can be summarized as follows:

- Innovate and offer services geared towards the social and environmental challenges in store by staying one step ahead of the game, studying the opportunities offered by new technologies and analyzing changes in lifestyles and habits.

- Promote the rational use of urban land by restoring buildings, which allows for multiple uses. This is achieved via an innovative space management model that optimizes the surface area of a building, thereby enhancing environmental management from an energy standpoint.
- Encourage a rational use of energy by keeping buildings in good working order, keeping utility consumption to acceptable levels and encouraging the use of renewable sources, whilst simultaneously ensuring the highest quality of service to create a satisfying experience for clients. This is of the utmost importance, given that approximately 50 per cent of the energy consumed within Europe is used to keep buildings operational. The NH Green Hotel Project is mostly related to this aspect.

6.8.1.3   The eco-innovation

The NH Green Hotel Project arose in response to an initiative that formed part of the chain's Sustainable Development Strategy to enhance the rational use of resources, particularly energy sources. Given that at that time the industry had no method of rewarding environmentally conscious behaviour, it was decided to approach the project from the technological innovation point of view and to develop an ad hoc solution.

The system consists of customizing the NH World key cards for guests' entry into the hotel rooms, thus:

- The system allowed guests to customize the conditions. They could mark their preferences regarding lighting and temperature when they checked-in and the room would be lit and heated to their tastes.
- Registering the conditions in terms of consumption, the system identified those guests whose use of the resources provided during their stay, could be considered above average as regards rational use of energy and sustainability.
- On the other hand, with the customized NH World card it was not necessary to issue a new card each time a guest visited the chain's hotels.

NH managers believed that this system was a further step in the customized service they provide to their clients, which characterizes, and therefore differentiates NH.

NH's strategic targets concerning sustainability were the reduction of energy and water consumption, as well as a drop in emissions and waste. The company believed that their guests judged their strategy positively and shared their concern about the sustainability of their operational models. NH also believed that guests should be involved in saving energy and therefore NH should invest in new technologies and innovative developments that respond to their needs. NH wanted to keep them informed about their energy consumption.

NH set up a partnership with Siemens, who shared the same concern about the NH concepts mentioned above, and therefore reached an agreement to develop the NH Green Hotel Project together.

6.8.2   Dimensions of eco-innovation

6.8.2.1   *Design dimensions of the NH Green Hotel Project*

Hotel Solution is a management system for hotel rooms (Hotel Room Management System, HRMS) with special features. The system provides integrated control of the hotel rooms directly from the reception desk. Efficient management by guests, the service staff and the energy supplier helps to reduce the costs of the hotel. This management system is directly linked to the hotel reservation system (FOS), ensuring a smooth operation of access control and indoor air conditioning control. It also improves security and energy efficiency from check-in to check-out. The system can be adapted to any hotel type, regardless of its complexity or size.

The HRMS comprises a control board at reception from which all rooms are operated and monitored. An overview of the rooms provides information about the guest and the status of each hotel room. Messages and alarms, such as 'Do not disturb', 'Service Call', 'SOS' and/or 'Intrusion' can be seen on the general overview screen, so that the hotel staff can respond immediately. The HRMS operators' post at reception is a standard PC with Windows XP as a reliable operating system and Sybase SQL.

The HRMS control board registers the temperature of the rooms at all times and displays them in charts. It also allows the temperature to be adjusted centrally, if so required by the guest. The system enables different temperature profiles, depending on the season, in different areas of the hotel, the orientation of certain hotel wings, energy groups, and so on.

If in low season, for example, certain rooms or complete wings are not used, the control board enables the heating to be switched off easily in these rooms and applies a special form of building protection. In the building protection mode, the temperature control works at a minimum (building protection), so that energy savings can be maximized.

Each room is equipped with a controller that incorporates all the main functions of the room, such as the air conditioning control, access control, energy management, blinds and lighting control, messages and alarms, etc. Once the system is set up and switched on, all the important parameters are stored in the non-volatile memory controller, so that all local functions can be performed completely by themselves, and no connection to the network will be necessary.

This eco-innovation can therefore be considered a computer management system tool applied to rationalize energy consumption and, thus, encourage economic savings and, indirectly, reduce levels of emissions of air pollutants resulting from lower levels of energy demand. Therefore, it is an addition of a new component (the computer control system) but without resulting in a major system (or even sub-system) change. Indeed, it is a purely technological innovation, without a marked behavioural component, i.e. unlikely to result in explicit behavioural changes by hotel guests. It appears to be a tool to encourage guests' loyalty, improve the image of the company (increasing revenues and market quotas) and reduce the costs of providing the service (energy costs), rather than an explicit search for a reduction in the environmental problems associated with the provision of the service.

6.8.2.2   User dimensions of the eco-innovation

User development.   This eco-innovation largely lacks a user development dimension. The reason is that it has not been developed by NH, although the idea of applying it seems to have come from the hotel. However, nor is it an 'on-the-shelf' technology – previously existing, developed by a supplier and ready to be applied by the customer (NH). Therefore, close collaboration between the technology supplier (Siemens) and NH appears to have taken place in order for this technology to have been implemented. This close supplier-user relationship is shared by many eco-innovations.[10]

User acceptance.   General concern about environmental sustainability and, thus, guests' interest in environmental problems may have played an important part in the implementation of the eco-innovation. In addition to the sustainability aspect, which is likely to be attractive for guests, and since it is a rather technological eco-innovation requiring very limited behavioural changes by guests, user acceptance is easy to attain. This does not mean that guest behaviour is not key in order to reduce energy consumption in the hotel. However, the tool is unlikely to trigger major (explicit) behavioural changes by the guests.

6.8.2.3 Product service dimensions in eco-innovation

Change in product-service deliverable.   Largely because of the aforementioned reasons, the NH Green Hotel Project does not involve major changes in the product service delivered and does not change the perception of the customer relation. If, to be radical, product service (or business model) innovation requires a redefinition of the product service concept and how it is provided to the customer (see Chapter 2), then this project cannot be considered a radical change in this regard.

Change in product-service process.   A major advantage for the firm is the customization and customer loyalty attained with the system. However, there is no change regarding the value chain and no drastic change in the manner the hotel service is organized and provided. This can be considered an advantage in the sense that no major organizational change on the part of the adopter is required (that is, drop-in eco-innovation), whereas company competitiveness may be enhanced.

6.8.2.4 Governance dimension of eco-innovation

As regards public governance, the existence of high energy prices on account of the implementation of policy measures leading to the internalization of environmental externalities into those prices would certainly encourage the adoption of energy-saving technologies. Given that NH operates in many countries with different legislations and diverse factors affecting energy prices, it is uncertain how this factor has influenced the adoption of this eco-innovation, although the existence of those policies would certainly provide a stimulus to be more energy-efficient, save costs and enhance competitiveness on the part of the hotel chain.[11]

As far as private governance is concerned, it is likely that no major changes at the level of corporate (and environmental) strategy or internal organization of NH were required. However, the internal strategy of NH aimed at reducing energy costs, building a sustainability image and encouraging the guests' loyalty (that is, aimed at improving its competitiveness) has been a key factor in the implementation of this measure. Technological cooperation between the supplier and user of the eco-innovation has been necessary to implement the technology.

6.8.3 Dashboard of Eco-Innovation and impacts on competitiveness and sustainability

On the basis of the above discussion, Table 6.14 summarizes the case of the NH Green Hotel Project innovation within the dimensions of the dashboard developed in Chapter 2. Scores are also provided to reflect how radical the change occurred in these dimensions was.

The impacts of the NH Green Hotel Project innovation on competitiveness and environmental sustainability can be summarized as follows in Table 6.15.

Table 6.14   Characterization of the NH Green Hotel Project eco-innovation

Dimensions of eco-innovation	Score (1–5)	NH Green Hotel Project
1 *Design of component addition*	3	This is the key aspect of the project, which is a computer management system tool applied to rationalize energy consumption.
2 *Design of sub-system change*	1	No change in the sub-system is involved.
3 *Design of system change*	1	No change in the system is involved.
4 *User development*	1	No development of the eco-innovation by the user has occurred, although there has been close cooperation with the technology supplier to adapt it to the user company.
5 *User acceptance*	2	The 'drop-in' nature of the eco-innovation makes user acceptance likely to be easy to obtain.
6 *Change in product service deliverable*	2	The NH Green Hotel Project does not involve major changes in the product service delivered and does not change the perception of the customer relation.
7 *Change in product service process*	1	Customization and customer loyalty attained with the system, although there is no change regarding the value chain.
8 *Governance change*	2	No major public governance aspect involved. As regards private governance, it is likely that no major changes at the level of corporate (and environmental) strategy or internal organization of NH were required.

Source: Authors' own table.

Table 6.15   Impacts of the NH Green Hotel Project innovation on competitiveness and environmental sustainability

Dimensions of eco-innovation	Impacts on competitiveness	Impacts on environmental sustainability
Design dimensions	• A more rational use of energy saves costs.	• A reduction of energy consumption reduces the environmental problems associated with energy production.
User dimensions	• User behaviour and acceptance of this eco-innovation is key to reducing energy consumption.	• Energy consumption and its associated environmental impacts directly depend on the behaviour of guests. This eco-innovation is unlikely to change user behaviour drastically.
Product service dimensions	• Customization and consumer loyalty may improve competitiveness but, otherwise, no change in the service provided.	• The environmental benefits depend on the rational use of energy stemming from the application of the technology.
Governance dimension	• No evidence of any link to public policies. Higher energy taxes would encourage the adoption of this technology by other hotel chains. However, no direct public governance element appears to have been involved in its adoption. The private governance dimension in the search for competitiveness has been key in this regard.	• The link between competitiveness and lower environmental problems associated with lower energy consumption makes the adoption of this system attractive from a business point of view, apparently without the need for the implementation of public policies.

Source: Authors' own table.

6.8.4   Conclusions

Given the overall (and increasing) scale of the hotel business worldwide, tackling the environmental impacts caused by this service activity should receive attention from a sustainability perspective. The NH Green Hotel Project provides an interesting (albeit limited) technological tool to address one dimension of these environmental impacts, i.e. those related to energy consumption.

This eco-innovation can be characterized as purely technological, and focused on the rational use of energy. It is mostly a component addition, 'drop-in' eco-innovation which requires few changes in the way the hotel business is run and even fewer in the behaviour of end-users (guests). However, this aspect, together with the fact that reductions in energy consumption can be achieved alongside an improvement in the image of the firm, enhancing the competitiveness of the company, is precisely what makes it attractive from a private governance point of view and makes the implementation of public policies an unnecessary condition for its adoption. Obviously, higher energy prices triggered by public policies aimed at internalizing the externalities of energy production and consumption would provide an additional incentive for its diffusion.

CHAPTER 7
Conclusion

A starting point of this book could be the dilemma of 'how to improve the quality of the environment without limiting economic activity' and its respective answer of focusing on **eco-innovation**. We have addressed the issue of eco-innovation from numerous angles, providing the reader with a general picture of what eco-innovation is and what factors lead to the success or failure of an eco-innovation.

One of the main messages of the book is that, despite many success stories, both public policy makers and businesses are at the bottom of the learning curve of how to deal with eco-innovation. It offers major opportunities for those who, in both the public and private realm, are able to address the whole innovation process in an effective way in conjunction with multiple stakeholders. This is a major challenge that requires new mind sets, perspectives and competences.

The chapters on barriers, governance and business provided background and practical guidance on how the eco-innovation can be dealt with. However, there are many ways of eco-innovating and in practice various factors influencing eco-innovation are likely to interrelate in multiple and even unexpected ways. This led us to an important conclusion; a thorough understanding of eco-innovation and its management and policy can benefit a great deal from empirical analysis which grasps the details of specific innovation types and the determinants of their development and diffusion. The case study methodology chosen in this book has proven particularly suitable for this purpose.

By means of case studies of successful eco-innovations, we hope that Chapter 6 provided the reader with a valuable insight into the eco-innovation process. We hope this was a useful addition to the first four more theoretical chapters – providing some meat on the bones, so to speak. Case studies show clear evidence that how and when the different dimensions of eco-innovation play a crucial role depends on both the innovation and the techno-institutional context in which it is developed and applied. Because the development and diffusion of eco-innovations is context and location specific, a comprehensive

understanding of the many drivers for and barriers to eco-innovation
is crucial. Indeed, technological infrastructure and socio-economic
institutional setting play a decisive role in the diffusion of eco-
innovations, which calls for active collaboration among policy makers, researchers, technology pioneers and incumbent industries.

Furthermore, we hope the case studies provided valuable insight
into the respective implications regarding competitiveness and sustainability, providing evidence that eco-innovations may mitigate the
traditionally perceived trade-off between competitiveness and environmental protection – confirming our initial hypothesis that eco-
innovation may indeed support both objectives and provide win-win
solutions. In Chapter 2, eco-innovation was defined as innovation
that improves environmental performance. It is worth repeating that
innovation is often a complex technological and social systemic
change process which consists of the invention of an idea for change
and its application in practice. Therefore, understanding its impacts
on competitiveness and sustainability is not a straightforward issue
and this complex process has different kinds of impacts on the system.
The process of innovating produces both tangible and intangible
impacts that improve capabilities and competences of engaged stakeholders to better address both competitiveness and sustainability.
Finally, the outcomes of eco-innovation have direct positive impacts
on competitiveness and sustainability. By addressing both the process
and outcome-oriented impacts of eco-innovation, we hope to have
shown the wealth of ways in which eco-innovation processes can trigger economic and environmental improvements in their different
dimensions (Table 7.1).

The *design* of both product and process eco-innovations supports
corporate efforts in efficiency improvements, cost management and
opening new markets, as well as reducing harmful impacts (emissions
and resource use) on the environment. Design is also the source of
new options, which is crucial in reshaping existing systems and managing societal transitions towards more sustainable paths.

Addressing *user* perspectives in the process of eco-innovation
brings innovation management closer to the markets and understanding of lead users, which help companies to become first movers for
building new markets. User-led eco-innovations have a better chance
of success in the market place. Furthermore, by addressing user needs,
eco-innovation can play a major role in mainstreaming sustainable
lifestyles by linking environmental aspects with other determinants of
competitive product and services.

Table 7.1   Implications of eco-innovation on competitiveness and sustainability

Dimension of eco-innovation	Competitiveness	Sustainability
Design	• Efficiency improvements • Cost management • Opening new markets • Increasing sales (revenues)	• Reducing harmful impacts, emissions and resource use • Re-designing existing systems • Transitions towards more sustainable paths
User	• Boosting innovations close to the market • Lead users and first movers for building new markets	• Mainstreaming sustainable lifestyles
Product-Service	• Renewal of business concepts • Knowledge intensive • Higher added-value	• Dematerialization • Immaterialization
Governance	• Horizontal coordination across policy fields • Encouraging a participatory approach in environmental policy • Wiring up the innovation system	• Mainstreaming environment, both in sectoral policies and business

Eco-innovation has a lot to do with revisiting existing corporate practices and exploring how things could be done better or even questioning the corporate mission. *Product service* dimensions offer opportunities for the renewal of business concepts, adding value by increasing knowledge intensiveness of products and services. This may have important implications for sustainability performance in terms of both dematerialization (reduced use of resources) and immaterialization (the move from resource-intensive products to immaterial services).

The *governance* of eco-innovation can benefit from the high status given to innovation in both policy and business recently. In this context, eco-innovation combines different policy fields and supports the horizontal integration and coordination of policies. Similarly, in business, eco-innovation processes enhance cooperation among different units and create new partnerships with the public sector, academia and businesses in different sectors. Indeed, the success of an eco-innovation in the market place is highly dependent on the engagement and participation of different stakeholders in its development. Thus eco-innovation can be a relevant tool for wiring up the innovation system. Eco-innovations may contribute to the renovation of the whole innovation system, taking into account social, ecological and economic aspects of the development. The long-term survival of the economic system depends on its ability to create and maintain sustainable economic processes, which do not involve short-term value creation at the expense of long-term wealth.

One of the main themes of the book has been to describe the variety of eco-innovations. We hope that the book helped the reader to find their bearings among the wealth of approaches to eco-innovating and to identify the approach most suitable for a specific situation in hand. We find it particularly relevant to seek to strike a balance between direct environmental impacts and the impacts on the longer-term transformation of the whole system. Some innovations, in particular component additions (end-of-pipe solutions) and sub-system changes (eco-efficiency solutions) are likely to have direct impacts on environmental performance. However, it may be just as important to consider how eco-innovation contributes to the transformation of the system they are part of, for instance the case of the Prius within the transport system or the EcoWorx backing having an influence on the carpet industry going green. In the case of the Prius, the hybrid synergy drive improves fuel efficiency but may also work as a crucial step towards the introduction of electric vehicles. Many expectations are placed on eco-innovations that deal with radical system level changes; finding new solutions in order to redirect existing systems towards a more sustainable path. Building the common visions that address eco-effectiveness and the future needs of society is a very ambitious but important starting point.

In other words, we need eco-innovations which develop and diffuse on different timescales. Some 'low hanging fruits' can easily be adopted now, while others require considerable joint efforts at the development and pre-commercialisation stages. Thus, it is worth exploring dual approaches in both policy and management to ensure incremental performance and environmental improvements in the short-term, as well as more systemic and radical changes in the longer term. This calls for a sensible balance between standardization (which allows cost reductions through economies of scale) and the maintenance of a certain degree of diversity, which can be expensive in the short-term, but cost-effective from a longer-term perspective. This is the case when the promotion of different eco-innovations allows them to exploit their potential for cost reductions and quality improvements, moving up their learning curves. The case studies in this book show that diversity characterizes eco-innovation and can play a major role in the transition towards a more sustainable and competitive economy.

If we wish to see eco-innovation making a difference, we have to be brave. Bold visions need to be converted into feasible plans that help share risks and bring in different stakeholders to work together. This is one of the biggest, if not the biggest, challenge for ourselves and for our children.

Notes

1 INTRODUCTION

1 WCED (1987) *Our Common Future* (Oxford University Press for the World Commission on Environment and Development).

2 Already in 1989, Pearce, D., Markandya, A. and Barbier, E. (1989) *Blueprint for a Green Economy* (London: Earthscan Publications Ltd.) identified more than one hundred definitions.

3 Hawken, P., Lovins, A. B. and Lovins, L. H. (1999) *Natural Capitalism: Creating the Next Industrial Revolution Natural Capitalism* (US: Back Bay Books); Schmidheiny, S. (1992) *Changing Course: A Global Business Perspective on Development and the Environment* (World Business Council for Sustainable Development).

4 Hawken, P. (1993) *The Ecology of Commerce* (New York: HarperCollins).

5 Walley, N. and Whitehead, B. (1994) 'It's Not Easy Being Green', *Harvard Business Review*, 72.3, 36–44.

6 Wagner, M. and Schaltegger, S. (2003) 'How Does Sustainability Performance Relate to Business Competitiveness?', *Greener Management International*, 44, Winter 2003, 5–16.

7 See for example: Xepapadeas, A. and De Zeeuw, A. (1999) 'Environmental policy and competitiveness: The Porter hypothesis and the composition of capital', *Journal of Environmental Economics and Management*, 37, 165–182; Simpson, R. D. and Bradford, R. L. (1996) 'Taxing variable cost: Environmental regulation as industry policy', *Journal of Environmental Economics and Management*, 30, 282–300; Palmer, K. W., Oates, W. E. and Portney, P. R. (1995) 'Tightening environmental standards: The benefit–cost or the no-cost paradigm', *Journal of Economic Perspectives*, 9(4), 119–132; Walley, N. and Whitehead, B. (1994) 'It's Not Easy Being Green', *Harvard Business Review*, 72(3), 36–44.

8 Luken, R. (1997) 'The Effect of Environmental Regulations on Industrial Competitiveness of Selected Industries in Developing Countries', *Greener Management International*, 19, 67–78.

9 Faucheux, S. and Nicolai, I. (1998) 'Les firmes face au développement soutenable: changement technologique et gouvernance au sein de la dynamique industrielle', *Revue d'Economie Industrielle*, 83, 127–145.

10 See for example: Sinclair-Desgagné, B. (1999) *Remarks on Environmental Regulation, Firm Behaviour and Innovation*, Scientific Series 99s–20 (Montreal: Cirano); Porter, M. and Van der Linde, C. (1995a) 'Green and Competitive: Ending the Stalemate', *Harvard Business Review*, September/October 1995, 120–134; Porter, M. and Van der Linde, C. (1995b) 'Toward a New Conception of the Environment–Competitiveness Relationship', *Journal of Economic Perspectives*, 9.4, 97–118; Shrivastava, P. (1995) 'Ecocentric Management for a Risk Society', *Academy of Management Review*, 20.1, 118–37; Porter, M. (1991) 'America's Green Strategy', *Scientific American*, 264.4, 96; Gabel, L. H. and Sinclair-Desgagné B. (1993) 'Managerial Incentives and Environmental Compliance', *Journal of Environmental Economics and Management*, 24, 940–55.

11 Porter and Van der Linde (1995a) op. cit.; Porter and van der Linde (1995b) op. cit.

12 Esty, D. and Porter, M. (1998) 'Industrial Ecology and Competitiveness: Strategic Implications for the Firm', *Journal of Industrial Ecology*, 2.1, 35–43; Shrivastava (1995) op. cit.

13 Jaffe, B., Peterson R., Portney R. and Stavins R. (1995) 'Environmental Regulation and the Competitiveness of US Manufacturing: What Does the Evidence Tell Us?', *Journal of Economic Literature*, 33, 132 –63.

14 WCED (1987) op. cit.

2   WHAT IS ECO-INNOVATION?

1 See, for example, Schmidheiny, S. (1992) *Changing Course: A Global Business Perspective on Development and the Environment* (World Business Council for Sustainable Development).

2 Frosch, R. A. and Gallopoulos, N. E. (1989) 'Strategies for Manufacturing', *Scientific American*, 261(3), 94–102; Côte, R. (1994) 'Designing and Operating Industrial Parks as Ecosystems', School for Resource and Environmental Studies, Dalhousie University, Canada; Graedel, T. E. and Allenby, B. R. (1995) 'Matrix approaches to abridged life cycle assessment', *Environmental Science & Technology*, 29(3), p. 134.

3 See, for example, Kurk, F. and Eagan, P. (2007) 'The value of adding design-for-the-environment to pollution prevention assistance options', *Journal of Cleaner Production*, XX, 1–5.

4 Braungart, M., McDonough, W. and Bollinger, A. (2007) 'Cradle-to-cradle design: creating healthy emissions: A strategy for eco-effective product and system design', *Journal of Cleaner Production*, 15, 1337–1348.

5 Hawken, P., Lovins, A. B. and Lovins, L. H. (1999) 'Natural Capitalism: Creating the Next Industrial Revolution', *Natural Capitalism* (US: Back Bay Books).

6 Andersen, M. M. (2008) 'Eco-innovation: Towards a taxonomy and a theory', paper for the *DRUID Conference*, Copenhagen.

7 See, for example, Dosi, G., Freeman, C., Nelson, R., Silverberg, G. and Soete, L. (eds) (1988), *Technical Change and Economic Theory* (London: Pinter); Arthur, B. (1994) *Increasing Returns and Path Dependence in the Economy* (Ann Arbor: University of Michigan Press); Nelson, R. R. and Winter, S. G. (2002) 'Evolutionary Theorizing in Economics', *Journal of Economic Perspectives*, 16(2), 23–46.

8 Nelson, R. and Sampat, B. (2001) 'Making Sense of Institutions as a Factor Shaping Economic Performance', *Journal of Economic Behaviour and Organization*, 44, 3154.

9 Berkhout, F. (2005) 'Technological Regimes, Environmental performance and innovation systems' in M. Weber and J. Hemmelskamp (ed.) *Towards Environmental Innovation Systems* (Berlin: Springer), 57–80.

10 Könnölä, T. and Unruh, G. C. (2007) 'Really Changing the Course: The Limitations of Environmental Management Systems for Innovation', *The Journal of Business Strategy and the Environment*, 16(8), 525–537.

11 Rothwell, R. and Gardiner, P. (1988) 'Re-innovation and robust designs: producer and user benefits', *Journal of Marketing Management*, 3(3), 372–387; Griffin, A. (1997) 'PDMA research on new product development practices: Updating trends, and benchmarking best practices', *Journal of Product Innovation Management*, 14, 429–458.

12 Rothwell, R. and Gardiner, P. (1988) 'Re-innovation and robust designs: producer and user benefits', *Journal of Marketing Management*, 3(3), 372–387; Griffin, A. (1997) 'PDMA research on new product development practices: updating trends, and

benchmarking best practices', *Journal of Product Innovation Management*, 14, 429–458.

13 See for example: Barbiroli, G. and Raggi, A. (2003) 'A method for evaluating the overall technical and economic performance of environmental innovations in production cycles', *Journal of Cleaner Production*, 11, 365–374; Kurk, F. and Eagan, P. (2007) 'The value of adding design-for-the-environment to pollution prevention assistance options', *Journal of Cleaner Production*, XX, 1–5; Fiksell, J. (1997) *Design for the Environment* (McGraw-Hill).

14 Schmidheiny (1992), op. cit.

15 Braungart, McDonough and Bollinger (2007), op. cit.

16 Schmidheiny (1992), op. cit.

17 Jaenicke, M. (2008) 'Ecological modernisation: new perspectives', *Journal of Cleaner Production*, 16(5), 557–565.

18 Frosch and Gallopoulos (1989), op. cit.; Côte (1994), op. cit.; Graedel and Allenby (1995), op. cit.; Socolow, R. (ed.) (1997), *Industrial Ecology and Global Change* (Cambridge University Press); Ayres, R. (1996) 'Creating industrial ecosystems: A viable management strategy?', *International Journal of Technology Management*, 12(5/6), 608.

19 McDonough, W. and Braungart, M. (2002) *Cradle to Cradle: Remaking the Way We Make Things* (NY: North Point Press); Braungart, McDonough and Bollinger (2007), op. cit.

20 McDonough and Braungart (2002), op. cit.; Braungart et al (2007), op. cit.

21 Von Hippel, E. (1988) *The sources of innovation* (New York: Oxford University Press).

22 Von Hippel, E. (2005) *Democratizing Innovation* (MIT Press).

23 Hienerth, C., Von Hippel, E. and Baldwin, C. Y. (2006) 'How User Innovations Become Commercial Products: A Theoretical Investigation and Case Study' *MIT Sloan Research Paper No. 4572–06; HBS Finance Working Paper No. 876967; Harvard NOM Working Paper No. 06–13*. Available at SSRN: http://ssrn.com/abstract=876967.

24 Riggs, W. and Von Hippel, E. (1994) 'Incentives to innovate and the sources of innovation: The case of scientific instruments', *Research Policy*, 23(4), 459–469.

25 Urban, G. I. and Von Hippel, E. (1988) 'Lead user analyses for the development of new industrial products', *Management Science*, 34(5), 569–582.

26 Luthje, C., Herstatt, C. and Von Hippel, E. (2005) 'User-innovators and "local" information: The case of Mountain Biking', *Research Policy*, 34: 951–965.

27 Rondinelli, D. A. and London, T. (2003) 'How Corporations and Environmental Groups Cooperate: Assessing Cross-Sector Alliances and Collaborations', *Academy of Management Executive*, 17(1), 61–76.

28 Urban and Von Hippel (1988), op. cit.

29 Ibid.

30 Midgely, D. (1977) *New Products Marketing* (New York: Halsted Press).

31 Stahel, W. R. and Jackson, T. (1993) 'Optimal Utilisation and Durability' in Jackson, T. (ed.) *Clean Production Strategies* (Boca Raton, Florida: Lewis Publishers), 261–291.

32 Halme, M., Anttonen, M., Kuisma, M., Kontoniemi, N. and Heino, E. (2007) 'Business models for material efficiency services: Conceptualization and application', *Ecological Economics*, 63, 126–137.

33 Markides, C. (2006) 'Disruptive innovation: in need of a better theory', *J. Prod. Innov. Manag.*, 23, 19–25.

34 Mont, O. (2002) 'Clarifying the concept of product-service system', *Journal of Cleaner Production*, 10(3), 237–245.

35 Williams, A. (2007) 'Product service systems in the automobile industry: contribution to system innovation?', *Journal of Cleaner Production*, 15 (2007), 1093–1103.

36 Goedkoop ,M .J., van Halen, J. G., te Riele , H. and Rommens, P. J. M. (1999) *Product Service Systems, Ecological and Economic Basics* (The Hague: Vrom EZ).

37 Linton, J. D., Klassen, R. and Jayaraman, V. (2007) 'Sustainable supply chains: An introduction', *Journal of Operations Management*, 25(6), 1075–1082.

38 Könnölä and Unruh (2007), op. cit.

39 The terms 'socio-technological transformation' (Geels, F. W. (2002) 'Technological transitions as evolutionary reconfiguration processes: a multilevel perspective and a case study', *Research Policy* 31(89), 1257–1274); 'system innovation' (Edqvist, C. (ed.) (1997) *Systems Innovation: Technologies, Institutions and Organisations* (London: Pinter Publishers)); and 'transition' (Rotmans, J., Kemp, R. and van Asselt, M. (2001) 'More evolution than revolution: transition management in public policy', *Foresight*, 3(1), 15–32) have also

been used to describe a similar kind of fundamental transformation processes of the co-evolution of technological and institutional systems.

40 See, for example, Kemp, R. and Soete, L. (1992) 'The greening of technological progress: An evolutionary perspective', *Futures*, June, 437–455; Jacobsson, S. and Johnson, A. (2000) 'The Diffusion of Renewable Energy Technology: An Analytical Framework and Key Issues for Research', *Energy Policy*, 28, 625–640; Unruh, G. C. (2000) 'Understanding Carbon Lock-in', *Energy Policy*, 28, 817–830; Kline, D. (2001) 'Positive Feedback, Lock-in, and Environmental Policy', *Policy Sciences*, 34, 95–107; Geels, F. W. (2002) 'Technological transitions as evolutionary reconfiguration processes: a multilevel perspective and a case study', *Research Policy*, 31(89), 1257–1274; Carlsson, B. and Jacobsson, S. (2004) 'Dynamics of Innovation Systems: Policy-making in a Complex and Non-deterministic World', *International Workshop on Functions of Innovation Systems*, Utrecht University; Frenken, K., Hekkert, M. and Godfroij, P. (2004) 'R&D Portfolios in Environmental Friendly Automotive Propulsion: Variety, Competition and Policy Implications', *Technological Forecasting and Social Change*, 71(5), 485–507; Foxon, T. J. et al (2005) 'UK innovation systems for new and renewable energy technologies: drivers, barriers and systems failures', *Energy Policy*, 33 (16), 2123–37; Carrillo-Hermosilla, J. (2006) 'A policy approach to the environmental impacts of technological lock-in', *Ecological Economics*, 58(4), 717–742; Carrillo-Hermosilla, J. and Unruh, G. C. (2006), 'Technology stability and change: an integrated evolutionary approach', *Journal of Economic Issues*, XL (3), 707–742.

41 Pérez, C. (1983) 'Structural Change and Assimilation of New Technologies in the Economic and Social Systems', *Futures*, 15(4), 357–775; Freeman, C. and Perez, C. (1988) 'Structural crisis of adjustment, business cycles and investment behaviour', in Dosi, G., Freeman, C., Nelson, R., Silverberg, G. and Soete, L. (eds), *Technical Change and Economic Theory* (London: Pinter Publishers), 38–66.; Unruh (2000), op. cit.

42 Paavola, J. (2007) 'Institutions and environmental governance: A reconceptualization', *Ecological Economics*, 63, 93–103.

43 Ibid.

44 Ibid.

45 Ostrom, E. (1990) *Governing the Commons: The Evolution of Institutions for Collective Action* (Cambridge: Cambridge

University Press); Sengupta, N. (2004) 'Common Mistakes about Common Property', *Tenth Biennial Conference of the International Society for the Study of Common Property in Oaxaca*, Mexico, 9–13 August.

46 Jørgensen, B. (2006) 'Technology and Innovation in Waste Management in the Arctic: Example of an Automated Waste Collection System in Stakkevollan, Tromsø, Norway', *The 12th Mayors Conference of WWCAM, 2006 Winter Cities Forum*, Changchun, China.

3   BARRIERS TO ECO-INNOVATION

1 Rennings, K. (2000) 'Redefining innovation: Eco-innovation research and the contribution from ecological economics', *Ecological Economics,* 32: 319–332; Del Río, P. (2004) 'Public policy and clean technology promotion: The synergy between environmental economics and evolutionary economics of technological change', *International Journal of Sustainable Development,* 7(2): 200–216.

2 Erdmann, G. (2005) 'Innovation, time and sustainability' in M. Weber and J. Hemmelskamp (eds), *Towards Environmental Innovation Systems* (Berlin: Springer), p. 199.

3 See, for example, Arthur, W. B. (1988) 'Competing technologies: an overview' in Dosi, G., Freeman, C., Nelson, R., Silverberg, G. and Soete, L. (eds) *Technical Change and Economic Theory* (London: Pinter), 590–607.

4 Carrillo-Hermosilla, J. (2006) 'A policy approach to the environmental impacts of technological lock-in', *Ecological Economics,* 58(4): 717–742; Carrillo-Hermosilla, J. and Unruh, G. C. (2006), 'Technology stability and change: An integrated evolutionary approach', *Journal of Economic Issues,* Vol. XL, No. 3: 707–42; Unruh, G. C. and Carrillo-Hermosilla, J. (2006) 'Globalizing Carbon Lock-in', *Energy Policy,* 34(10): 1185–1197; Könnölä, T., Unruh, G. C. and Carrillo-Hermosilla, J. (2006). 'Prospective voluntary agreements for escaping techno-institutional lock-in', *Ecological Economics,* 57(2): 239–252; Del Río, P. and Unruh, G. C. (2007) 'Overcoming the lock-out of renewable energy technologies in Spain: the cases of wind and solar electricity', *Renewable and Sustainable Energy Review,* 11(7), 1498–513.

5 Carrillo-Hermosilla, J. and Könnölä, T. (2008) 'Towards a sustainable development through eco-innovation' in R.A. López (ed.),

Progress in Sustainable Development Research (New York: Nova Science Publishers), 1–34.

6 Barriers to eco-innovations cannot only be interpreted in terms of direct obstacles (that is, factors explicitly impeding their development and adoption) but also to more 'passive' hindering factors in terms of lack of drivers for the development or adoption of eco-innovations.

7 Del Río, P. (2002) *Industry, Technological Change and Sustainable Development: Patterns Of Adoption of Cleaner Technologies in the Paper Industry*, unpublished PhD thesis (in Spanish) (Madrid: Universidad Autónoma de Madrid); Del Río, P. (2005) 'Analysing the factors influencing clean technology adoption: a study of the Spanish pulp and paper industry', *Business Strategy and the Environment*, 14: 20–37.

8 Del Río, P. (2005), op. cit.

9 See, in this respect, the overview of the literature between 1990 and 2007 carried out by Montalvo, C. (2008) '*General wisdom concerning the factors affecting the adoption of cleaner technologies: A survey 1990–2007*', *Journal of Cleaner Production*, 16(1), 7–13; Del Río, P. (2007) 'An overview of the empirical literature on the determinants of innovation and adoption of sustainable technologies', in R. A. López (ed.), *Progress in Sustainable Development Research* (New York: Nova Science Publishers), 37–71; Del Río, P. (2008) 'The empirical analysis of the determinants for environmental technological change: A research agenda', *Ecological Economics* (forthcoming), identifies knowledge gaps in and proposes several lines of future research.

10 Kemp, R. and Volpi, M. (2008) '*The diffusion of clean technologies: a review with suggestions for future diffusion analysis*', *Journal of Cleaner Production*, 16(1), 14–21.

11 According to the authors, endogenous factors refer to information transfer, improvements in the technology and price reductions as a result of learning processes, economies of scale and competition between suppliers). Exogenous factors include changes in the price of energy, income changes and changes in regulatory framework.

12 Montalvo (2008), op. cit.

13 Ashford, N. (2005a) 'Government and environmental innovation in Europe and North America' in Weber, M. and Hemmelskamp, J. (eds) *Towards Environmental Innovation Systems* (Germany: Springer), 159–174.

14 There are multiple sources of risks. For example, according to Montalvo (2008, op. cit., p. 3) sources of risk and uncertainty include 'the likelihood or unlikelihood of appropriating the benefits

of innovations, the timing and trade-offs of investments in relation to business cycles, the age of current production processes and the possible economic benefits rendered by adoption of newer and untested technologies'. Del Río (2005, op. cit., p. 8) observes that there are regulatory uncertainties, uncertainties related to the drastic changes that adoption may cause in firms, market uncertainties and technical uncertainties. For the European Commission (2004, Commission's Communication on 'Stimulating technologies for Sustainable Development: an Environmental Technologies Action Plan for the European Union', COM(2004) 38 final, 28.1.2004) uncertainty is related to likely legislation, standards and targets, trends in consumer behaviour, how law enforcers will react to new technologies, reliable information (economic and environmental) on environmental technologies and their likely evolution compared to other relevant alternatives and on the extent to which the public sector will demand environmental technologies through purchasing.

15 Ibid.

16 However, other authors claim that the relationship between firm size and eco-innovation follows a U-shape: the largest and the smallest firms are the most environmentally innovative (Hemmelskamp, J. (2000) *Environmental Taxes and Standards: An Empirical Analysis of the Impact on Innovation* in: Hemmelskamp, J., Leone, F. and Rennings, K. (eds) *Innovation-oriented Environmental Regulation: Theoretical Approaches and Empirical Analysis* (Heidelberg, Germany: Physica Verlag), 303–330.

17 Kemp and Volpi (2008), op. cit., p. 17.

18 Del Río (2005), op. cit.

19 Seroa da Motta empirically assesses the relevance of foreign ties (origin of capital) on environmental performance, showing a positive relationship (Seroa da Motta, R. (2006) 'Analyzing the environmental performance of the Brazilian industrial sector', *Ecological Economics*, 57: 269–281).

20 Wagner also considers the variable 'firm legal structure', that is, whether the company is in sole proprietorship or not. However, a priori, it is difficult to find any causal relation between this variable and eco-innovation (Wagner, M. (2008) 'Empirical influence of environmental management on innovation: evidence from Europe', *Ecological Economics*, 66(2–3), 392–402).

21 Garrod, B. (1998) 'Are economic globalization and sustainable development compatible? Business strategy and the role of the

multinational enterprise', *International Journal of Sustainable Development* 1(1), 43–62.

22 For example, in an empirical analysis of Portuguese firms, Conceicao et al show that development of environmental innovation is positively associated with the firm's exports share (Conceicao, P., Heitor, M. and Vieira, P. (2006) 'Are environmental concerns drivers of innovation? Interpreting Portuguese innovation data to foster environmental foresight', *Technological Forecasting & Social Change*, 73, 266–276).

23 Berkhout, F. (2005) 'Technological Regimes, Environmental performance and innovation systems: Tracing the links' in M. Weber and J. Hemmelskamp (eds) *Towards Environmental Innovation Systems* (Berlin: Springer), 57–80.

24 Kemp and Volpi (2008), op. cit.

25 Smolny, W. (2003) 'Determinants of Innovation Behaviour and Investment: Estimates for West-German Manufacturing Firms', *Economics of Innovation and New Technology*, 12, p. 449.

26 Horbach, J. (2008) 'Determinants of Environmental Innovation – New Evidence from German Panel Data Sources', *Research Policy*, 37(1), p. 165.

27 Ibid.

28 Doonan, J., Lanoie, P. and Laplante, B. (2005) 'Determinants of environmental performance in the Canadian pulp and paper industry: an assessment from inside the industry', *Ecological Economics* 55(1), 73–84.

29 Luken, R. and Van Rompaey, F. (2008) 'Drivers for and barriers to environmentally sound technology adoption by manufacturing plants in nine developing countries', *Journal of Cleaner Production*, 16(1), 67–77

30 Montalvo (2008), op. cit, p. 10.

31 Ibid.

32 Ibid., p. 5.

33 Koefoed, M. and Buckley, C. (2008) 'Clean technology transfer: A case study from the South African metal finishing industry 2000–2005', *Journal of Cleaner Production*, 16(1), 78–84.

34 Visser, R., Jongen, M. and Zwetsloot, G. (2008) 'Business-driven innovations towards more sustainable chemical products', *Journal of Cleaner Production*, 16(1), 85–94.

35 Fresner, J. Sage, J. and Wolf, P. (2002) 'A benchmarking of 50 Austrian companies from the galvanizing and painting sector: Current implementation of cleaner production options and active environmental management' (ERCP, Cork, Ireland).

36 Sartorius, C. (2008) 'Promotion of stationary fuel cells on the basis of subjectively perceived barriers and drivers', *Journal of Cleaner Production*, 16, 171–180.

37 Cagno, E. and Trucco, P. (2008) 'Cleaner technology transfer in the Italian galvanic industry: economic and know-how issues', *Journal of Cleaner Production*, 16(1), 32–36.

38 These authors showed that the ease of acquisition of the know-how to implement the BAT depended on: 1) the ease of access to information/training on the new technique, and the relative cost of access to the know-how; 2) the difficulty in transferring into the company the know-how necessary to implement and manage the new technique. The difficulty faced by galvanic companies in adopting BATs was the result of poor access to the know-how needed to implement the techniques. Although obtaining information on the different BATs was easy (thanks to the information provided by industrial associations), the implementation of those BATs was hindered by the unavailability of technical skills within the company.

39 Ashford (2005a), op. cit.

40 Ibid.

41 Ibid.

42 Ibid.

43 Yüksel, H. (2008) 'An empirical evaluation of cleaner production practices in Turkey', *Journal of Cleaner Production*, 16(1), 50–57.

44 Many authors have proposed taxonomies on the environmental strategies followed by the firms. According to Faucheux et al (1998), firms which do not react to new environmental challenges follow an inactive (or passive) strategy and those firms which see environmental issues as an additional cost that should be minimized (and not as a business opportunity) follow a defensive (or reactive) strategy and usually invest a significant amount of money and efforts to challenge environmental regulation. Finally, proactive firms mostly view environmental issues as a business opportunity and usually anticipate the implementation of environmental regulation (Faucheux, S., Nicolai, I and O'Connor, M. (1998) 'Globalisation, competitiveness, governance and environment: What prospects for Sustainable Development?' in Faucheux, S., Gowdy, J. and Nicolai, I. (eds) *Sustainability and Firms: Technological Change and the Changing Regulatory Environment* (Cheltenham (UK): Edward Elgar), 1–40).

45 As shown by Del Río (2005), op. cit.

46 Visser et al (2008), op. cit.
47 Rogers, E. M. (1995) *Diffusion of Innovations* (New York: Free Press).
48 ADL (2005) 'The Innovation High Ground', Arthur D. Little, http://www.adl.com/ (home page), date accessed 14 November 2008.
49 Montalvo (2008), op. cit.
50 Doonan et al (2005), op. cit.
51 Wagner (2008), op. cit.
52 Ibid., p. 3.
53 Montalvo (2008), op. cit., p. 59.
54 Del Río (2002, 2005), op. cit.
55 Frondel, M., Horbach, J. and Rennings, K. (2005) 'What triggers environmental management and innovation? Empirical evidence from Germany', *European Congress of Environmental and Resource Economics*, Bremen.
56 Horbach, J. (2005) 'Methodological aspects of an indicator system for sustainable innovation' in J. Horbach (ed.) *Indicator Systems for Sustainable Innovation* (Heidelberg: Physica-Verlag), 1–20.
57 See Del Río (2008), op. cit., and Chapter 4.
58 Könnölä, T. and Unruh, G. C. (2007) 'Really Changing the Course: The Limitations of Environmental Management Systems for Innovation', *The Journal of Business Strategy and the Environment*, 16(8), 525–537.
59 See Del Río (2008), op. cit., in this regard.
60 Ibid.
61 Kivimaa, P. (2007) 'The Determinants of Environmental Innovation: the impacts of Environmental Policies on the Nordic Pulp, Paper and Packaging Industries', *European Environment*, 17: 92–105.
62 Visser, R., Jongen, M. and Zwetsloot, G. (2008) 'Business-driven innovations towards more sustainable chemical products', *Journal of Cleaner Production*, 16(1), S85–94.
63 Lanjouw, J. and Moddy, O. (1996) 'Innovation and the international diffusion of environmentally responsive technology', *Research Policy*, 25, 549–571.
64 Del Río (2007, 2008), op. cit.
65 This is one of the reasons that the European Commission has implemented the Environmental Compliance Assessment Programme (ECAP) in order to tackle the information needs of SMEs regarding ways to comply with environmental regulation by cco-innovating.
66 Del Río (2005), op. cit.

67 Luken and Van Rompaey (2008), op. cit.

68 Berkhout (2005), op. cit.

69 The relevance of the user-supplier relationship in encouraging eco-innovation has been empirically tested and confirmed (see Dupuy, D. (1997) 'Technological change and environmental policy: The diffusion of environmental technology', *Growth and Change*, 28, 49–66; and Van Dijken, K. et al (1999) *Adoption of Environmental Innovations* (Dordrecht, the Netherlands: Kluwer Academic Publishers)).

70 European Commission (2004), op. cit.

71 Luken and Van Rompaey (2008), op. cit.

72 Cabezudo, S., Cadenas, A. and Del Río, P. (2000) 'Las fuerzas del cambio empresarial en medio ambiente', *Ekonomi Gerizan*, 7, 155–174.

73 Wagner (2007), op. cit., empirically shows a positive influence of eco-labelling on environmental product innovations.

74 Luken and Van Rompaey (2008), op. cit.

75 Visser, R., Jongen, M. and Zwetsloot, G. (2008) 'Business-driven innovations towards more sustainable chemical products', *Journal of Cleaner Production*, 16(1), 85–94.

76 Luken and van Rompaey (2008), op. cit.

77 Del Río (2002, 2005), op. cit.

78 Bergmann, A., Hanley, N. and Wright, R. (2006) 'Valuing the attributes of renewable energy investments', *Energy Policy*, 34(9), 1004–1014.

79 European Commission (2004), op. cit.

80 Carrillo-Hermosilla and Könnölä (2008), op. cit.

81 Montalvo (2008), op. cit.

82 Ashford, N. A. (2005b) 'Pathways to Sustainability: Evolution or Revolution?' in M. van Geenhuizen, D. V. Gibson, and M. V. Heitor (eds) *Regional Development and Conditions for Innovation in the Network Society* (Purdue University Press), 35–59.

83 Horbach (2008), op. cit.

84 Faucheux S. and Nicolai I. (1998) 'Les firmes face au développement soutenable: changement technologique et gouvernance au sein de la dynamique industrielle', *Revue d'Economie Industrielle*, 83: 127–145.

85 Del Río (2005), op. cit.

86 Luken and Van Rompaey (2007), op. cit., p. 4, explicitly consider this variable in their empirical study. The authors classify environmentally sound technologies (clean and pollution abatement

technologies) into three categories according to their degree of complexity: Lower order of technological complexity (including input material change and better process control); medium order of technological complexity (equipment modification, on-site reuse and useful by-products) and higher order of technological complexity (major technology change and product modification).

87 Cagno and Trucco (2008), op. cit.

88 Del Río (2002, 2005), op. cit.

89 Del Río (2002), op. cit.

90 Kemp, R. (1994) 'Technology and the transition to environmental sustainability', *Futures*, 26(10), 1023–46; Dupuy (1997), op. cit.; Del Río (2008), op. cit.

91 Kerr, S. and Newell, R. (2001) 'Policy-induced technology adoption: evidence from the US lead phasedown', *Journal of Industrial Economics*, 51(3), 317–343.

92 Jaffe and Stavins found that adoption decisions were more sensitive to up-front cost considerations than to longer term operating expenses. The costs of the technology had a significant and negative impact on adoption and this influence was three times as large as that of energy prices. In much the same vein, Anderson and Newell (2003) observed that 40 per cent of plants were more influenced by the impact of initial costs than by annual cost savings – especially for SMEs (Jaffe, A. B. and Stavins, R. N. (1995) 'Dynamic incentives of environmental regulations: The effects of alternative policy instruments on technology diffusion', *Journal of Environmental Economics and Management*, 29, S43–S63).

93 Kemp and Volpi (2008), op. cit.

94 Colombo, M. G. and Mosconi, R. (1995) 'Complementarity and cumulative learning effects in the early diffusion of muliple technologies', *Journal of Industrial Economics*, 43(1), 13–48.

95 Del Río (2002, 2008), op. cit.

96 Ashford (2005a), op. cit.

97 Ibid.

98 Berkhout (2005), op. cit.

99 Del Río (2005), op. cit.

100 Berkhout (2005), op. cit.

101 Ibid.

102 Unruh, G. C. (2000) 'Understanding Carbon Lock-in', *Energy Policy*, 28, 817–30;

103 Erdmann (2005), op. cit.

4 POLICY STRATEGIES TO PROMOTE ECO-INNOVATION

1 For an overview of the aforementioned literature, see Del Río, P. (2002) *Industry, Technological Change and Sustainable Development: Patterns Of Adoption of Cleaner Technologies in the Paper Industry*, unpublished PhD thesis (in Spanish) (Madrid: Universidad Autónoma de Madrid); and Del Río, P. (2008) 'The empirical analysis of the determinants for environmental technological change: A research agenda', *Ecological Economics* (forthcoming).

2 Before the introduction of an environmental policy, firms do not pay for the negative environmental externality they are responsible for and therefore the privately optimal level of pollution is above the socially optimal level (Johnstone, N. and Labonne, J. (2006) 'Environmental policy, management and R&D', OECD Economic Studies, No. 42, 2006/1). On the other hand, industry tends to under-invest in research, development, and demonstration (RD&D) generally, compared to the societal returns of that RD&D (see Griliches, Z. (1992) 'The Search for R&D Spillovers', *Scandinavian Journal of Economics*, 94, 29–42).

3 There are exceptions to this general statement, however. For example, there is a rationale to use regulation to push certain cleaner consumer products with short pay-back periods which nevertheless do not get adopted into the market. This is the case with regards to more energy-efficient light bulbs. Indeed, this seems to be the approach to stimulate their uptake in some EU countries and California. In this case, the use of economic instruments which would increase the cost of electricity, providing an indirect incentive to adopt the more efficient alternatives would probably not be effective, unless the price of electricity increased significantly, which would lead to other problems.

4 Volleberg, H. (2007) 'Differential Impact of Environmental Policy Instruments on Technological Change: A Review of the Empirical Literature', TI 2007–042/3, Tinbergen Institute Discussion Paper (Amsterdam); Del Río, P. (2007) 'The empirical literature on the determinants for the adoption of sustainable technologies: An overview and lessons for future research' in López, R. (ed.). *Progress in Sustainable Development Research* (New York: Nova Science Publishers), 37–71; Del Río (2008), op. cit.

5 Kneese, A.V. and Schulze, C. L. (1975) *Pollution, Prices and Public Policy* (Washington D.C.: Brookings).

6 Gunningham, N. (2007) 'Reconfiguring environmental regulation: Next-generation policy instruments' in Parto, S. and Herbert-Copley, B. (eds) *Industrial Innovation and Environmental Regulation: Developing Workable Solutions* (Tokyo: United Nations University Press), p. 202.

7 The neoclassical approach to technology policy is built on Arrow's analysis of market failure (Arrow, K. J. (1962) 'Economic welfare and the allocation of resources for invention' in Nelson, R. (ed.) *The Rate and Direction of Inventive Activity* (Princeton: Princeton University Press), 609–625). According to this analysis, a completely competitive and decentralized market will provide a sub-optimal level of knowledge. This justifies public intervention either to create knowledge or to establish intellectual property rights. In neoclassical microeconomics a state with a welfare maximizing goal (under conditions of unbounded rationality) and perfect information on its environment and the consequences of its decisions, should be able to correct market failures efficiently and bring the economic system to a Pareto optimal equilibrium. The role assigned to the state is therefore corrective in nature (Moreau, F. (1999) 'The role of the State in an Evolutionary Microeconomics', Working Paper du Laboratoire d'Econométrie no 99–1, Conservatoire National des Arts et Métiers, Paris, p. 5). The evolutionary approach to technological change suggests taking a broader view of technology policy than that put forward by the neoclassical approach. The fundamental difference lies in the fact that evolutionary economics is based on the assumption of a single stable equilibrium for the economic system. The existence of multiple alternative equilibriums gives a new rationale to the state's intervention in the economy, in that coordination of the decisions by individual agents may be necessary in order to seek convergence between the particular and general interests. In the evolutionary approach, the main question is not optimization and equilibrium, but endogenous change, evolution and economic development (Llerena, P. and Matt, M. (1999) 'Inter-organizational collaborations: The theories and their policy implications' in A. Gambardella and F. Malerba (eds) *The Organization of Economic Innovation in Europe* (Cambridge University Press), 179–201). The focus of attention has ceased to be on the market failure per se and has become the improvement in competitive performance and the promotion of structural change (Mowery, D. and Rosenberg, N. (1989) 'New developments in US technology policy: Implications for competitiveness and international trade policy', *California*

Management Review, 32, 107–124). Thus, the role assigned to the State ceases to be corrective and becomes adaptive, insofar as it is more concerned with influencing the process than imposing a particular result (Metcalfe, J. S. (1995) 'Technology systems and technology policy in an evolutionary framework', *Cambridge Journal of Economics*, 19(1), 25–46: p. 31).

8 Parto and Herbert-Copley (2007), op. cit., p. 293.
9 Oosterhuis, F. (2006) 'Innovation dynamics induced by environmental policy', IVM Report E-07/05 (Amsterdam), p. 15.
10 Del Río, P. (2004) 'Public policy and clean technology promotion: The synergy between environmental economics and evolutionary economics of technological change', *International Journal of Sustainable Development*, 7(2), 200–216.
11 Kivimaa, P. and Mickwitz, P. (2006) 'The challenge of greening technologies: Environmental policy integration in Finnish technology policies', *Research Policy*, 35, 729–744.
12 Kemp, R. (2007) 'Integrating environmental and innovation policies' in Parto and Herbert-Copley (2007), op. cit., 258–82.
13 Kemp, R. (2000) 'Technology and Environmental Policy: Innovation effects of past policies and suggestions for improvement', OECD, Paris; Del Río (2004), op. cit.
14 Norberg-Bohm, V. (1999) 'Stimulating green technological innovation: An analysis of alternative policy mechanisms', *Policy Sciences*, 32, p. 32.
15 Oosterhuis (2006), op. cit., p. 21.
16 Kemp (2007), op. cit., p. 266.
17 Kemp (2000), op. cit.
18 Gunningham (2007), op. cit., p. 220.
19 Kemp (2007), op. cit., p. 265.
20 Ashford, N. (1993) 'Understanding Technological Responses of Industrial Firms to Environmental Problems: Implications for Government Policy' in Fischer, K. and Schot, J. (eds). *Environmental Strategies for Industry* (Island Press), 277–307.
21 Del Río (2008), op. cit.
22 Gunningham (2007), op. cit.
23 For example, information and monitoring requirements can empower social actors if environmental information about is easily accessible and sufficient to allow for meaningful interpretation of the data (ibid., p. 221).
24 Von Hippel, E. (1988) *The sources of innovation* (New York: Oxford University Press).

25 See Taylor, M. R., Rubin, E. S. and Hounshell, D. (2005) 'Control of SO_2 Emission from Power Plants: A Case of Induced Technological Innovation in the U.S.', *Technological Forecasting and Social Change*, 72(6), 697–718.

26 Oosterhuis (2006), op. cit.

27 Norberg-Bohm, V. (2000) 'Technology Commercialization and Environmental Regulation: Lessons from the U.S. Energy Sector' in J. Hemmelskamp, K. Rennings, and F. Leone (eds) *Innovation-Oriented Environmental Regulation: Theoretical Approaches and Empirical Analysis* (Heidelberg: Springer/Physica-Verlag), 193–220.

28 Del Río (2004, 2008), op. cit.; Jaffe, A. B., Newell, R. G. and Stavins, R. N. (2002). 'Environmental policy and technological change', *Environment and Resource Economics*, 22(1–2), 41–69.

29 CCC (2006) 'Clean, Clever and Competitive: Advice of the Eminent People Group', http://cleanclevercompetitive.com/

30 BLUEPRINT (2003) 'Blueprints for an Integration of Science, Technology and Environmental Policy', STRATA Project, Contract Nr.: HPV1-CT-2001-00003, http://www.blueprint-network.net/

31 Frondel, M., Horbach, J. and Rennings, K. (2004) 'End-of-Pipe or Cleaner Production? An Empirical Comparison of Environmental Innovation Decisions Across OECD Countries', ZEW Discussion Paper No. 04–82, Mannheim, Centre for European Economic Research (ZEW).

32 Oosterhuis (2006), op. cit.

33 This view that there is a 'natural' tendency for environmental technology to develop from abatement (end-of-pipe) to 'integrated' (clean) technologies is, however, challenged by Berkhout, F. (2005) 'Technological Regimes, Environmental performance and innovation systems: Tracing the links' in M. Weber and J. Hemmelskamp (eds) *Towards Environmental Innovation Systems* (Berlin: Springer), 57–80.

34 Del Río (2008), op. cit.

35 Kemp (2007), op. cit, p. 263.

36 Moreau (1999), op. cit.

37 Kemp, R. (1997) *Environmental Policy and Technical Change* (Cheltenham, UK, and Brookfield, US: Edward Elgar), p. 241.

38 Godard, O. (1993) 'Stratégies industrielles et conventions d'environment: De l'univers stabilise aux univers controversies', *Insee Méthodes*, 39–40, 175–86.

39 Del Río (2008), op. cit.
40 The 'Narrow window dilemma', underlined by Paul A. David, high-lights the briefness of the period during which a policy maker may pilot with success a dynamic economic system. In such a system, any delay in the implementation of public policy measures could prove fatal to the policy maker's goals (David, P. A. (1987) 'Some new standards for the economics of standardization in the information age' in Dasgupta, P. and Stoneman, L. (eds) *The Economic Theory of Technology Policy* (London: Cambridge University Press).
41 Sartorius, C. (2008) 'Promotion of stationary fuel cells on the basis of subjectively perceived barriers and drivers', *Journal of Cleaner Production*, 16(1), 171–180.
42 Del Río (2008), op. cit.
43 Norberg-Bohm (2000), op. cit.
44 Ashford, N. (2005) 'Government and environmental innovation in Europe and North America' in Weber, M. and Hemmelskamp, J. (eds) *Towards Environmental Innovation Systems* (Berlin: Springer), 159–174.
45 Barton, J., Jenkins, R., Bartzokas, A., Hesselberg, J. and Knutsen, H. (2007) 'Environmental regulation and industrial competitiveness in pollution-intensive industries' in Parto and Herbert-Copley (2007), op. cit., p. 51.
46 Fukasaku, Y. (2005) 'The need for environmental innovation indicators and data from a policy perspective' in M. Weber and J. Hemmelskamp (eds) *Towards Environmental Innovation Systems* (Berlin: Springer), 251–267.
47 Malerba, F. (2002) 'Sectoral systems of innovation and produc-tion', *Research Policy*, 31(2), 247–264.
48 Del Río (2002), op. cit.; Del Río, P. (2005) 'Analysing the factors influencing clean technology adoption: a study of the Spanish pulp and paper industry', *Business Strategy and the Environment*, 14, 20–37 Del Río (2008), op. cit.
49 Norberg-Bohm (1999), op. cit.
50 Montalvo, C. (2003) 'Sustainable production and consumption systems-cooperation for change – Assessing and simulating the willingness of the firm to adopt/develop cleaner technologies: The case of the In-Bond industry in northern Mexico', *Journal of Cleaner Production*, 11, p. 421.
51 Del Río (2008), op. cit.
52 Ashford (1993), op. cit.
53 Jaenicke, M., Blazejczak, J., Edler, D. and Hemmelskamp, J. (2000) 'Environmental Policy and Innovation: An International

Comparison of Policy Frameworks and Innovation Effects' in Hemmelskamp, J., Rennings, K. and Leone, F. (eds) *Innovation-Oriented Environmental Regulation* (Heidelberg: Physica Verlag), 125–152.

54 Del Río (2004), op. cit.

55 Del Río (2008), op. cit.

56 Requate, T. (2005) 'Dynamic incentives by environmental policy instruments – a survey' *Ecological Economics*, 54, 175–195.

57 See, among others: Ashford, N., Ayers, C. and Stone, F. (1985) 'Using regulation to change the market for innovation', *Harvard Environmental Law Review*, 9, 419–466; Ashford (2005), op. cit.; Murphy, J. and Gouldson, A. (2000) 'Environmental policy and industrial innovation: Integrating environmental and economy through ecological modernisation', *Geoforum*, 31, 33–44; Taylor, M. R., Rubin, E. S. and Hounshell, D. (2005) 'Control of SO_2 Emission from Power Plants: A Case of Induced Technological Innovation in the U.S.', *Technological Forecasting and Social Change*, 72(6), 697–718; Kemp (2000), op. cit.; and Frondel, Horbach and Rennings (2004), op. cit. A notable exception is Montalvo (2003, op. cit.) who discovers that negative impacts on the willingness to develop clean technology from stringent environmental regulation can be expected.

58 Frondel, Horbach and Rennings (2004), op. cit.

59 Ashford (1993), op. cit.

60 Gunningham, N. (2007) 'Reconfiguring environmental regulation: Next-generation policy instruments' in Parto, S. and Herbert-Copley, B. (eds) *Industrial Innovation and Environmental Regulation: Developing Workable Solutions* (Tokyo: United Nations University Press), p. 218.

61 Van Soest, D. P. and Bulte, E. H. (2001) 'Does the Energy-Efficiency Paradox Exist? Technological Progress and Uncertainty', *Environmental and Resource Economics*, 18(1), 101–112.

62 Kemp (2000), op. cit.

63 Del Río (2004), op. cit.

64 Ashford (1993), op. cit.

65 Bernauer, T., Engels, S., Kammerer, D. and Seijas, J. (2006) 'Explaining Green Innovation – Ten Years after Porter's Win-Win Proposition: How to Study the Effects of Regulation on Corporate Environmental Innovation?', ETH Zurich, Center for Comparative and International Studies (Zurich).

66 Norberg-Bohm (1999), op. cit.

67 Del Río (2008), op. cit.

68 Ashford (1993), op. cit.
69 COM (2004) 'Stimulating Technologies for Sustainable Development: An Environmental Technologies Action Plan for the European Union', http://eur-lex.europa.eu/LexUriServ/ site/en/ com/2004/com2004_0038en01.pdf
70 Jaenicke et al (2000), op. cit.
71 Ibid.
72 Clayton et al (1999), op. cit., p. 31.
73 Del Río (2004), op. cit.
74 Calleja, I. and Delgado, L. (2004) 'European Environmental Technologies Action Plan (ETAP)', *Journal of Cleaner Production*, 16S1, 181–183.
75 Ibid.
76 Blazejczak, J. and Edler, D. (2000) 'Elements of Innovation-friendly Policy Regimes: An International Comparative Study for the Paper Industry' in Hemmelskamp, J., Rennings, K. and Leone, F. (eds) *Innovation-oriented Environmental Regulation: Theoretical Approaches and Empirical Analysis* (Heidelberg and New York: Physica Verlag), 175–192.
77 Oosterhuis (2006), op. cit., p. 39.
78 Clayton, A., Spinardi, G. and Williams, R. (1999) 'Policies for cleaner technology. A new agenda for government and industry', *Earthscan*, p. 27.
79 Wallace, D. (1995) 'Environmental policy and industrial innovation', Royal Institute of International Affair (London, U.K).
80 Oosterhuis (2006), op. cit., p. 39.
81 Ibid.
82 Parto and Herbert-Copley (2007), op. cit.
83 We refer to 'hard' instruments as those of the command-and-control type, which use regulation as a 'stick', that is, an obligation to do something falls on firms (either in the form of adoption of a certain technology, reduction of emissions by a certain percentage or avoidance of emissions and discharges to the environment which surpass its capacity to absorb them). Another set of hard instruments are some types of economic instruments, which put a price on those discharges (taxes and tradable permits). The latter can also be ambitious or lenient. In the case of taxes, stringency depends on the tax level. In the case of tradable permits, it depends on the ambition of targets (which in turn determines the number of permits to be issued and, thus, their price) and on the method of allocating those permits (that is, whether they are auctioned or grandfathered).

84 See for example: Roedliger-Schluga, T. (2004) 'The Porter hypothesis and the economic consequences of environmental regulatio' (Cheltenham, UK: Edward Elgar); Ashford (2005), op. cit.; Kemp (1997, 2007), op. cit.; Del Río (2008), op. cit.

85 Kemp (2007), op. cit., p. 266.

86 Clayton et al (1999), op. cit.

87 Gunninham (2007), op. cit., p. 208.

88 Clayton et al (1999), op. cit.

89 Mazzanti, M. and Zoboli, R. (2006) 'Economic instruments and induced innovation: the European policies on end-of-life vehicles', *Ecological Economics*, 58(2), 318–337; IPTS (2004) 'Promoting environmental technologies: Sectoral analyses, barriers and measures', Institute for Prospective Technological Studies, European Commission, Report EUR 21002 EN.

90 A recent special issue of the Journal Cleaner Production (2008, number 16) is devoted to 'sustainability and supply chain management'. An overview is offered by Seuring, S. and Müller, M. (2008) 'From a literature review to a conceptual framework for sustainable supply chain management', *Journal of Cleaner Production*, 16(15), 1699–1710. The originality of the paper by Mazzanti and Zoboli (2006, 'Economic instruments and induced innovation: the European policies on end-of-life vehicles', *Ecological Economics*, 58(2), 318–337) mainly lies in the analysis of the impact of environmental regulation on different stages of the supply chain of a product, where there are relationships between various manufacturing industries with different interests in innovation. IPTS (2004, op. cit.) also establishes that supply chains can play an important role in sectors where prices of raw materials are high and that in these sectors a higher degree of adoption of clean technologies can be expected. In addition, inter- and intra-trade across the supply chain and the power relations that it implies is an issue. The capacity to engage and influence suppliers of technologies, materials and other inputs is a strong determinant of innovation, particularly in industrial sectors close to large chains of retailing.

91 Yap, N., Devlin, J., Chao, C. and Ton, S. (2007) 'Corporate environmental innovation and public policy: case studies from Taiwan' in Parto and Herbert-Copley (2007), op. cit. According to these authors (p. 45), a corporate synergy system 'is a mechanism though which a group of manufacturing companies work together to achieve certain production of management goals. It is established among firms linked by supply chains and usually consists of a central firm and its manufacturing suppliers or satellites'.

92 Graedel, H. and Allenby, B. (1995) *Industrial Ecology* (New Jersey: Prentice Hall); Norberg-Bohm (1999), op. cit.

93 Norberg-Bohm (1999), op. cit.

94 Ashford (2005), op. cit., p. 7.

95 Ibid. This author observes that in the US coordinated facility-based permitting, while not commonplace, is increasingly implemented to meet this criticism, as they are some of the 'regulatory' reinvention strategies discussed below. In Europe, some VAs are multi-media in nature, but others continue to be single-media (or energy) focused. However, there have also been multimedia approaches at the levels of European countries, such as the Integrated Pollution Control Law in the UK, as well as at EU level, such as the Integrated Pollution Prevention and Control (IPPC) Directive.

96 Del Río (2008), op. cit.

97 Rothwell, R. (1992) 'Industrial innovation and government environmental regulation', *Technovation*, 12(7), 447–458; Norberg-Bohm (1999), op. cit.

98 OECD (1999) *Technology and Environment: Towards Policy Integration* (Paris: Organisation for Economic Co-operation and Development), p. 20.

99 Ashford (1993), op. cit.

100 Herbert-Copley, B. (2007) 'To the limits ... and beyond? Environmental regulation and innovation in the Canadian pulp and paper industry' in Parto and Herbert-Copley (2007), op. cit., 115–137.

101 Oosterhuis (2006), op. cit.

102 See also Requate (2005), op. cit.

103 Kemp (2000), op. cit.

104 For example, this would be the case if each kWh of electricity from clean sources (that is, renewable energy) was subsidized.

105 This has been empirically shown by Kemp (1997, op. cit.) for the Dutch case.

106 In the context of 'subsidies' it should also be taken into account that the elimination of environmentally harmful subsidies could have a significant, positive role on eco-innovation.

107 UNESCAP (2008) 'The role of various environment-related measures', http://www.unescap.org/drpad/vc/orientation/M5_3.htm, date accessed 16 November 2008.

108 Toffel, M. W. (2003) 'Closing the loop: product take-back regulations and their strategic implications', *International Journal of Corporate Sustainability*, 10(9), 161–172.

109 Türpitz, K. (2003) 'The determinants and effects of environmental product innovations', *Greening of Industry Network International Conference*, October 12–15 (San Francisco).

110 Yap et al (2007), op. cit.

111 Del Río (2004), op. cit.

112 Jaffe et al (2002), op. cit.

113 See Driesen, D. (2003) 'Does Emission Trading Encourage Innovation?', *Environmental Law Reporter*, 33, 10094–10108; Kemp (2000), op. cit.

114 Kemp (2007), op. cit.

115 Yüksel, H. (2008) 'An empirical evaluation of cleaner production practices in Turkey', *Journal of Cleaner Production*, 16(1), 50–57.

116 Del Río (2008), op. cit.

117 See Rennings, K., Ziegler, A., Ankele, K. and Hoffmann, E. (2006) 'The influence of different characteristics of the EU enviromental management and auditing scheme on technical environmental innovation and economic performance', *Ecological Economics*, 57(1), 45–59; and Rehfeld, K., Rennings, K. and Ziegler, A. (2007) 'Integrated product policy and environmental product innovations: An empirical analysis', *Ecological Economics*, 61(1), 91–100.

118 See Frondel et al (2005), op. cit.; Murphy and Gouldson (2000), op. cit.

119 Könnölä and Unruh (2007), op. cit.

120 As suggested by Yap et al (2007), op. cit.

121 Kemp (1997), op. cit.

122 Könnölä et al (2006), op. cit.

123 Ibid.

124 Könnölä, T., Unruh, G. and Carrillo-Hermosilla, J. (2007) 'Toward prospective voluntary agreements: reflections from a hydrogen foresight project', *Journal of Cleaner Production*, 15(3), pp. 259–265.

125 Andersen, P., Joergensen, B., Eerola, A., Koljonen, T., Loikkanen, T., and Eriksson, E. A. (2005) 'Building the Nordic Research and Innovation Area in Hydrogen', Summary Report, Nordic H2 Energy Foresight, http://www.h2foresight.info/ (home page), date accessed 25 November 2008.

126 Norberg-Bohm, (1999), op. cit., p. 23.

127 Gunningham (2007), op. cit., p. 210.

128 Norberg-Bohm (1999), op. cit., p. 16.

129 Other instruments include innovation waivers (see Kemp (2000), op. cit.) and protection of intellectual property rights – which is particularly effective for the invention stage (see Norberg-Bohm (1999), op. cit.).

130 Public funding can be provided for basic research, applied research and experimental development of technologies. This can be done in universities, public and private research centers or in companies (Yap et al (2007), op. cit.).

131 See, among others, Norberg-Bohm (2000, op. cit.) and Yap et al (2007, op. cit.) for empirical evidence in the US and Taiwan, respectively.

132 Note that investment subsidies for the adoption of cleaner technologies have already been included in the environmental policy category.

133 Johnstone, N. and Labonne, J. (2006) 'Environmental policy, management and R&D', OECD Economic Studies No. 42, 2006/1.

134 Rothwell (1992), op. cit.

135 One type of information provision is Environmental Technology Verification (ETV) programs, which originate in the US but which are also part of the European Environmental Technology Action Plan (ETAP). Their purpose is to accelerate market acceptance of innovative technologies by providing users with accessible, understandable, and credible information about the performance of eco-innovations, substantially reducing the uncertainty for purchasers (Calleja and Delgado (2008), op. cit., p. 182).

136 Ashford (2005), op. cit.

137 Yap et al (2007), op. cit.

138 Del Río (2002, 2004), op. cit.; Kemp (2000, 2007), op. cit.

139 Könnölä et al (2007).

140 Del Río (2002, 2004), op. cit.

141 Könnölä et al (2007), op. cit.

142 Carrillo-Hermosilla, J. (2004) 'Technology and the environment: an evolutionary approach to sustainable technological change', IE Business School Working Paper Series 02/04.

143 See OECD (1999), op. cit.; and Luiten and Blok (2004), op. cit.

144 Kemp (2007), op. cit., p. 7.

145 Kemp (2000), op. cit.

146 Oosterhuis (2006), op. cit.

147 See the European Environmental Compliance Assessment Programme (ECAP) http://ec.europa.eu/environment/sme/.

148 Del Río (2004, 2008), op. cit.
149 Calleja and Delgado (2008), op. cit.
150 Ibid., p. 182.
151 Rotmans, J., Kemp, R. and van asselt, M. (2001) 'More Evolution than Revolution: Transition Management in Public Policy', *Foresight*, 3 (1), 15–31.
152 Ibid., p. 22.
153 The above are deemed the most policy-relevant distinctions, but others could have been considered as well. For example, measures could be more effective for the promotion of cross-sectoral eco-innovations while others should better be directed at sector-specific eco-innovations. In addition, effective measures to boost technological eco-innovations may differ from those to encourage non-technological eco-innovations.
154 See, among others: Cleff, T. and Rennings, K. (2000) 'Determinants of environmental product and process innovation: Evidence from the Mannheim Innovation Panel and a follow-up telephone survey' in J. Hemmelskamp, F. Leone and K. Rennings (eds) *Innovation-oriented Environmental Regulation: Theoretical Approaches and Empirical Analysis* (Heidelberg: Physica Verlag), 331–347.

5 BUSINESS STRATEGIES FOR ECO-INNOVATION

1 Schmidheiny, S. (1992) *Changing Course: A Global Business Perspective on Development and the Environment* (World Business Council for Sustainable Development).
2 Porter, M. and Van der Linde, C. (1995) 'Toward a New Conception of the Environment–Competitiveness Relationship', *Journal of Economic Perspectives*, 9.4, 97–118; Von Weizsäcker, E., Lovins, A. B. and Lovins, L. H. (1997) *Factor Four: Doubling Wealth – Halving Resource Use* (London: Earthscan).
3 Decanio, S. J. (1993) 'Barriers within firms to energy-efficient investments', *Energy Policy*, 21(9), 906–14.
4 ISO (2006) 'The ISO Survey 2006', http://www.iso.org/iso/survey2006.pdf, date accessed 14 November 2008.
5 Kuisma, M., Lovio, R. and Niskanen, S. (2001) 'Hypotheses on the impact of environmental management systems in industry', Ministry of the Environment, Finland, Helsinki (in Finnish); Hertin, J., Berkhout, F., Tyteca, D. and Wehrmeyer (2003) "Are

"soft" policy instruments effective? Establishing the link between environmental management systems and the environmental performance of companies', *Berlin Conference on the Human Dimension of Global Environmental Change*, 5–6.

6 IMPRESS (2003) 'The Impact of Clean Production on Employment in Europe: An Analysis using Surveys and Case Studies', TSER Progamme, Contract SOE-1-CT-98-1106, 2003, http://www.impress.zew.de/, date accessed 14 November 2008.

7 ADL (2005) 'The Innovation High Ground', Arthur D. Little, http://www.adl.com/ (home page), date accessed 14 November 2008.

8 Schmidheiny (1992), op. cit.

9 Fussler, C. and James, P. (1996) *Driving Eco-Innovation: A Breakthrough Discipline for Innovation and Sustainability* (London: Pitman Publishing), p. 364.

10 McDonough, W. and Braungart, M. (2002) *Cradle to Cradle: Remaking the Way We Make Things* (New York: North Point Press); Braungart, M., McDonough, W. and Bollinger, A. (2007) 'Cradle-to-cradle design: creating healthy emissions: A strategy for eco-effective product and system design', *Journal of Cleaner Production*, 15, 1337–48.

11 Frosch, R. A. and Gallopoulos. N. E. (1989) 'Strategies for Manufacturing', *Scientific American*, 261(3), 94–102; Côte, R. (1994) 'Designing and Operating Industrial Parks as Ecosystems', School for Resource an Environmental Studies, Dalhousie University, Canada; Graedel, T. E. and Allenby, B. R. (1995) 'Matrix approaches to abridged life cycle assessment', *Environmental Science & Technology*, 29(3), p. 134A; Socolow, R. (1997) *Industrial Ecology and Global Change* (New York: Cambridge University Press); Ayres, R. (1996) 'Creating industrial ecosystems: A viable management strategy?', *International Journal of Technology Management*, 12 Issue 5/6, p. 608.

12 McDonough and Braungart (2002), op. cit.

13 Braungart et al (2007), op. cit.

14 Anastas, P. T. and Zimmerman, J. B. (2003) 'Design through the Twelve Principles of Green Engineering', *Env. Sci. and Tech.*, 37(5), 95–101; Segars, J. W., Bradfield, S. L., Wright, J. J. and Realff, M. J. (2003) 'EcoWorx, Green Engineering Principles in Practice', *Environ. Sci. Technol.*, 37(23), 5269 –5277.

15 Linstone, H. A. (2007) 'The rise and fall of corporate R&D: Out of the dusty labs', *Technological Forecasting and Social Change*, 74(4), 558–562.

16 Smits, R. (2002) 'Innovation studies in the 21st century: Questions from a user's perspective', *Technological Forecasting and Social Change*, 69(9), 861–883.

17 Von Hippel, E. (2007) 'Harvard Business Review List of Breakthrough Ideas for 2007', *Harvard Business Review*, 85(2), 20–54.

18 Von Hippel, E. (1988) *The Sources of Innovation* (Oxford University Press).

19 Ibid.

20 Von Hippel, E. (2005) *Democratizing Innovation* (MIT Press).

21 Montalvo, C. (2008) 'General wisdom concerning the factors affecting the adoption of cleaner technologies: A survey 1990–2007', *Journal of Cleaner Production*, 16(1), 7–13.

22 Koefoed, M. and Buckley. C. (2008) 'Clean technology transfer: a case study from the South African metal finishing industry 2000–2005', *Journal of Cleaner Production*, 16(1), 78–84.

23 Visser, R., Jongen, M. and Zwetsloot, G. (2008) 'Business-driven innovations towards more sustainable chemical products', *Journal of Cleaner Production*, 16(1), 85–94.

24 European Commission (2004), Commission's Communication on 'Stimulating technologies for Sustainable Development: an Environmental Technologies Action Plan for the European Union', COM(2004) 38 final, 28.1.2004.

25 Cagno, E. and Trucco, P. (2008) 'Cleaner technology transfer in the Italian galvanic industry: economic and know-how issues', *Journal of Cleaner Production*, 16(1), 32–6.

26 Ashford, N. A. (2005) 'Pathways to Sustainability: Evolution or Revolution?' in M. van Geenhuizen, D. V. Gibson, and M. V. Heitor (eds) *Regional Development and Conditions for Innovation in the Network Society* (Purdue University Press), 35–59.

27 Montalvo (2008), op. cit.

28 Ibid.

29 Berkhout, F. (2005) 'Technological Regimes, Environmental performance and innovation systems: Tracing the links' in M. Weber and J. Hemmelskamp (eds) *Towards Environmental Innovation Systems* (Berlin: Springer), 57–80.

30 The relevance of the user-supplier relationship in encouraging eco-innovation has been empirically tested and confirmed. In its study of Canadian chemical firms, Dupuy (1997, 'Technological change and environmental policy: The diffusion of environmental

technology', *Growth and Change*, 28, 49–66) showed that the link between technologically specialized suppliers (as information providers and close collaborators in technology implementation) and users was strong, favouring the diffusion of environmental technologies. User-producer and customer-producer relationships were the most relevant factors for clean technology adoption in the study by Van Dijken et al (1999, *Adoption of environmental innovations* (Dordrecht, the Netherlands: Kluwer Academic Publishers)).

31 European Commission (2004), Commission's Communication on 'Stimulating technologies for Sustainable Development: an Environmental Technologies Action Plan for the European Union', COM(2004) 38 final, 28.1.2004.

32 Tukker, A. (2004) 'Eight types of product-service system: Eight ways to sustainability? Experiences from SusProNet', *Business Strategy and the Environment*, 13(4), 246–60; Williams, A. (2007) 'Product service systems in the automobile industry: contribution to system innovation?', *Journal of Cleaner Production*, 15(11–12), 1093–1103.

33 Wagner, M. (2008) 'Empirical influence of environmental management on innovation: evidence from Europe', *Ecological Economics*, 66(2–3), 392–402.

34 Ibid.

35 Del Río, P. (2005) 'Analysing the factors influencing clean technology adoption: a study of the Spanish pulp and paper industry', *Business Strategy and the Environment*, 14, 20–37.

36 Visser et al (2008), op. cit.

37 However, it has been suggested that a 'small wins capability' can assist employee based eco-innovations by overcoming entrenched industry institutional practices and precedents (Griffiths, A. B. and Haigh, N. L. (2004) 'Co-ordinating small wins as an effective mechanism for implementing firm level eco-innovations', *64th Annual Meeting of the Academy of Management*, New Orleans, 6–11 August). The concept of small wins refers to the work of Karl Weick in understanding and making large complex social problems manageable. A 'small win is a concrete, complete, implemented outcome of moderate importance. By itself, one small win may seem unimportant. A series of small wins at small but significant tasks, however, reveals a pattern that may attract others, deter opponents' (Weick, K. (1984) 'Small wins: Redefining the scale of social problems', *American Psychologist*, 39, p. 43).

38 Tushman, M. and Anderson, P. (1997) *Managing strategic inno-vation and change: A collection of readings* (New York: Oxford University Press), p. 656.
39 Ibid.
40 Hawken, P., Lovins, A. B. and Lovins, L. H. (1999) *Natural Capitalism: Creating the Next Industrial Revolution Natural Capitalism* (US: Back Bay Books).
41 Powell, W. and DiMaggio, P. (1991) *The New Institutionalism in Organisational Analysis* (Chicago, IL: The University of Chicago Press).
42 Tushman, M. and O'Reilly, C. A. (1997) *Winning Through Innovation* (Boston: Harvard Business School Press).

6   ECO-INNOVATIONS IN PRACTICE

1 Eisenhardt, K. M. (1989) 'Building theories from case research', *Academy of Management Review*, 14(4), p. 548
2 Cook, T. D. and Campbell, D. T. (1976) 'The design and conduct of quasi-experiments and true experiments in field settings' in M. D. Dunnette (ed.) *Handbook of Industrial and Organizational Psychology* (Chicago: Rand McNally), 223–336; Patton, M. Q. (1990) *Quality Evaluation and Research* (Thousand Oaks, CA: Sage).

Case study 1: Ecocement

1 Faced with increasingly strong legislative and stakeholder pres-sure, the Cement Sustainability Initiative (CSI) was established in 1999 by ten of the world's leading cement companies under the auspices of the Geneva-based World Business Council for Sustainable Development (WBCSD) (Klee, H. and Coles, E. (2004) 'The Cement Sustainability Initiative: Implementing Change Across a Global Industry', *Corporate Social Responsibility and Environmental Management*, 11, 114–120). Today the CSI project is comprised of 18 major cement producers who believe there is a strong business case for the pursuit of sus-tainable development. Collectively these companies account for more than 40 per cent of the world's cement production, ranging in size from very large multinationals to smaller local producers (CSI (2008), www.wbcsdcement.org (home page), date accessed 3 June 2008).

2 EU (2007) 'Hearing on the Evolution of the European Cement Industry', European Economic and Social Committee Consultative Commission on Industrial Change, Brussels, 30 May (DI 56/2007).

3 Taiheiyo (2008) 'Ecocement', Taiheiyo Cement Co., http://www. taiheiyo-cement.co.jp/english/ (home page), date accessed 3 June 2008.

4 A second Ecocement plant opened in July 2006, the Tokyo Tama Ecocement Facility in the town of Hinodemachi, Nishitama, Tokyo. The facility accepts about 94,000 tons of municipal-waste incinerator ash each year from the 25 cities and 1 town in the Tama region of Tokyo Prefecture and manufactures 133,000 tons of Ecocement (Taiheiyo (2007), 'Taiheiyo Cement Corporate Social Responsibility Report', Taiheiyo Cement Co., http://www.taiheiyo-cement.co.jp/english/ (home page), date accessed 3 June 2008).

5 Taiheiyo (2008), op. cit.

6 *Asia Pulse* (1997) 'Tokyo municipalities to build ash-recycling cement plant', 10 July.

7 Hydraulic cement is a combination of limestone, clay, and Portland cement, which is the main component in concrete. Hydraulic and Portland cement products include mixtures that harden with the addition of water. Since concrete is an important component of every large construction project, the mixture of hydraulic and Portland cement products is an extremely precise and carefully controlled process. To make Portland cement, dry materials are crushed to a specific size and proportioned to make a specific chemical mixture. The materials are blended using either a dry or wet process, producing a dry fine grey powder which is then used to make other blended hydraulic cements (GlobalSpec (2008), http://materials.globalspec.com/, date accessed 3 June 2008).

8 Ampadu, K.O. and Torii, K. (2001). 'Characterization of eco-cement pastes and mortars produced from incinerated ashes', *Cement and Concrete Research*, 31, 431–436.

9 Vigon, B. (2002) 'Toward a sustainable Cement Industry – Substudy 9: Industrial Ecology in the Cement Industry', An Independent Study Commissioned by the WBCSD.

10 Taiheiyo (2008), op. cit.

11 Ampadu and Torii (2001), op. cit.

12 Taiheiyo (2008), op. cit.

13 Vigon (2002), op. cit.
14 WBCSD (2001) 'Taiheiyo Cement Corporation: Using urban waste for "eco-cement"', WBCSD, http://www.wbcsd.org (home page), date accessed 28 May 2008.
15 *Japan Chemical Week* (1997) 'Ecocement Pioneered Using Ash As Raw Material', 4 November.
16 The cement industry is recognized by some European governments as an essential part of their waste management policy (CEMBU-REAU (2008), the European Cement Industry Association, http://www.cembureau.be (home page), date accessed 28 May 2008).
17 *The Daily Yomiuri/Yomiuri Shimbun* (2001) 'Towards a "material balance"', 15 January.
18 Placet, M. and Fowler, K. (2002) 'Toward a Sustainable Cement Industry – Substudy 7: How Innovation Can Help the Cement Industry Move Toward More Sustainable Practices', An Independent Study Commissioned by the WBCSD.

In addition to the indicated references, this case study used the following internet sources:
http://www.jsa.or.jp/eng/news/letter/v5i1.pdf
http://en.wikipedia.org/wiki/Cement

Case study 2: Automated vacuum system for waste collection

1 Envac (2008) http://www.envac.net, Envac Centralsug home page, date accessed 13 May 2008.
2 Envac (2008), op. cit.
3 Oppent (2008) http://www.oppent.com, Oppent home page, date accessed 13 May 2008.
4 PneuLogix (2008) http://www.pneulogix.com, PneuLogix home page, date accessed 13 May 2008.
5 Oppent (2008), op. cit.
6 PneuLogix (2008), op. cit.
7 Jørgensen, B. (2006) 'Technology and Innovation in Waste Management in the Arctic. Example of an Automated Waste Collection System in Stakkevollan, Tromsø, Norway' *The 12th Mayors Conference of WWCAM, 2006 Winter Cities Forum*, Changchun, China.
8 Envac (2008), op. cit.
9 Ibid.
10 Oppent (2008), op. cit.
11 Envac (2008), op. cit.

12 Iriarte, A., Gabarrell, X. and Rieradevall, C. (in press) 'LCA of selective waste collection systems in dense urban areas', *Waste Management*.
13 Envac (2008), op. cit.
14 Ibid.

Case study 3: High-Speed Train System

1 Boyd, L. and Pritcher, L. (2008) 'Brief History of the U.S. Passenger Rail Industry', http:// library.duke.edu/digitalcollections/ adaccess/rails-history.html, date accessed 26 November 2008.
2 Keating, O. (2007) 'High-speed Rail', http://www.o-keating.com/ hsr/, date accessed 26 September 2008.
3 European Commission (2008) 'EU Energy and Transport in Figures', Luxembourg.
4 CNT (2006), 'High-speed Rail and Greenhouse Gas Emissions in the U.S.', Center for Neighborhood Technology, http://www.cnt. org/climate/high-speed-rail, date accessed 26 September 2008.
5 Keating (2007), op. cit.
6 CNT (2006), op. cit.
7 Ibid.
8 García, A. (2008) 'Consumo de energía y emisiones del ferrocarril: Situación actual y posibilidades de mejora', conference presentation at the *Jornada Anual 2008 de la Cátedra Rafael Mariño de Nuevas Tecnologías Energéticas*, Universidad Pontifica Comillas, Madrid, 29–30 May
9 Ibid.

In addition to the indicated references, this case study used the following internet sources:
http://www.guardian.co.uk/world/2008/feb/02/spain.railtravel
http://www.altavelocidad.org/index_en.htm
http://www.eurostar.com/
http://en.wikipedia.org/wiki/AVE

Case study 4: EcoWorx™, carpet backing

1 This case background has benefited greatly from valuable information provided by Gregory C. Unruh.
2 Shaw Green Edge (2008), http://www.shawgreenedge.com (home page), date accessed 3 July 2008.
3 Biehl, M., Edmund Prater, E., Matthew, J. and Realff, M. J. (2007) 'Assessing performance and uncertainty in developing carpet

reverse logistics systems', *Computers & Operations Research*, 34, 443–63.

4 Shaw Green Edge (2008), op. cit.

5 CARE (2007), Carpet America Recovery Effort Annual Report, http://www.carpetrecovery.org/pdf/annual_report/07_CARE-annual-rpt.pdf, date accessed 3 July 2008.

6 Shaw Contract Group (2008), http://www.shawcontractgroup.com (home page), date accessed 3 July 2008.

7 See Shaw (2008), http://www.shawfloors.com (home page), date accessed 3 July 2008.

8 Biehl et al (2007), op. cit.

9 See http://www.carpetrecovery.org/index.php

10 Biehl et al (2007), op. cit.

Case study 5: Carbon Capture and Storage (CCS)

1 Davison, J. (2007) 'Performance and costs of power plants with capture and storage of CO2', *Energy*, 32, 1163–1176.

2 European Commission (2008) 'Proposal for a Directive of the European Parliament and of the Council on the geological storage of carbon dioxide and amending Council Directives 85/337/EEC, 96/61/EC, Directives 2000/60/EC, 2001/80/EC, 2004/35/EC, 2006/12/EC and Regulation (EC) No 1013/2006', Brussels, 23.1.2008 COM(2008) 18 final, p. 2.

3 Klaasen, G. (2008) 'The economics of EU carbon capture and storage policy', *16th Annual Conference of the European Association for Environmental and Resource Economics*, Gothenburg, 26–28 June.

4 For example, using simulations with the PRIMES model, Klaasen (2008, op. cit.) shows that CCS is a cost-effective instrument for meeting the EU 20 per cent reduction in GHG and the 20 per cent renewable target for 2020, as part of a package including renewables, energy efficiency measures and reductions in non-CO_2 greenhouse gases. The author finds that, if CCS were not enabled under the EU ETS, the additional costs of meeting the 20 per cent GHG and 20 per cent targets (and 30 per cent reduction in 2030) would be 60 billion euros per year in 2030 or 40 per cent higher in 2030.

5 See, among others, IPCC (2005), *IPCC special report on Carbon Dioxide Capture and Storage*, prepared by working group III of the Intergovernmental Panel on Climate Change, Metz, B., O. Davidson, H. C. de Coninck, M. Loos, and L. A. Meyer (eds)

(Cambridge (UK): Cambridge University Press) (available in full at http://www.ipcc.ch); IEA (2006), *Storing CO2 Underground*, Paris; Pacala, S. and Socolow, R. (2004) 'Stabilization Wedges: Solving the Climate Problem for the Next 50 Years with Current Technologies', *Science*, 305, 968–972. IPCC (ibid.) highlights the important contribution of CCS to the emissions reductions portfolio (including renewable energy, nuclear, energy efficiency and shift from coal to gas) required to reach those targets according to two integrated assessment models (MESSAGE and MiniCAM). This increases by the end of the period (2095). Notwithstanding, the IPCC (ibid., p. 45) anticipates that 'the actual use of CCS is likely to be lower than the estimates of economic potential indicated by these energy and economic models because the results are typically based on an optimised least-cost analysis that does not adequately account for real-world barriers to technology development and deployment, such as environmental impact, lack of a clear legal or regulatory framework, the perceived investment risks of different technologies, and uncertainty as to how quickly the cost of CCS will be reduced through R&D and learning-by-doing. Models typically employ simplified assumptions regarding the costs of CCS for different applications and the rates at which future costs will be reduced'.

6 Wright, I., Ashworth, P., Xin, S., Di, L., Yizhong, Z., Liang, X., Anderson, J., Shackley, S., Itaoka, K., Wade, S., Asamoah, J. and Reiner, D. (2007) 'Public Perception of Carbon Dioxide Capture and Storage: Prioritised Assessment of Issues and Concerns. Summary for Policy-Makers', commissioned by the International Energy Agency Working Party on Fossil Fuels, funded by the UK Department of Trade and Industry, p. 4.

7 European Commission 2008a, op. cit.

8 Johnson, T. and Keith, D. (2004) 'Fossil electricity and CO_2 sequestration: How natural gas prices, initial conditions and retrofits determine the cost of controlling CO_2 emissions', *Energy Policy*, 32(3), p. 357.

9 Ibid., p. 368.

10 The traditional power generation sector in Europe has appreciated this characteristic and is certainly in favour of this technology, as shown by the statements of the European industry association (see Eurelectric (2008) 'Eurelectric Position Paper on Carbon Capture & Storage', March 2008, Brussels), which regards CCS 'as a crucial means of tackling climate change'.

11 IPCC (2005), op. cit, p. 19.
12 Wright et al (2007), op. cit., p. 4.
13 European Commission (2008), op. cit., p. 1.
14 IEA (2005) 'Projected Costs of Generating Electricity – 2005 Update', Paris, p. 189.
15 European Commission (2008), op. cit., p. 1.
16 IPCC (2005), op. cit.
17 Ibid.
18 Coninck, H.C. and Groenenberg, H. (2008) 'Effective EU and Member State policies for stimulating CCS', International Journal on Greenhouse Gas Control, 2, 653–664.
19 According to IPCC (2005, op. cit., p. 21): (1) 'Research phase' means that the basic science is understood, but the technology is currently at the stage of conceptual design or testing at the laboratory or bench scale, and has not been demonstrated in a pilot plant. (2) 'Demonstration phase' means that the technology has been built and operated at the scale of a pilot plant, but further development is required before the technology is ready for the design and construction of a full-scale system. (3) 'Economically feasible under specific conditions' means that the technology is well understood and used in selected commercial applications, for instance if there is a favourable tax regime or a niche market, or processing in the order of 0.1 $MtCO_2$ yr-1, with few (less than 5) replications of the technology. (4) 'Mature market' means that the technology is now in operation with multiple replications of the technology worldwide.
20 According to Johnson and Keith (2004, op. cit., p. 372), new coal plants with CCS become competitive near $75/tC whereas the option of retrofitting existing coal-fired capacity for post-combustion carbon capture is uncompetitive below $300/tC.
21 According to the World Energy Outlook 2006 (IEA (2006), op. cit.), its potential would only be 12 per cent of overall emissions reductions in 2050.
22 According to IPCC (2005, op. cit., p. 21), only industrial separation (natural gas processing, ammonia production), pipeline and Enhanced Oil Recovery (EOR) can be considered mature. Another ten CCS components are not mature, but in different stages of pre-maturity (research, demonstration and economically feasible under specific conditions). See note 21 for definitions of these stages.
23 Rubin et al (2007) criticize the estimates of CCS costs in the literature: 'A number of recent studies have estimated CCS costs based

on technologies that are either currently commercial or under development. Relatively few studies are published in peer-reviewed journals. For the most part, they focus on coal-based power plants, which are a major source of CO_2 emissions. Most studies consider only CO_2 capture costs and do not include the costs of transport and storage. While some studies also have reported ancillary benefits of CO_2 capture, such as improved capture of criteria air pollutants (like sulphur dioxide, SO_2), a more complete picture of the environmental and resource implications of CO_2 capture is largely lacking in the current literature' (Rubin, E., Chen, C. and Rao, A. (2007) 'Cost and performance of fossil fuel power plants with CO2 capture and storage', *Energy Policy*, 35, p. 4444).

24 IPCC (2005), op. cit.
25 Several variables influence the costs and uncertainty regarding those costs. Carbon dioxide avoidance costs are likely to be sensitive to assumptions about the costs of CO_2 transport and storage, fuel costs, discount rate, load factor and coal type (Davison, 2007, op. cit.). Fuel costs are particularly variable at present. The dynamics of plant dispatch are also likely to influence CO_2 mitigation costs (Johnson and Keith, 2004, op. cit.).
26 Rubin et al (2007), op. cit.
27 These results indicate that the omission of transport and storage costs (as in most studies to date) can lead to incorrect conclusions about the relative total cost of different power systems (Ibid.).
28 Davison (2007), op. cit.
29 Groenenberg and Coninck (2007, op. cit.) report costs between €20/tCO_2 and €60/tCO_2.
30 Røine, K., Tvinnereim, E. and Hasselknippe, H. (eds) (2008) *Carbon 2008 – Post-2012 is Now* (Copenhague: Point Carbon). Interviewed more than 4,000 actors in the EU ETS. Expected prices are in the region of €24 in 2010 and €35 in 2020.
31 IPCC (2005, p. 44) shows that the increased CO2 production resulting from the loss in overall efficiency of the power plant due to the additional energy required for capture, transport and storage lead to a larger amount of CO2 produced per kWh relative to the reference plant without capture. For specific data for the energy penalty in CCS plants attached to different types of power plants, see Davison (2007, op. cit.).
32 Rubin et al (2007), op. cit, p. 4451.
33 According to IPCC (2005, op. cit., p. 41), the cost of CCS for all electricity systems can be reduced by about 0.01–0.02 USD/kWh when using Enhanced Oil Recovery (EOR) with CO_2

storage because the EOR revenues partly compensate the CCS costs.

34 European Commission (2008), op. cit., p. 3. Although the accidental release of CO_2 might occur when storing and transporting CO_2, the European Commission (op. cit., p. 5) states that 'for properly selected, managed and decommissioned sites, the risk of leakage, and a fortiori of irreversible consequences, is in fact low'. Catastrophic leakage of CO_2 from storage is not regarded as a serious risk by experts (Wright et al (2007), op. cit.).

35 Wright et al (2007), op. cit., p. 3.

36 Markides, C. (2006) 'Disruptive innovation: In need of a better theory', *J. Prod. Innov. Manag.*, 23, 19–25.

37 Wright et al (2007), op. cit., p. 5.

38 Ibid., p. 8.

39 However, Klaasen (2008, op. cit.) argues that, since dynamic efficiency and local benefits are likely to be small, there is little evidence to justify going beyond the carbon market. This is so because he shows (making simulations with the PRIMES model) that: 1) the impact on learning of the additional deployment is small and impacts on achievement of global climate objectives and export potential would be correspondingly low; 2) impacts on air quality, employment and security of supply relative to the market-based option are also small (ibid., p. 17).

40 Groenenberg and Coninck (2008), op. cit.

Case study 6: Hybrid Synergy Drive

1 HybridCars.com (2008), http://www.hybridcars.com/history/history-of-hybrid-vehicles.html, date accessed 27 October 2008.

2 Cobb, J. (2003) 'The Greening of Suburbio', *The New Cork Times*, November 30 http://query. nytimes.com/gst/fullpage.html?res=9A01E5D6133AF933A05752C1A9659C8B63, date accessed 27 October 2008.

3 This is a world wide, official figure TMC.

4 Indeed, the term 'Hybrid Synergy Drive, HSD' refers to the synergy between thermal and electric engines in order to achieve the greatest performance while reducing environmental impacts.

5 IPCC (2001), 'Third Assessment Report', Geneva.

6 Ishitani, H., Baba, Y. and Kobayashi, O. (2000) 'Well to wheel energy efficiency of fuel cell electric vehicles by various fuels', Japan Society of Energy and Resources, *Energy and Resources*, 21(5), 417–425.

7 However, some authors contest the fuel economy performance of the Prius (see, for example, Phillips (2007) '*Warning: Toyota Prius Falls Short of Fuel Efficiency Expectations*' http://www.zaphu.com/2007/09/27/warning-toyota-prius-falls-short-of-fuel-efficiency-expectations/).

8 Méndez (2005) 'El sector de la automoción y el medio ambiente', XV Foro de la Automoción, 20 April.

9 Lee, J., Gemba, K. and Kodama, F. (2006) 'Analyzing the innovation process for environmental performance improvement', *Technological Forecasting and Social Change*, 73(3), 290–301.

10 Corporate Average Fuel Economy (more information about CAFE standards can be found in http://www.epa.gov/fueleconomy/420f04053.htm#cafe, date accessed 27 October 2008).

11 IPCC (2007) 'Fourth Assessment Report', Geneve.

12 EEA (2003) 'Europe's Environment: The Third Assessment', environmental assessment report No. 10. European Environment Agency, Copenhagen.

13 Rowley (2007a) 'Toyota's Next Hybrid?', *Business Week*, 25 June.

14 Phillips (2007), op. cit.

15 Smith, G. (2004) 'Emission impossible: At last a green mobile that doesn't look like something an elephant sat on', *The Guardian*, 27 January.

16 Rego, J. and Stempel, J. (2007) 'The Prius Effect', Brand Neutral, http://mek1966.googlepages.com/Prius_Effect.pdf, p. 8.

17 IEA Hybrid Website (2006), http://www.ieahev.org/hybrid.html, date accessed 27 October 2008.

18 Kaho, T. (2007) 'Decade of the Toyota Prius Hybrid', http://www.hybridcars.com/carmakers/toyota.html, date accessed 27 October 2008.

19 Rowley, I. (2007b) 'The Trouble with Hybrids', *Business Week*, 8 June.

20 Rowley (2007b), op. cit.

21 Méndez (2005), op. cit.

22 Smith (2004), op. cit.

23 For example, Kaho (2007, op. cit.) argues that its distinctive futuristic and aerodynamic design with a high-tech appeal prompts many buyers to choose the Prius, since others know they're piloting an environmentally positive car at a glance.

24 Car Research (2006), 'On test: Toyota Prius (2004–2008 model)', 20 August.

25 Smith (2004), op. cit.

26 Car Research (2006), op. cit.

27 For example, the Prius takes full advantage of the latest light-weight materials technology. Everything from its bodyshell to the accelerator has been designed to be as lightweight as possible to enhance its driving performance (Smith (2004), op. cit.).

28 EEA (2003), op. cit.

29 All these calculations are provided by Tarboton, R. (2004) 'Economy drive', *The Guardian*, 9 August. It is assumed that the Prius costs around £2000 more than their petrol counterpart.

30 *Business Week* (2007) 'Why Hybrids Are Such a Hard Sell', 19 March.

31 White, J. (2006) 'GM, Toyota Bet Hybrid Green', *The Wall Street Journal*, 11 December.

32 Lave, L. and MacLean, H. (2002) 'An environmental-economic evaluation of hybrid electric vehicles: Toyota's Prius vs. its conventional internal combustion engine Corolla', Transportation Research Part D 7, 155–162.

33 2001 oil prices were used.

34 Lave and MacLean (2002).

35 Ibid.

36 Méndez (2005), op. cit.

37 Rowley (2007a), op. cit.

38 Ibid.

39 Rowley (2007b), op. cit.

40 Brand Neutral (2007), op. cit.

41 In a conventional engine, there's a trade-off between power and efficiency. But the Prius' hybrid system combines different power sources to maximize each one's strength – the high-speed power of an internal combustion engine and the clean efficiency, ultra-low running costs and low-speed of an electric motor (Smith, 2004, op. cit.).

42 Markides, C. (2006) 'Disruptive innovation: In need of a better theory', *J. Prod. Innov. Manag.*, 23, 19–25.

43 White (2006), op. cit.

44 HybridCars.com (2008), op. cit.

45 Anonymous (2006) 'Commitment at the Top', http://www.theenvironmentsite.org/guides/green-garage/guide-to-buying-a-green-car/, date accessed 27 October 2008.

46 See, for example, Rowley (2007b).

47 Lave and McLean (2002), op. cit.

48 In the US, different states have implemented different types of policies. In addition, some cities in the US and elsewhere (for example, London) encourage the uptake of the hybrid cars. A very

complete overview in the case of the US is provided by http://www.hybridcars.com/incentives-laws.html (date accessed 27 October 2008).

49 In the UK, a reduced vehicle excise duty (£70 in 2004) was applied to hybrids. In Colorado, the purchase of hybrid electric vehicles is exempted from the sales tax. Reduced vehicle registration charges are awarded to hybrids in the district of Columbia.

50 An example is the energy bill in the US on 8 August 2007, which effectively gave a break to US manufacturers by extending what could be a tax credit of as much as $3,400 per car to purchasers of the first 60,000 hybrids sold by a company, with the credit phasing out after that. However, this does not benefit the Prius, since Toyota has already sold more than 60,000 hybrids (Brooke, J (2005) 'Challenges ahead for Toyota hybrids', *International Herald Tribune*, 7 September).

51 For example, this has been the case of the cities of Los Angeles, Santa Mónica and San José in California.

52 For example, the Prius has been made exempt from the London congestion charge.

53 This is the case for example in Florida or California, although not for all hybrids in this later case.

54 For example, the Energy Saving Trust, a UK group working to reduce carbon dioxide emissions awards £700 for hybrid purchasers, or the provincial government of Manitoba (Canada), which will give $2,000 cash to anyone who buys an eligible hybrid car.

Case study 7: Green Hotel Project

1 This case study has benefited greatly from the valuable information provided by NH Hotels.

2 Of course, other environmental impacts should be taken into account, including visual intrusion, biodiversity loss and land occupancy.

3 This involves working with suppliers to green the supply chain (ITP (2008) 'Going Green: Minimum Standards toward a Sustainable Hotel', International Tourism Partnership, London, http:// www. tourismpartnership.org/downloads/Going%20Green.pdf, date accessed 19 November 2008).

4 Ibid.

5 INESC (2008), http://www.inescc.pt/urepe/chose/energy.htm, date accessed 19 November 2008.

6 On average, America's 47,000 hotels spend $2,196 per available room each year on energy (about 6 per cent of all operating costs). Through a strategic approach to energy efficiency, a 10 per cent reduction in energy consumption would have the same financial effect as increasing the average daily room rate by between $0.62 and $1.35 (Energy Star (2008) 'Hotels: An Overview of Energy Use and Energy Efficiency Opportunities', U.S. Environmental Protection Agency and the U.S. Department of Energy, www.energystar.gov/ia/business/challenge/learn_more/Hotel.pdf, date accessed 19 November 2008).

7 INESC (2008), op. cit.

8 EPA (2008) 'National Action Plan for Energy Efficiency – Sector Collaborative on Energy Efficiency: Hotel Energy Use Profile', U.S. Environmental Protection Agency, http://epa.gov/cleanenergy/documents/sector-meeting/4bii_hotelenergy.pdf, date accessed 30 October 2008.

9 The geographical breakdown for the sales figures is: Spain (39 per cent), Germany (21 per cent), Benelux (28 per cent), rest of Europe (6 per cent) and America (5 per cent) (NH (2008), Information for Shareholders and Investors, http://corporate-information.nh-hotels.com/eng/key_figures.jsp, date accessed 19 November 2008).

10 See, for example, Del Río (2005) 'Analysing the factors influencing clean technology adoption: A study of the Spanish pulp and paper industry', *Business Strategy and the Environment*, 14, 20–37, for an analysis in the pulp and paper sector.

11 Note that energy prices may be high or low depending on other factors apart from taxes, including fuel costs, cost-pass-through rates into prices, etc.

In addition to the references listed, this case study used the following internet sources:

http://www.tourismpartnership.org/
http://www.un.org/esa/sustdev/mgroups/success/1999/tour6.htm
http://ec.europa.eu/environment/ecolabel/product/pg_tourism_en.htm
http://www.globalstewards.org/hotel.htm
http://www.ecoholidaying.co.uk/
NegativeEffectsTourismEnvironmentalAspects.tml

Index

3M, 112

absorptive capacity, 36, 37, 113
    see also technological
        capability / capacity /
        competency
age of the firm, 35
Alcan, 96
Alstom, 152
ambidextrous organization, 42,
    122
American Chemical Society, 109
Asnaes Power Station, 105
automated vacuum waste
        collection system, 23–5,
        126, 138–47, 233
automobile / car, 9, 10, 13, 15,
        16, 18, 19, 20, 67, 74, 75,
        108, 109, 117, 127, 148,
        149, 151, 152, 177–88,
        206, 230, 239, 240
    catalytic converters, 9, 12, 16,
        95
    internal combustion engine,
        12, 16, 178, 179, 182,
        184, 241
AVE (Alta Velocidad Española),
        151, 153, 234
    see under trains

Belgium, 149
best available technologies
        (BAT), 38, 72, 114, 212

biocompatibility, 14, 104
    see also biomimicry
biodegradability, 14, 107,
        108, 162
    see also end-of-cycle product;
        open / closed loop
        systems; recycling
biomimicry, 6
    see also biocompatibility
Blueprint Report, 57, 219
Boeing, 17
bottom-up processes, 22, 30
    compare top-down processes
BP, 118
Brundtland Report, 1

calcium carbonate (limestone),
        131–3, 232
calcium oxide (incineration ash),
        129–33, 136, 137
carbon (CO2) emissions, 9, 12,
        13, 15, 16, 60, 95, 102,
        105, 118, 120, 121, 127,
        128, 133, 136, 137, 151,
        153, 166–76, 179, 180,
        183, 185, 187, 207, 208,
        215, 235–42
    see also global warming;
        greenhouse gas
carbon capture and storage
        (CCS), 13, 60, 127,
        166–76, 235–9
    see also carbon sequestration

DATE DUE

MAY 1 2 2010